Words of Life

250 Bible Readings

Andrew Goldsmith

ISBN: 9798398578874

CONTENTS

1

INTRODUCTION

"Anyone who listens to my teaching and follows it is wise,
like a person who builds a house on solid rock."
(Matthew 7:24, NLT)

God describes his own word – the Bible – in various ways. It is food for our soul, light for our path, and a sharp weapon that cuts deeply. It is truth. It is pure, perfect, delightful and so good. It is like a seed with incredible potential. It is life-giving and life-shaping, breathed out by the Living God for us to receive and obey. It carries God's good news, brings his revelation of himself and his glorious purposes through Christ, and by the Spirit it illuminates for us the pathway to life.

The Lord Jesus calls us to follow his building instructions. Every house is made of a range of materials to a certain design, even if it is scratched together or endlessly modified. He looks on our lives with the steadfast and relentless love of God and longs for us to build well. He knows the best materials – the very words of life – and what a secure and renewed life he offers us. It is like building a house on solid rock.

This book is to help you explore that Book, the Bible.

It includes 250 Bible reflections drawing from both the Old and the New Testaments. That's 250 different building blocks from which to choose as we set our lives on the Rock. (It's also one for each weekday of a year with weekends 'off' and two weeks to catch up.)

They are arranged in three broad sections. The first section draws mainly from the Old Testament (90 readings), exploring God in his beauty and wisdom, and leading us to anticipate the coming King. The second section focuses on our glorious Lord and Saviour, Jesus Christ, and comes mainly from the Gospels and the New Testament (60 readings). The third and final section explores various aspects of our new life in Christ, the experience of God's people and the grounds of our faith, drawing from across the whole Bible (100 readings).

May we choose well, build well, and enjoy what God has in store for us through his word – life, even eternal life, and life in all its secure and joyful fullness with Jesus.

2

THE KING IN HIS BEAUTY: THE OLD TESTAMENT

Your eyes will see the king in his beauty
and view a land that stretches afar.
(Isaiah 33:17)

To read through the Old Testament is to travel with God's people through their turbulent history as nomads and slaves, as wanderers in the desert, as warriors and worshippers, as pilgrims and rebels, under wicked rulers and wayward kings and godless empires. It's a varied experience filled with memorable drama and the foundations for knowing God.

The Old Testament also offers us the riches of their faith experience: the word of the Lord through the prophets, the revelation of God's character, knowledge of the God who saves and speaks, and the wisdom of seeing his kindness and steadfast love amidst the chaos or uncertainty of their lives. Abraham, Job, Ruth, Hannah, David, Zechariah and others reveal for us what Isaiah movingly refers to as 'the king in his beauty.'

This is what lifts the story of God's people from being merely a story of adversity or human struggle to being food for our souls and light for our path: God is with them, the LORD Almighty is their refuge and strength, and he is revealed here that we might behold him more fully and clearly too.

Drawn from this land that stretches afar, across the Old Testament, the following 30 reflections help us to see something of the king in his beauty.

Genesis 15:1	God is our Reward
Genesis 35:29	Reconciliation
Genesis 45:7	Boldness as God's remnant
Exodus 3:13-15	The Divine Name
Exodus 19:5-6	Treasured possession
Exodus 20:2-3	God saves before he commands
Exodus 31:2-5	God of all gifts
Exodus 34:5-7	Compassionate and gracious God
Joshua 4:6-7	A memorial – 'Remember, remember'
Ruth 2:12	Our refuge
2 Samuel 7:22	How great You are
2 Chronicles 20:15	The battle is the LORD's
Job 16:19-21	Our Advocate in heaven
Job 26:14	The whisper and thunder of God
Isaiah 12:3-4	Deep and life-giving wells
Isaiah 25:7-8	The Lord will wipe away our tears
Isaiah 40:28-31	Strength to the weary
Isaiah 61:3-4	Oaks of righteousness
Jeremiah 11:4-5	"Amen, Lord"
Lamentations 3:21f	New every morning
Ezekiel 1:25-28	High, holy and awesome
Ezekiel 34:15-16	The LORD our Shepherd
Ezekiel 36:24-27	A new heart, a new spirit
Daniel 12:1-3	From dust to glory
Hosea 2:14-15	Gateway of hope
Hosea 11:1-4	Led by God's loving kindness
Joel 2:28-29	The Spirit on all God's people
Micah 6:8	Act justly, love mercy, walk humbly
Zechariah 4:6	By the Spirit's power
Zechariah 7:9-10	God's heart for the needy

God is our Reward

*After this, the word of the L*ORD *came to Abram in a vision: "Do not be afraid, Abram. I am your shield, your very great reward."*
(Genesis 15:1)

Abram would receive many promises from God, stunning in their scope, surprising given his age and circumstances. He would be promised countless offspring (literally, so many you can't count them), a glorious reputation, a homeland, and that one of his offspring – a seed – would bring blessing to the nations. These are wonderful promises indeed and form the shape of God's story of salvation and grace towards Abram/Abraham and his family, to Israel as a people, then to all believers through Christ.

But the words of Genesis 15:1 are significant too. They are deeply personal promises to Abram, before any children or descendants appear, long before a land or people are established. God speaks before he takes another step.

God offers him divine reassurance: 'Do not be afraid.' Fear is banished, despite the presence of the living God, indeed, because of the presence of the living God! Abram doesn't know the future, but that's ok: the Lord knows.

This is personal to Abram but the promises are to each believer still, repeated often - do not be afraid. God is with us, always.

God then promises security, protection: 'I am your shield.' Not a guarantee of a trouble-free life, but surely a guarantee of God's vigilant care and protection, of rescue from harm, of the Defender over our soul. Abram would live under God's shield, even when he made terrible choices or endured loss.

The reward of faith is here too; God himself is our very great reward. The prize for Abram was real in earthly, human terms – family, descendants, honour, security, land and a future. But it was greater than that, richer and more lasting, altogether more wonderful: all these would be in God's timing, with God's presence and with the friendship of God forever, even beyond death.

By faith, he is our very great reward too. His company is the prize. Earthly blessings are real and good, but many won't last; He will. His presence, protection and prize are ours in Christ Jesus.

Reconciliation

Then he breathed his last and died and was gathered to his people, old and full of years. And his sons Esau and Jacob buried him.
(Genesis 35:29)

The Bible is full of stories of family conflict. Every family has a degree of 'trouble', with those who don't relate well or hold a grudge, those who have fallen out or don't make contact, some who are ready to pick a fight or are just a bit more distant. Thankfully, this is rarely the full story and a happy family is also a great joy.

Jacob and Esau were NOT a model of a happy family. They are famous for their falling out, the betrayal and trickery of Jacob, the threats of violence from Esau and the years spent apart. Even at their reunion, Jacob schemes and pivots to keep big brother out of reach.

The Bible reflects their actual story, not editing out the mess they made or experienced. And it also reflects the activity of God, even when Jacob literally fights with the LORD! Many a Christian has that experience of ignoring God, rebelling against his nudges to do something that is inconvenient or costly, or even flatly denying his commands at times. But Jacob went one better (or worse) and wrestled with God.

Yet, for all that, for fallouts between the brothers and the faults of Isaac along the way, this verse speaks of the tender mercy of God. The brothers bury their father, Isaac. Here at the end of a long life, the warring factions of the distrusting siblings are together.

God is able to reconcile us to himself, the most improbable of all reconciliations. So he is also able to show his tender mercy and kindness in our families, to heal hurts, to prompt forgiveness, to renew friendship, or simply bring us into the same space as one another. God is able, and God is always on the side of what is good.

Boldness as God's remnant

"But God sent me ahead of you to preserve for you a remnant on earth and to save your lives by a great deliverance." (Genesis 45:7)

The word 'remnant' – a remainder, people who are left after others are lost or move on – is a word that appears throughout the Bible. God speaks of a 'remnant' in terms of his own people: Israel, God-fearers, believers, followers and the church.

In Genesis 6-8, Noah was saved despite the flood. God preserved Noah and his family as a remnant. At the end of Genesis we read how the Lord preserved Joseph despite his brothers' wickedness, despite Potiphar's wife's lies and accusations, despite being stuck in an Egyptian prison and then despite famine striking the nations around the Nile. Through the wilderness years, most of the Israelites perished but God preserved and even grew their numbers in that desolate place. In times of oppression or exile, God preserved his people there too. And God will preserve his church.

In Acts 15:17, the remnant include 'the Gentiles who bear my name', who 'seek the Lord' (quoting Amos 9:11-12). God's people come from all nations, cultures, tribes or backgrounds and God will continue to preserve for himself a 'remnant on earth' as he did in Joseph's day. Joseph was rejected by men but raised up for a 'great deliverance'. We can be confident of our great deliverance, not through Joseph's saving plans but through Jesus' great saving death and resurrection.

In the face of outward pressure, distraction or persecution, internal conflict, criticism or sin, God has preserved and will preserve his church. So let us rejoice and rely on him, and serve him faithfully and boldly.

The Divine Name

Moses said to God, "Suppose I go to the Israelites and say to them, 'The God of your fathers has sent me to you,' and they ask me, 'What is his name?' Then what shall I tell them?"

God said to Moses, "I AM WHO I AM. This is what you are to say to the Israelites: 'I AM has sent me to you.' "

God also said to Moses, "Say to the Israelites, 'The LORD, the God of your fathers—the God of Abraham, the God of Isaac and the God of Jacob—has sent me to you.' This is my name forever, the name by which I am to be remembered from generation to generation.

(Exodus 3:13-15)

Moses wants reassurance, some sense of the qualities, significance or credit rating of the God he is taking with him into the presence of mighty Pharaoh of Egypt. What can the God from the fire, the voice from the burning bush, offer Moses and the Israelites? What will he be to them, that his name would convey or represent?

God reveals his name as 'I AM WHO I AM'. Not a title as much as a promise: what God will do and be to them rather than merely who he is. For who could fathom the living God?

The promise of this Name is of God's true and enduring presence with them. Wherever they go, 'I AM'. Whatever they face, 'I AM'. Whatever they need from him, he will fully deliver.

It is not a promise of a faltering presence that comes and goes, or a shadow of his true nature that might prove inadequate for God's plans for them. It is a statement of the intensity of his presence. He will be fully with them, for all that they need, for all of their lives, for all God's purposes in and through them to be fulfilled.

This is the LORD, Yahweh, God of promises, God who keeps his promises. He spoke to Moses of this being his name forever, a name to remember and be remembered by.

The experience of their forefathers was to be their experience: God had demonstrated his faithfulness and would continue to do so. Now we can know that God's promises receive their 'yes' in his Son, the Lord Jesus Christ, who promised to be with his disciples always (Matthew 28:20). The living God is with us, to be remembered, praised and relied on in our generation too.

Treasured possession

"'Now if you obey me fully and keep my covenant, then out of all nations you will be my treasured possession. Although the whole earth is mine, you will be for me a kingdom of priests and a holy nation.' These are the words you are to speak to the Israelites."
(Exodus 19:5-6)

When the Lord spoke to Israel in the wilderness, having rescued them from Egypt, he had saved them to be his people but said they were his 'treasured possession' – a sense of being saved up by God as something of great value to him. Now he wanted them to be 'on show' to the world. Israel was to be an example to everyone of the God they served and to whom they belonged, to reveal God's greatness, mercy, love, wisdom … his glory.

God said that the whole earth is his, but they in particular were where his focus was, with his love and his purposes. They were to represent God to the world, as a kingdom of priests, a nation set apart for God's purposes and blessing.

Today, the whole earth is still his! But now he also sees **us**, the church, those who belong to Christ by faith, as a chosen people, a kingdom of priests, a holy nation, belonging to God (1 Peter 2:9), that through us the world might see and know Jesus and his glory for themselves.

Look around at **the church**, the body of believers, and see what God has done in uniting this varied group of people around Christ Jesus. So diverse in background, interests, personality, appearance and age, yet one in Christ and God's treasured possession.

Know also that **you** are treasured by God, and ask him to help you live well for him where he has placed you.

God saves before he commands

"I am the LORD your God, who brought you out of Egypt, out of the land of slavery. You shall have no other gods before me."
(Exodus 20:2-3)

God saves before he commands. He saves before we respond with any good deeds or positive changes in our character. Saving grace comes first, not anything we do, and is a gift from God.

The words today come from the start of the Decalogue, the Ten Commandments. Before declaring these foundational commands for what a good and God-honouring life is that we are to live, before anything about what WE are to do, God reminds his people what HE has done.

He is their God. Theirs. They belong to him, as his precious possession. He loves them and has compassion on them, as he did back in Egypt before Moses was even born. They were being cruelly oppressed as a nation of slaves, lacking dignity, hope or protection. But God heard and acted, he moved in mercy and power. He brought them out of Egypt, delivered them from destruction, rescued them from slavery. He saved them from evil and death and for his blessing and new life. He brought them to himself to lead, nurture and bless. All this HE did, they didn't earn it or add to it.

This is the pattern of grace. Grace comes before the Law, not the Law before grace. It is the same in what God has done in Christ: he saved us from sin, evil and death by his own mercy and power, through what HE has done and nothing from ourselves (Ephesians 2:8-9).

Having been saved, Israel then, and believers now, are prompted out of love for God to live new lives, to change, to grow in Christ-likeness, to obey God's law.

May we rejoice in the grace shown towards us, the free gift, and gladly seek to obey God. For he is the Lord who saved us.

God of all gifts

"See, I have chosen Bezalel son of Uri, the son of Hur, of the tribe of Judah, and I have filled him with the Spirit of God, with skill, ability and knowledge in all kinds of crafts—to make artistic designs for work in gold, silver and bronze, to cut and set stones, to work in wood, and to engage in all kinds of craftsmanship." (Exodus 31:2-5)

In the book of Exodus, we read how God established his people into a new community after rescuing them from Egypt – from slavery, drudgery, hard labour and a hopeless past into a bright, free, purposeful and hopeful future. Imagine being part of that vast multitude, free to live, to work, to start a new life!

As they began their life together, God put worship at the heart of their life, with the mobile worship venue – the tabernacle, a holy Tent of Meeting – as a focal point. And God provided detailed instructions.

Today's verses tell of a master craftsman, Bezalel, gifted with 'skill, ability and knowledge ... to engage in all kinds of craftsmanship.' At the heart of their life was not simply a functional space, but crafted and curated works of art showing beauty, skill and knowledge. These also are gifts of God's Spirit. They still are.

As you go about your day, recognise how the Lord continues to give good gifts so that people can design, make, paint, cook, compose, draw, build, write, forge and engineer all kinds of things. Many of them are useful (the page or screen you are reading this on). Many of them are deliberately beautiful, whether they are meant to be 'useful' or not.

Look around today, and give thanks for the Giver, as we appreciate the gifts and the beauty and design in what God has provided.

Compassionate and gracious God

*Then the L*ORD *came down ... and proclaimed his name, the L*ORD*. And he passed in front of Moses, proclaiming, "The L*ORD*, the L*ORD*, the compassionate and gracious God, slow to anger, abounding in love and faithfulness, maintaining love to thousands, and forgiving wickedness, rebellion and sin." (Exodus 34:5-7)*

When people sign off an official letter or email, they will often include below the main text their job title or role, perhaps their qualifications or accreditation. You are unlikely to get a letter from a hospital doctor calling you to an appointment which just ends with, "Thanks, Mary xx" or a tax payment request on a postcard from "Jim in Newcastle." If you do, best ignore them!

How would the Lord of all the cosmos, the Almighty, the God of Heaven, sign off his 'post', I wonder?

Exodus 34 gives us one of the clearest reminders of how the LORD would proclaim who he is. His 'name' is who he is, what he is like, not simply a title. And the 'signature' he leaves us with is his character: compassionate and gracious, slow to anger, abounding in love and faithfulness, maintaining love to thousands, and forgiving wickedness, rebellion and sin.

This is what our God is like. It is not all he has to say, all that he is, but the fact that this form of words is repeated often, tells us how the LORD wants us to take this to heart (e.g. Numbers 14:18; 2 Chronicles 30:9; Nehemiah 9:17; Jonah 4:2).

Our God is altogether beautiful and wonderful. He delights to show his compassion to us, exercising the surprising and amazing grace of his favour, so we receive what we don't deserve (and don't receive what our sins do deserve). When we look to him in loving trust, we find this is who he is.

When we encounter him, we find what the people of God have always found, that patiently he waits for us to come to him and he works in us despite weakness, failure and erratic faithfulness on our part, whereas he is slow to anger, not impulsive or erratic. To those who turn to him, we find his love is a secure place and forgiveness is real for any wrongdoing.

He is still the same: yesterday, today and forever he is compassionate and gracious.

A memorial – 'Remember, remember'

"In the future, when your children ask you, 'What do these stones mean?' tell them that the flow of the Jordan was cut off before the ark of the covenant of the LORD. When it crossed the Jordan, the waters of the Jordan were cut off. These stones are to be a memorial to the people of Israel forever." (Joshua 4:6-7)

Do you remember when bonfire night occurs? 'Remember, Remember, the fifth of November. Gunpowder, treason and plot.' Ironic that we can easily remember the date of a potential terrorist act!

Memorials and remembrance help fix important events in our mind, as well as, for example, the people involved in wars. They are a lasting reminder of significant times, perhaps of great victory, often of great sacrifice and loss. Memorials often involve huge expense – they are tended with care, treated with respect and speak from the past into the present.

The people of God in the Bible built their own memorials at times. They piled up stones to recognise that they had met with God in particular places and heard his voice or knew his protective power.

This text comes from Joshua's experience of the Lord's dramatic provision. God made a way for his people through the water into a new home, into a new life and a hopeful future. A miraculous way, an act of power and grace by the Lord. So they set up stones to remind the next generation: see what the Lord has done here; he's a faithful and powerful God, who brought us through and gave us life.

We don't tend to build memorials in our worship services when we gather as a church. We do however have other tangible reminders: bread and wine, the water of baptism, the cross. These remind us what the Lord Jesus Christ has done for us, of his grace and mercy and power in the past, which extend into the present as we put our faith in him.

Each time we share in the communion meal we 'take, eat, drink' and 'do this in remembrance' of our Saviour and Lord. In doing so we proclaim again his glory and our hope, that God is faithful to his promises. He will bring us through life, through death, and into new life.

Remember Jesus Christ .... (2 Timothy 2:8)

Our refuge

"May the LORD repay you for what you have done. May you be richly rewarded by the LORD, the God of Israel, under whose wings you have come to take refuge." (Ruth 2:12)

These beautiful words from Boaz to Ruth are from a man in a position of power and security, with a settled home and community, to a woman with none of these. Ruth was homeless with no income or provider and a foreigner to the people of Israel. A very insecure future it seemed. How she would long for that sense of security, stability, well-being and belonging.

Boaz sees with the eyes of faith that she already has these things – from God. She has found refuge 'under his wings'. Then Boaz acts to provide and protect her; he is God's 'hands and feet' here.

The actions of Boaz honour Ruth for what she has done, for her own selflessness and care towards Naomi despite her own grief. Ruth has lost much in caring for Naomi but Boaz prays with confidence that she will gain much more under the Lord's care and blessing. The Lord Jesus would remind his disciples of this too, that God sees what we might have lost in this life and yet how much we gain in finding new life with him (Matthew 19:29).

May you know the Lord as your refuge, that you can come to him with any need or concern, and he would only want you to know peace, the security and well-being of your soul. May you know the care of others, their listening and love, and see God's kindness in that. May you know that there is no safer place than to find refuge in God, and take time to seek his company and protection today.

How great You are

"How great you are, O Sovereign LORD? There is no one like you, and there is no God but you, as we have heard with our own ears."
(2 Samuel 7:22)

The words from 2 Samuel come from a prayer. King David is responding to God who has promised a blessing on the family and house of David – his family line, his descendants – which will last forever. But this great promise came with a condition of sorts: David would not get to build the temple, his son would. Solomon would have the honour and personal glory of building a 'house' for God; David would not have that honour.

But David is still king. He had the choice: would he bow to God's words, believe in the promises of God for something not yet in his control or even in his lifetime (blessing on his descendants, the assurance of a lasting kingdom), or would he go for the prestige and personal glory within his grasp? Would he choose to build the temple anyway? He had the means, power and desire to do so.

What we find in this prayer is his heart's response revealed. Would David be *'full of God'* or would he be *'full of himself'*? The latter is a spiritually dangerous place, ultimately foolish. David is spared this by seeking after God again, meeting with him humbly in prayer.

David's prayer embraces God as 'Sovereign LORD', the one who truly reigns and has the right to rule his life. He recognises the goodness of God, the wisdom and power seen in history and in God's promises: 'There is no one like you, and there is no God but you.'

God's promises work out whether we choose to embrace them or not, and when we do choose them, we get to share in the goodness of them – the blessing – and not miss out. David's prayer calls us to be 'full of God' and avoid being 'full of ourselves' when we have our own gain, comfort, status or desires in mind and these dictate our choices. David's actions were wise in laying his hopes and fears before God, seeking him and not seeking to control.

God is great indeed, he is always good and desires our greatest good. Whatever the cost, it is wise and for our good to go with his words and ways, and humbly seek to follow.

The battle is the Lord's

He said: "Listen, King Jehoshaphat and all who live in Judah and Jerusalem! This is what the LORD says to you: 'Do not be afraid or discouraged because of this vast army. For the battle is not yours, but God's." (2 Chronicles 20:15)

God is the Creator, our Redeemer, a Promise-Maker and Promise-Keeper, our Father, and more. The Bible gives him various titles, and he is known by what he does. He is also a Warrior, the Lord of Hosts. The legions of angels that Jesus could call on, the army of Heaven, is an unseen but unimaginably powerful force.

Spiritual battles don't involve conquering land, bombing buildings, funding missile defences or stealth aircraft. They are far more 'everyday' and also unseen.

Our spiritual battles may be with doubt or discouragement, with difficult personal conflict or a breakdown of trust. It may be seeking to bring about positive change in a workplace, relating to a boss we don't like, handling stress in a godly way, resisting gossip, or holding on to God through times of physical or emotional pain. It may be shaped by our fears, our sin, our apathy, or the actions of others.

Spiritual battles are felt deeply but won't make the news. They are no less real.

In our battles, God is ever-present. He remains steadfast, unshaken, loving and full of grace and truth. He offers us his armour (Ephesians 6) and his strength.

But at times he will simply say, "The battle is not yours, but mine." We need not carry the weight of it or assume the outcome rests on us alone, for the Lord fights for us and against our enemies.

So, *'Do not be afraid or discouraged.'*

Our Advocate in heaven

"Even now my witness is in heaven. My advocate is there on high. My friends scorn me, but I pour out my tears to God. I need someone to mediate between God and me, as a person mediates between friends." (Job 16:19-21)

Have you ever felt misunderstood? Perhaps you tried to do something you thought was helpful and it turned out to be unhelpful or was simply rejected. Or you tried to offer comfort or advice and it came across all wrong or caused an eruption! Or it's a situation, which is delicate, complicated, and personal and you don't know where to begin to share it.

At times we all need someone to listen to us, perhaps without offering advice. At other times we need the wisdom of others to help us know what to do next, or what **not** to do. Or perhaps we have made a mistake or been a source of real harm and we need forgiveness.

Good news! We have a witness in heaven, an Advocate on high. One who stands for us, between us and God. Job didn't know his name but we can: Jesus Christ, the Son of God.

He stands always in God's presence to intercede, to represent, to pray. He hears our prayers and truly knows us.

He has also given us an Advocate, another Counsellor, a Comforter, to be with us: God the Holy Spirit.

So we may still be misunderstood, making mistakes, wondering what to do and at times needing someone to say: Stop! But rest in this confidence, that we have someone to whom we can take it all, who will see through the mess, handle our sins and those against us, and listen all day, every day. One full of wisdom and love who can help us to grow, learn, change and be a blessing in these tough situations.

What a friend we have in Jesus.

The whisper and thunder of God

"And these are but the outer fringe of his works; how faint the whisper we hear of him! Who then can understand the thunder of his power?" (Job 26:14)

The Book of Job is often sidelined or ignored with the impression that it's either a depressing read, one epic complaint, or just long! It starts and ends with a story of Job and his family; the central part is Job and his 'miserable comforters' or friends in conversation. It also has some of the most stunning words in the whole Bible to portray the sheer majesty and power of God, as the Creator in particular. Miss it, and miss out.

In today's verse, Job has been reflecting on the Lord's supreme power. Look up, behold the sun and moon. See the vastness and variety of the skies; consider the breadth and power of the sea. Try it today – marvel at the scale, beauty, variety and the implied power!

And Job says these are just *'the outer fringe of his works'* – just the hint of the edge of God's power, majesty and glory! These are like a faint whisper of the reality of God.

'Who then can understand the thunder of his power?'

For all the intimacy and joy of our experience of God – in singing, in gathered worship, in private prayer, in our tears, the goodness of life's precious moments – these are just the hint of the intimacy and joy to come.

For all the sense of God's power in history, revealed in the Scriptures, seen in creation, these are like faint whispers next to the deep thunder of his awesome greatness.

How great is our God, who rules over all and holds us in his hands.

Deep and life-giving wells

With joy you will draw water from the wells of salvation. In that day you will say: "Give thanks to the LORD, call on his name; make known among the nations what he has done, and proclaim that his name is exalted." (Isaiah 12:3-4)

As you read the Bible, you can't help but notice that the physical surroundings become part of the prayers, prophecies and songs – mountains, deserts, fields, rivers, etc. They are part of the actual landscape but also become part of the story. God reveals his glory or speaks his commands on mountains; he leads and feeds people in deserts; the fields become a sign of his provision; the rivers a picture of his blessings flowing to us and to the world.

In today's verses, Isaiah borrows another familiar landmark: a well. No kitchen taps in the ancient world, no coffee machines. If you want a drink, go to the well. Draw from it all that you need. Be refreshed, sustained; you and your family, your flocks and herds.

In John's Gospel, a well becomes a place to encounter Jesus in his thirst who then offers life-giving water, a new spring to flow in our hearts from him (John 4). By the well, the Son of God addresses the Samaritan woman in her greater need, honours her questions and points her to new life.

Isaiah isn't inviting us to water either but to a life-transforming source: the wells of salvation. The source of eternal life, of God's renewing and restoring grace in our lives. The well we are invited to is God, to come the LORD himself. Then 'give thanks to the LORD, call on his name,' because in him we find salvation: the forgiveness of sins, the new life from above, the adoption into God's family, the presence of God with us, a future hope secured.

Well, well!

The Lord will wipe away our tears

On this mountain he will destroy the shroud that enfolds all peoples, the sheet that covers all nations; he will swallow up death forever. The Sovereign LORD will wipe away the tears from all faces; he will remove the disgrace of his people from all the earth. The LORD has spoken. (Isaiah 25:7-8)

Our God is awesome in power yet full of tenderness. He rules over the affairs of nations but draws near to us in our intimate needs and in our sorrow. There is no God like the Lord.

Today's words remind us that even death will be overcome; the final enemy we each face that 'enfolds all peoples' and none escape, will be stripped of its power. This, of course, was achieved through Jesus who died our death, carrying our sins, who went down into the grave and defeated death itself to rise again, gloriously alive, as conqueror of sin and death. He has dealt with it; 'he will swallow up death forever' is a promise we can trust as we put our lives into the hands of Christ Jesus.

He has ultimate power over death; it will not have the final word for those in Christ.

But he is also tender towards us as we grieve in this life, as we feel the shadow and pain of death, or shame over our sins and wrongdoing. Whether grief or shame or pain, whatever prompts tears: 'The Sovereign LORD will wipe away the tears' from our faces.

Whatever you carry in hurt, sorrow, fear or shame, he is able to receive it, to bring healing and fresh comfort. He is the LORD and he is able.

Strength to the weary

*Do you not know? Have you not heard? The L*ORD *is the everlasting God, the Creator of the ends of the earth. He will not grow tired or weary, and his understanding no one can fathom. He gives strength to the weary and increases the power of the weak. Even youths grow tired and weary, and young men stumble and fall; but those who hope in the L*ORD *will renew their strength. They will soar on wings like eagles; they will run and not grow weary, they will walk and not be faint.*
(Isaiah 40:28-31)

Chapter 40 of Isaiah is an extended song or declaration in praise of God for his supremacy over all things, his sovereignty over all of history and rule over the nations and their leaders. Leaders will be swept away like mere chaff in a whirlwind; people are like grasshoppers in comparison to the one who stretches out the cosmos like a giant canopy (verses 22-24).

Well might he say: "To whom will you compare me? Or who is my equal?" says the Holy One. (v. 25)

No one is the answer. No one compares to him in strength, power, scope, insight, beauty, glory, holiness, wisdom or justice. How good that we can trust the affairs of history as a whole or the details of our lives to a God like this.

Yet as the people of Isaiah's day looked at their circumstances, they wondered if this amazing God had perhaps taken his eye off the ball, grown tired or disinterested in them, or maybe he despaired of their constant failure to be faithful. They were exiled from home after generations of rebellion, idolatry, wickedness and rejection of God's promises. Would God help?

The answer to their doubts and questions is remarkable, touching and encouraging. Not only is the Lord himself tireless and his wisdom beyond our understanding, so we can trust him when we don't understand, but he also sustains his people. He is our strength.

He sees and knows that even those who feel young or strong will stumble or fall; faith will seem tough at times, God may seem distant, serving God well might be draining our reserves. But he enables us to persevere by being renewed with his strength, not ours alone. By grace, he enables us to soar with fresh freedom and energy, to run the race with perseverance, to keep on walking without losing heart.

God is our strength, his strength is seen in our weakness, and his grace is sufficient to renew and empower us afresh.

Oaks of righteousness

They will be called oaks of righteousness, a planting of the LORD for the display of his splendour. They will rebuild the ancient ruins and restore the places long devastated; they will renew the ruined cities that have been devastated for generations. (Isaiah 61:3-4)

If anyone were to check my phone and the photos on there, they might wonder why there are so many of **trees**. But I love trees! There is something about the variety, the strength of them, the way they provide shelter, the grandeur of some and sheer size of others, their sky-reaching lines and changing nature through the seasons. No? Just me?

A tree that is dying or lacking nutrients can be sustained by the health and protection of the surrounding trees. Recently the 'Wood Wide Web' has been discovered, how trees communicate via a highly complex underground fungal network. Their own social media!

God also loves trees, he invented them, and the Bible speaks of a tree often as a picture of that which is strong, steadfast, upright, glorious even. In today's verses, the prophet Isaiah tells of how the Lord will transform the lives of the poor, the blind, the captive, the broken-hearted (verses 1-2) and he will make THEM to be 'oaks of righteousness, a planting of the LORD, for the display of his splendour.'

God will take the very people who seemed spiritually lost, blind to his grace and his ways, captive to sin, or broken-hearted by life's trials, and make THEM the focus of his triumph – strong and majestic trees to show what he has done. And THEY will be the means to renew and restore the land, the lost cities, and the broken places. (Jesus preached this same promise of God's favour through him in Luke 4.)

God is still growing that which is strong and secure, people of faith planted in Christ, rooted well in God's word and his love. We can be a testimony to his work, 'oaks of righteousness', with weaker trees sustained and protected by the strong perhaps as God grows the church. All part of God's kingdom and his means to serve his kingdom, a thriving 'forest' to renew our society and proclaim God's good news.

Treemendous.

"Amen, Lord"

"I said, 'Obey me and do everything I command you, and you will be my people, and I will be your God. Then I will fulfill the oath I swore to your ancestors, to give them a land flowing with milk and honey'—the land you possess today."
I answered, "Amen, Lord." (Jeremiah 11:4-5)

The prophet Jeremiah receives very direct commands from the Lord God at this point, whilst he still lives within very challenging circumstances. The people are physically vulnerable under a foreign power, removed from their familiar comfort zones of home and culture, facing an uncertain future, and giving Jeremiah a hard time by rejecting him and his message.

No wonder Jeremiah complains honestly and often!

The commands of God, the 'word of the LORD' to his chosen prophet, carry divine power in that they are surely true and good even in such a hard place and with seemingly insurmountable problems. So Jeremiah is able to hold onto the promises in them: in short, 'do this, and I will bless you.' In this case, the promise of God's assured presence and protection and the provision of a generous and good land, 'flowing with milk and honey'.

What is Jeremiah's response?

Does he point to the problems? Does he ask for a timescale? Does he question whether this is realistic? No – he simply says, "Amen, Lord."

In the original Hebrew, apparently this is just the one word to God: 'Amen'. 'Agreed.' Just a one - word answer! Sometimes, that is all that is needed from us to God. A direct answer of faith: uncomplicated, without reservation, not knowing the full details or outcome.

God generously tends to provide us with more wisdom, more details, the input of friends or our own experience. He graciously helps us, moves our will to want to obey more readily when it is still costly, inconvenient, demanding or the outcome is unclear. But sometimes he simply says, I want you to trust, to obey, to do this.

And then the answer 'Amen, Lord' may be all that we can offer or all that is needed. In such obedience, we can also know true joy.

May you know the joy of simple trust, the glad heart that says, 'Amen, Lord.'

New every morning

Yet this I call to mind and therefore I have hope: Because of the LORD's great love we are not consumed, for his compassions never fail. They are new every morning; great is your faithfulness.

I say to myself, "The LORD is my portion; therefore I will wait for him." The LORD is good to those whose hope is in him, to the one who seeks him; it is good to wait quietly for the salvation of the LORD.

(Lamentations 3:21-26)

The Lamentations of the prophet Jeremiah are five chapters of rich and heartfelt reflections on suffering. Carefully structured as a poem, it offers a resource for national lament for the Israelites over the fate of Jerusalem, but also for the personal grief of the individual. The tone of the book is one of being overwhelmed with sorrow. By including this in the Bible, it reminds us that the God who rules over history and who speaks to us is one who knows our hurts, tears, deep grief and desolations.

These words from chapter 3, the heart of the book, are like a fresh ray of sunlight into the prevailing darkness, like a new dawn after deep night. There has been precious little note of hope so far amidst honest grief and the depths of sorrow.

True grief honestly expressed is a healthy emotion and part of our healing. God is no less present in the dark as in the light (Psalm 139:12), his love and light cannot be fully extinguished whatever we face.

So here we see the precious hope in each new morning, even in the worst of times God's great love cannot be obscured, his compassions never fail, because his faithfulness is great indeed. Indeed, he is completely faithful: he will always be with and for his people.

Therefore we can have hope, and put our hope in him. We can find rest in his love, mercy, presence and faithfulness. We can look up with faith and know confidently that he still sustains his people through Christ our Saviour, our great high priest (Hebrew 4:16).

We can lay our grief and needs before this God of infinite compassion; our soul can 'wait quietly for the salvation of the LORD.'

High, holy and awesome God

Then there came a voice from above the expanse over their heads as they stood with lowered wings. Above the expanse over their heads was what looked like a throne of sapphire, and high above on the throne was a figure like that of a man. ... Like the appearance of a rainbow in the clouds on a rainy day, so was the radiance around him.

This was the appearance of the likeness of the glory of the LORD. When I saw it, I fell facedown, and I heard the voice of one speaking.
(Ezekiel 1:25-28)

Some things we experience are inexpressible. We can't put them into words. We can try, but the words fall short of doing justice to the experience, the detail, the impact and the reality.

We might relate to this from trying to describe an event which left us reeling with joy, surprise or awe: the birth of a child, healing from a terrible illness, a beautiful mountain view, a sporting triumph or a success in some way against all the odds. Or maybe from an encounter with God in his kindness, grace, forgiveness and love.

Ezekiel had a day like this. He saw the heavens opened and 'visions of God' (v. 1). He attempts to convey what he has seen and is drawn to **who** he has seen: the LORD in his beauty, majesty and glory.

'Glory' conveys immense worth, great weightiness and substance, true beauty, splendour and power. The God of all glory has these to the greatest extent. He has holy glory in all that he is and does, and Ezekiel is struggling to put words to this. We can pick out just two aspects of this vision: altitude and light.

Ezekiel sees storms, lightning and clouds in the sky. In the clouds and fire are fantastic holy creatures, themselves glorious and beautiful, high above the earth, and the spirit of God moving powerfully over the earth. Above these are 'an expanse, sparkling like ice, and awesome.' (v. 22) Immeasurably great and high and wide. And yet, even further above this is a throne and one like a man: the unimaginable altitude of God's dwelling above Ezekiel.

God is high and holy, but still reveals himself to Ezekiel and now through Christ.

The vision is also full of light, colour and radiance. God is full of beauty, there is no darkness in him. For all the justified awe and fear of Ezekiel's encounter, we are reminded that God's holiness is unapproachable unless we are made holy. We are invited to gaze and even to know a good God, high and holy, who speaks still.

The LORD our Shepherd

"I myself will tend my sheep and have them lie down, declares the Sovereign LORD. I will search for the lost and bring back the strays. I will bind up the injured and strengthen the weak, but the sleek and the strong I will destroy. I will shepherd the flock with justice."
(Ezekiel 34:15-16)

God is revealed in the Old Testament as a Father to his children, a refuge and strength to the weak, a warrior without rival, Yahweh the promise-making and promise-keeping LORD. He is our provider, ruler, shelter and rescuer. To Moses he is revealed as 'compassionate and gracious, slow to anger, abounding in love and faithfulness' (Exodus 34:6). He is also no pushover; he will not tolerate injustice and he loves his people.

Ezekiel confronts the religious leaders of his day for their abuse of power, their pride and greed, their self-serving desire for their own status and riches. They show indifference towards God's people, even oppressing the faithful. God will not tolerate this indefinitely.

With strong words of rebuke and judgement, the LORD himself condemns such behaviour. He stands against corrupt, abusive or unfaithful leaders still, those in the world but in the church especially. Those who teach and lead will be judged more strictly (James 3:1; Romans 2:21; Revelation 2:2,20).

The remarkable promise here and wonderful insight into the character of God is not that he will send better shepherds. Thankfully, there are many faithful, godly, kind leaders of God's people in every generation and upright, compassionate leaders in civic roles too. The great word of hope to Israel is not simply better leaders but that the LORD himself will be their shepherd.

In words that echo elsewhere (Psalm 23; Micah 5:4; Isaiah 40:11), the LORD promises to lead his people and do so rightly – with justice. He will make them lie down, tend to their needs, restore them. He will also directly oppose those concerned for their own status or full of their own importance, those invested in their popularity and indifferent to the needs of the flock. The 'sleek and the strong' self-interested leaders of Israel had forgotten the true Shepherd. He loves his people and will not stand idly by.

In Jesus we meet that good Shepherd in person (John 10:11). He still pursues those who are lost and wandering, heals the hurting and opposes the proud. We can entrust ourselves to him.

Renewed hearts

'I will gather you from all the countries and bring you back into your own land. I will sprinkle clean water on you, and you will be clean; I will cleanse you from all your impurities and from all your idols. I will give you a new heart and put a new spirit in you; I will remove from you your heart of stone and give you a heart of flesh. And I will put my Spirit in you and move you to follow my decrees and be careful to keep my laws.' (Ezekiel 36:24-27)

Many religions include rituals and practices which relate to getting clean, such as the washing of hands, the bathing in a sacred river, the use of holy water. In Christianity, as we pass through the water in baptism it is a symbol of how we are made clean.

The need to get clean is a natural instinct, however the desire to be clean on the inside is not natural but needs our spiritual eyes to be opened to see it. God graciously comes to us and reveals our inner life in need of the deep clean, that inner renewal of the heart and mind, of our will and desires, purifying us from sin's penalty.

No detergent, 10-step programme, anti-virus software or mindfulness guru can sort out the root issue: we need a new heart. The problem is deep-seated. But God knows us inside out and looks on us with compassion and power, as the Lord Jesus does throughout the gospels.

The promises to Ezekiel put all the emphasis on what God will do rather than what we can do. We are unable to clean our hearts by ourselves; our place is to come before God in humble faith, in repentance and looking for his mercy.

In a seven-fold string of commitments, the LORD God states his intention for the complete rescue of our situation by a heart transplant: removing a heart of stone (dead to God) and giving us a heart of flesh (alive to him). Spiritual transformation is offered to us.

The outcome of God's plan is that we are made clean, holy. We are set free from the grip and corruption of looking to idols for our help and instead we look to him. We are renewed, restored, with a new 'heart and spirit'. And he will work in our heart and mind by his Spirit, producing glad desires to live in obedience to his ways.

What God promised Ezekiel is the reality for every Christian today. To be 'washed ... sanctified ... justified in the name of the Lord Jesus Christ and by the Spirit of our God.' (1 Corinthians 6:11) Come and be clean, come be renewed, come for a heart alive to his Spirit.

From dust to glory

But at that time your people—everyone whose name is found written in the book—will be delivered. Multitudes who sleep in the dust of the earth will awake: some to everlasting life, others to shame and everlasting contempt. Those who are wise will shine like the brightness of the heavens, and those who lead many to righteousness, like the stars for ever and ever. (Daniel 12:1-3)

God holds in store a promise for his people: eternal life, a life blessed by the God of eternity, a life of lasting joy and in his presence.

The Old Testament is full of confident expectation in life beyond death for those known to the Lord, even if there is mystery for those before Christ of what it is like, where, and how God enables this. It is a sure hope though, not vague positive thinking or mere superstition. God's people will be 'delivered', saved, made whole and free.

Daniel has a vision behind the scenes of history, a sense of God's activity in his present, near future and perhaps far future. He sees that God knows those who truly belong to him, who stand with God by faith, and as a covenant-keeping God he will stand by them. He calls them righteous on account of their faith in him.

Their names are recorded 'in the book', a heavenly register. Jesus himself said his disciples are to 'rejoice that your names are written in heaven.' (Luke 10:20) This book of life records names and deeds; God's judgement will be full and true (Revelation 20:12-15).

Daniel sees that to lie in the dust is not the end: those in Christ will rest in peace but will indeed rise in glory. We will all rise, physically resurrected, and stand in the place of judgement. God will oversee a great division between the righteous and the unrighteous, those who trusted him by faith and rested on his love, and those who turned from him and loved their own way. Our actions in life will be known.

God's own will rise to everlasting life and forever shine like the heavens, like the stars. God's people will enjoy the light of God's presence, reflect the light of his love, be glorified with him forever. Those who are his are described as 'wise'; the greatest wisdom in this life is to choose Christ and life from him, and then to shape a life around his will and ways. Such a life has an impact, bringing others to seek after God, leading them to righteousness.

Resurrection and eternal life, welcomed into a forever home, clothed in the light and glory of Christ's righteousness, your name known to the Lord, blessed for eternity. May this be your confident hope too.

The gateway of hope

"But then I will win her back once again. I will lead her into the desert and speak tenderly to her there. I will return her vineyards to her and transform the Valley of Trouble into a gateway of hope. She will give herself to me there, as she did long ago when she was young, when I freed her from her captivity in Egypt." (Hosea 2:14-15, NLT)

The LORD God promised ancient Israel, his chosen but unfaithful people, that he still had a good future for them. He would remain faithful to his promises, as always, and was able to bring blessing from the most unpromising situations.

These verses from the prophet Hosea picture a stunning and wonderful reversal of fortune for Israel. He would bring them from a desert back to vineyards: from a place of barren, harsh struggle to a place of plenty, growth and provision. He describes this change for his beloved people as transforming 'the Valley of Trouble into a gateway of hope', and Israel's response as a glad surrender: 'She will give herself to me' – the wife returns to her loving Husband.

Do you find yourself in a desert place, a time of struggle in life or faith? Are there challenges and demands which could wear you down, strains in relationships, guilt over the past, or sorrow and grief perhaps – a 'valley of trouble'? The Lord is still active in the desert places, still able to bring you blessing, and turn this valley into 'a gateway of hope', the path into renewed life.

Give yourself to him, in the valley, and hold on to the hope he still offers. He is faithful and loving, always.

Led by God's loving kindness

"When Israel was a child, I loved him, and out of Egypt I called my son. But the more I called Israel, the further they went from me. They sacrificed to the Baals and they burned incense to images.

It was I who taught Ephraim to walk, taking them by the arms; but they did not realize it was I who healed them. I led them with cords of human kindness, with ties of love; I lifted the yoke from their neck and bent down to feed them." (Hosea 11:1-4)

Jesus instructs his disciples to address God as our Father - that is the privilege of all God's children by faith in Christ. The scriptures reaffirm this Fatherhood of God in both the Old and New Testaments and this title is for us to address him by. But he is neither male nor female; it is a title not a biological or gender identity. He is our Father in heaven and we experience this in how he shows his authority, leadership care and protection over his family.

He is also full of tenderness and mercy. Jesus speaks of his care over Jerusalem as like a hen over her chicks (Matthew 23:27). The Lord speaks of his motherly comfort over her child (Isaiah 66:13). God's parenting skills encompass all that is good, true, loving, kind, strong and necessary in the best of earthly parents, both a father and a mother.

Hosea's words capture something of God's tender care of his people as being similar to a parent teaching a little one to walk; unsteady and faltering they need support, direction and help. God's loving kindness is reflected in our lives wherever we express human kindness, in the support and care of children or adults, of family or strangers.

God is the source of all good gifts and Hosea calls the bruised people of God of his time to find healing, help, loving kindness and the relief of their burdens from the living God.

We can come to God our Father and to our Lord Jesus Christ, who have shown us great mercy in rescuing us from sin and bringing us into God's family. The loving kindness of God does not stop there though: we are saved from sin but saved for new life, to enjoy God's friendship and to show and tell of his kindness and grace to those we encounter today. Many more need his love, to be lifted up from the burdens of sorrow or injustice or anxiety, and enjoy walking securely with God.

The Spirit on all God's people

"I will pour out my Spirit on all people. Your sons and daughters will prophesy, your old men will dream dreams, your young men will see visions. Even on my servants, both men and women, I will pour out my Spirit in those days." (Joel 2:28-29)

God is abundantly generous. He doesn't do things by halves. Look at the absurd but deliberate abundance of Creation: some 360 types of hummingbird, more than 25,000 types of orchid. He gives life to billions of people, to the bewildering array of animals. He cares and sees.

He is not stingy with resources for spiritual life either but pours it out, as if from a limitless fountain. He doesn't drip feed his Holy Spirit over a few people (the 'most qualified' of disciples) but lavishly pours out his Spirit on all those who know him, on every single Christian.

So we can be confident that God has given us and will give us all that we need to fulfil his good purposes for our lives. His kingdom has no budget, no recession, no limit. His Holy Spirit flows to God's people and fills them.

Sometimes his activity is seen in powerful and dramatic ways of healing, courage under pressure, a breakthrough with a person or someone coming to faith for the first time. Often we know him in the everyday reality that he is with us, as he promised, in the gentle encouragement or kind word, and in the countless good things we enjoy.

What Joel heard as a promise to men and women of faith is seen in the church at large today, enabled and empowered by God, blessed and led by the Spirit, who shapes us where we work, rest, play and dream.

Thank you Lord, pour out your Spirit on us today.

Act justly, love mercy, walk humbly

He has showed you, O man, what is good. And what does the LORD require of you? To act justly and to love mercy and to walk humbly with your God. (Micah 6:8)

Imagine if every government aspired to this: to act justly, to love mercy and to walk humbly with the true God. Can you imagine what a difference that would make to the tone, the direction, the priorities and the impact? Imagine if any business, office environment, team, church ministry or home managed to echo these words clearly, joyfully and consistently – what a blessing that would be!

It's hard to imagine perhaps, even though we see wonderful examples at times, and hopefully see it in church life too. But it's also easier to point the finger away from ourselves and apply this famous verse to other people. We all want justice but it can easily become low-level anger, revenge, settling of scores or reputation management. That's why justice is tied to mercy.

In God's kingdom, justice is a priority – the right ordering of his world for good and against evil, and right relationships between people. So we work, plan and pray for justice and against injustice. But we are never to lose sight of mercy. Mercy looks on ourselves and sees we won't always get it right, and looks on others with similar patience and compassion.

So we seek to live and act justly, to do what is right. That is often costly and tough. Justice isn't easy. No wonder we are called to love mercy, to delight to be merciful and hold back from harshness, to be slow to anger and resist unjust criticism.

And in all this, the LORD is with us. In the mess or frustration of an unjust world, he's here. We can walk with him, humbly, for HE is the Lord (not us) and is able to lead us in this broken and beautiful world.

By the Spirit's power

So he said to me, "This is the word of the LORD to Zerubbabel: 'Not by might nor by power, but by my Spirit,' says the LORD Almighty."
(Zechariah 4:6)

One of the plainest realities about God is this: He speaks. He spoke Creation into being, he spoke in history, he spoke to and through his people and his Son, through prophets and apostles. He still speaks through his Word, the Bible. Behind all these, in all these, is the Spirit of God speaking what is good and true.

They are also words of power, they change things. He still speaks through the Bible, in our conscience, in the silence, in our struggles, through godly people, through the events of history, even in dreams.

Today's verse is a reminder that in his wisdom he often speaks to us something that we need to hear repeatedly: "This is not all down to you." We do not need to rely on our **own** resources, wits, money or energy to achieve the good things **God** has planned. We don't need to rely on ourselves. In fact, it's not wise to do so; that's a path to exhaustion and disappointment.

Rather, there is a greater power at work on our behalf for God's purposes: ***the Spirit of God***.

Where God wants to bring about change (the change of our attitudes or in the heart of another person, the growing faith in a child or a spouse, the deeper sense of real forgiveness in our own lives, spiritual fruit in the church, lives changed by the gospel through the church, greater justice in the world, etc.), guess what? It isn't resting – ultimately – on our abilities or efforts! It's not by OUR might or power, but by the Spirit.

His power brought creation into being, divided seas, made the Sun stand still and raised the Son from the grave. His power, his Spirit, is still at work to see God's kingdom come.

We pray, plan and work to see this kingdom in our lives, homes, community and nation. Today let's look to and rely on the Spirit's power – more of his power, even in our weakness.

God's heart for the needy

This is what the LORD Almighty says: 'Administer true justice; show mercy and compassion to one another. Do not oppress the widow or the fatherless, the alien or the poor. In your hearts do not think evil of each other.' (Zechariah 7:9-10)

Wherever you begin, you won't get far in reading through the Old Testament and not come across this clear emphasis: God's heart for the needy. It is everywhere: in the experience of God's people, in the protections and instructions of the law, in the protests and commands of the prophets, in the prayers of the Psalms and the wisdom of Proverbs.

In hundreds of texts, the character of God is revealed in this way, that he sides with and has deep compassion for those who lack power, status, earthly protection or security, and therefore are often more vulnerable to injustice and oppression.

He commands and expects his people to act with justice towards the poor or the vulnerable (Isaiah 1:17), to be open-handed and generous (Deuteronomy 15:11), to defend their rights and work to rescue them from evil or those who oppress (Psalm 82:3-4; Proverbs 31:9), and in all this be mindful that God is their Maker and ours, to whom we will give account (Proverbs 14:31; 17:5; 22:2).

Zechariah presents four commands: administer true justice; show mercy and compassion; do not oppress; do not think evil of others.

True justice protects the vulnerable, it does not criminalise those seeking refuge and it does not favour those with power.

Mercy and compassion require action not indifference, as the parable of the Good Samaritan illustrates. Compassion moves us to respond not merely shrug.

Oppressing the poor is seen, for example, with land grabs, harsh taxation, discrimination with access to legal representation or public services, unjust trade or harsh working conditions.

To think evil of others might include when we demonise the 'other', labelling or blaming the stranger or foreigner, maligning the motives of those seeking help. The LORD knows our hearts and words.

God stands behind his words, he looks with love on all he has made. How might we live differently? How are our hearts challenged?

3

SONGS OF FAITH: THE PSALMS

Blaise Pascal was a French mathematician, scientific pioneer, philosopher and Christian. He spoke of a 'God-shaped vacuum in the heart of each man which cannot be satisfied by any created thing but only by God the Creator, made know through Jesus Christ.' We are naturally searching for God. He also described chess as the 'gymnasium for the mind'. Quite the wordsmith!

With the Book of Psalms, that search finds great treasure. Here we can enter a rich encounter with the living God. And here is a gymnasium for the soul.

The Psalms are both songs and prayers – written for the community of faith – for gathered worship and prayer. They have been used as such for millennia and no doubt will continue to do so until the Lord returns. As with all God's word, they are timeless. They also speak to the individual believer, framed as they are in the hopes, struggles, heart-cries of faith and joy, of anger and despair, reflecting the spiritual depths of the ancient writers, enabling us to explore these as we engage with God today.

Here is a selection from 30 of the Psalms, spanning 1 to 150. May you find here something new of the fullness of knowing God through Jesus Christ, may your be heart filled and encouraged, and may this strengthen and stretch your spiritual muscles in this ancient and fabulous gym.

The life God in which God delights

Psalm 1

Blessed is the man who does not walk in the counsel of the wicked or stand in the way of sinners or sit in the seat of mockers.

But his delight is in the law of the LORD, and on his law he meditates day and night. He is like a tree planted by streams of water, which yields its fruit in season and whose leaf does not wither. Whatever he does prospers.

Not so the wicked! They are like chaff that the wind blows away. Therefore the wicked will not stand in the judgment, nor sinners in the assembly of the righteous.

For the LORD watches over the way of the righteous, but the way of the wicked will perish.

The first Psalm. The gateway to the whole treasure trove, wondrous grand palace and densely rich forest of the 150 Psalms. This is the threshold into the breadth of the Psalms' worship of the living God, its teaching of the walk of faith and the heart-filling and emotion-stretching range of all that lies beyond this first prayer.

It both beckons us in and also sets out the key orientation or priority: there is a good and godly life to be found, a flourishing new and eternal life with the Lord, but it comes from actively choosing to reject the worthless deceptions of worldly voices and values and instead listen to him, drawing our life from his word. One way to death, another to life. Choose well.

The entrance begins with the invitation to set our life like a well-watered tree, shunning the folly of the world's falsehoods, the worthless or ungodly distractions for the life-giving wisdom, nourishment, power and goodness of God and his words. Here is life!

A disciple going God's way is like a tree with good roots, ever flourishing, sustained through storms or droughts, bearing fruit in their life and offering shelter for others. Delighting in God and his words, we are branches of the true vine, ever fruitful, with God's life within us (John 15:1-8).

May God root us in his love and his word, sustain us through days of tears and bless us with joyful hope and his Spirit's encouragement. May he bring lasting growth in us and blessing through our lives.

Body and soul cry out

Psalm 6:2-5

Be merciful to me, LORD, for I am faint;
O LORD, heal me, for my bones are in agony.
My soul is in anguish.
How long, O LORD, how long?
Turn, O LORD, and deliver me;
save me because of your unfailing love.
No one remembers you when he is dead.
Who praises you from the grave?

A recent bestselling book presented a fascinating study of the interaction between our physical and emotional well-being and trauma, entitled *The Body Keeps the Score*, by Bessel van der Kolk. Our bodies can reflect our state of mind, our inner emotions, just as our emotional or spiritual states of well-being are affected by physical health. Feeling nervous? Our hands go cold, our tummy rumbles. Feeling excited? Our pulse races, muscles tense. Grief affects our appetite, shock can make us numb, joy can make us cry!

The Psalms are full of links between how we feel in our bodies and what is going on in our thoughts, our spirit. God has made us like this, our bodies are both valuable and vulnerable; they can tell us how we are more than we sometimes recognise.

Today's Psalm reflects that: the writer feels fear in his bones. Deep concern, dread or worry. He reaches out, looks up, knowing God is not simply full of power but also of steadfast love. He looks to God for mercy, physical relief perhaps, and so can we.

And in this life, this physical earthly life, even when our bones are shaking, worries mount up or we live with pain, the Lord is near and worthy of our praise. Who can give him praise from the dead? We can. We can praise him today.

How majestic is your Name

Psalm 8

O LORD, our Lord, how majestic is your name in all the earth!

You have set your glory above the heavens. From the lips of children and infants you have ordained praise because of your enemies, to silence the foe and the avenger.

When I consider your heavens, the work of your fingers, the moon and the stars, which you have set in place, what is man that you are mindful of him, the son of man that you care for him?

You made him a little lower than the heavenly beings and crowned him with glory and honour. You made him ruler over the works of your hands; you put everything under his feet: all flocks and herds, and the beasts of the field, the birds of the air, and the fish of the sea, all that swim the paths of the seas.

O LORD, our Lord, how majestic is your name in all the earth!

Consider the majesty of **God** in creation. When have you experienced awe and wonder at what you see, where you stand, at the scale or beauty of creation?

Consider how small **we** are, consider our weakness and vulnerability in comparison to the vast reach of the cosmos. Humanity stands before God, finite and fragile, yet we are the centre of the focus of his love within all he has made.

Consider **Christ**, through whom all this was made and for whom it was made, and to whom all things will give praise when creation is restored. For now, even the stones will cry out if we don't!

Consider how God **speaks** – through the reflected power, majesty, beauty and awe of creation, through his Word, and through his Son. May we listen well, serve gladly and obediently, and give praise to the God over all, who has done great things.

Why pray?

Psalm 9:10-11 *Those who know your name will trust in you, for you, LORD, have never forsaken those who seek you. Sing praises to the LORD, enthroned in Zion; proclaim among the nations what he has done.*

Why pray? Why can we pray for anything with confidence that we will be heard, and heard with clarity and mercy and kindness, and know that God might be inclined to act? Why pray at all?

Because the Lord has already shown his character. Because he is on the throne, not us. Because we can look back and see what he has done.

David wrote this Psalm having experienced the Lord's help already. He had concrete evidence of God's kindness and power, his righteousness in bringing about the downfall of evil and corruption, of leading and protecting his people, of Goliath's proud boasts amounting to nothing. David could look back on his own life and to Abraham, Jacob, Moses, Joshua and others and see: the Lord delivers on his promises.

So why can we pray? Because he is the Lord, he is still the only one on the throne; he is still building his kingdom and inviting people into it. He is still a 'stronghold for the oppressed' who does not forsake his own.

We pray because of who he is, what he is like, what he has done and what he has promised. We can pray because we can look back at the glorious Son of God, what he has done for us, his promises and saving power.

We can pray with confidence 'may your kingdom come.'

The eyes of the LORD

Psalm 11:4-5

The Lord is in his holy temple; the Lord is on his heavenly throne.
He observes the sons of men; his eyes examine them.
The Lord examines the righteous,
but the wicked and those who love violence his soul hates.

We live in a world with much moral confusion, political upheaval, what passes for wisdom but lacks truth, and many who are resistant or indifferent to God. It can be very unsettling. When it gets personal – in a family or in the workplace – it can even be distressing.

Much of the New Testament speaks to the church under pressure, facing similar circumstances to ours 2000 years ago, and calls them to faith, hope and love. To stand firm, to hold fast and to keep their eyes on Jesus. Many of the Old Testament prophets had the same urgent message.

Psalm 11 has a similar call with a note of great confidence: look at who is on the throne. Above the entire cosmos is the Lord – above the mess, the confusion (including within the church where it craves worldly approval) and the wars and abuses. Above the plain wickedness in this world at times, there is One on the throne. It is not about how **removed** he is, but about who **rules**. It doesn't portray the Lord as **inactive** but so **attentive**.

The gaze of the Lord is on the world, to behold, test and finally judge. He will deal with the righteous and the wicked. God truly loves what is good, but he truly hates is evil. Justice will be done.

So we take heart. Look up. See by faith who loves us, and his gaze is on his people.

Safe ground, God's promises

Psalm 12:3-7

May the LORD cut off all flattering lips and every boastful tongue that says, "We will triumph with our tongues; we own our lips—who is our master?"

"Because of the oppression of the weak and the groaning of the needy, I will now arise," says the LORD. "I will protect them from those who malign them."

And the words of the LORD are flawless, like silver refined in a furnace of clay, purified seven times.

O LORD, you will keep us safe and protect us from such people forever.

Psalm 12 is written in a world where truth and integrity seem scarce, even unknown, and God's people could feel at the mercy of lies, injustice, corruption, fake news and more. Perhaps David was surrounded by plots, rumours, bad advice and religious prophets more concerned with ease and popularity than God's plain truth.

But the Lord hears, as so often he hears the 'groaning' of his people, and he will respond.

'I will now rise up', says the Lord. His response is certain and decisive. It is not 'now', in this moment; we still wait for the kingdom to come in all its fullness. Not immediate, but 'now' conveys that his coming is so certain as to be present.

Compared to the attractive half-truths, subtle spin, outright lies, empty promises or delusions of this world, his Word is so good. Compared to the emptiness from some in politics, false teachers of religion or Bible-less pulpits, conspiracy theorists, unreliable journalists or deliberate scammers, his Word is so pure, true, reliable, life-giving.

This Word from above is sufficient to give us a secure ground on which to build (John 1:1-2). This Word will come in judgement on the world, certain and decisive, just not yet.

As Jesus said, 'Then you will know the truth, and the truth will set you free.' Set on his secure foundation, we are free to live for God, to live at peace knowing what is true and what matters, and to live securely in an uncertain world.

God's holy presence

Psalm 15:1-3 (NLT)

Who may worship in your sanctuary, L ORD? Who may enter your presence on your holy hill?

Those who lead blameless lives and do what is right, speaking the truth from sincere hearts.

Those who refuse to gossip or harm their neighbours or speak evil of their friends.

The presence of God is a holy presence. Moses was commanded to take his shoes off. Joshua fell down on his face. Daniel was speechless. The apostle John had to be lifted up. The temple mob who came to arrest Jesus fell before him.

It's a presence that topples idols and brings death to those who attempt to storm into it while indifferent to sin and the need for holiness. His presence is a place of joy and security for those invited in by grace.

It's a holy space yet amazingly God has invited us to come in, to enter, for he can make us clean. In Christ he has ripped through the curtain, broken the dividing wall and has gone through the heavens ahead of us.

Today's Psalm calls us to not take this lightly. We are still to live holy lives, if we claim to know a holy God with us. This calls us to a holy 'walk with God' that does what is right, speaks the truth, resists slander and unjust criticism, and shuns evil towards others.

God is holy. He invites us to be near but transforms us as we abide with him. May the world see this in us too.

Darkness to light

Psalm 18:28 *You, O LORD, keep my lamp burning; my God turns my darkness into light.*

A recurring pattern in the Bible is this: God can turn a situation around. What seems impossible for us is not for him. What seems hopeless for us is the very place where God is still working for good, still present and active. God may be silent, he is never absent.

That power to transform our experience or our everyday reality is captured here in Psalm 18 too. King David wrote for others to use this as a prayer or a song, so we can use this today.

'You, O LORD, keep my lamp burning' – God sustains that which would otherwise run out: our energy levels, our compassion, our patience, our hope, our love and our faith. His resources are infinite where ours are not, so he keeps the 'lamp burning'. A lamp would need tending to keep the oil levels sufficient, to check that the wick was not too long and ensure that the lamp had not blown out. God tends and cares for our soul; he will not break us but knows we are fragile at times.

'My God turns my darkness into light' – the Lord doesn't simply offer his presence, his friendship. He also has transforming power. He can radically change how we are and how we feel. Sometimes he changes circumstances (he heals us, provides a job, brings new resources or relationships improve), but more often than not he changes our perspective too – from 'darkness to light'.

May we know the presence and favour of the Lord today, and the friendship of Jesus who is the light of the world.

The heavens declare

Psalm 19:1-4

The heavens declare the glory of God; the skies proclaim the work of his hands.

Day after day they pour forth speech; night after night they display knowledge.

There is no speech or language where their voice is not heard.

Their voice goes out into all the earth, their words to the ends of the world.

The starry sky at night. A sharp sunrise or a mellow golden-red sunset. A full moon. The vastness of the sky when we are in an open space or on a hilltop. These 'speak', says the psalmist. They impress not just our eyes and cameras but our hearts and minds too.

With beauty, awe and wonder, the view as we look up declares God's glory, for this is his handiwork. The infinite variety of the skies, by day or night, and the sheer scale of the cosmos, remind us how small and limited we are and how vast and powerful God is, and how he also delights in beauty, artistry, detail and sheer splendour. THIS is glorious because **HE** is. And it tells us that he exists, he IS.

The language of creation is speaking to all of God's greatness, power and reality, his eternal power and divine nature (Romans 1:20). Only through his written Word do we then find who he is, what he has promised and done in Christ, and what it means to be secure in the love of his Son. The same Psalm tells us that God's word revives our soul, gives us a heart full of joy and light of understanding and direction to the eyes. These trustworthy and precious words endure (vv. 7-10).

May many more hear those words, words of God's glory and grace, spoken to the ends of the earth. May many have ears to hear.

Unshakeable love

Psalm 21:3-7

You welcomed him with rich blessings and placed a crown of pure gold on his head. He asked you for life, and you gave it to him—length of days, for ever and ever. Through the victories you gave, his glory is great; you have bestowed on him splendour and majesty. Surely you have granted him eternal blessings and made him glad with the joy of your presence. For the king trusts in the LORD, through the unfailing love of the Most High he will not be shaken.

There is a sense of absolute confidence and certainty about this Psalm, expressed most clearly in verse 7. The unfailing or steadfast love of the Lord is his confidence; he will not be moved.

Most things in life are not certain. Famously, death and taxes are unavoidable. Most things are subject to the impact of circumstances, health, weather, hard work, sin, opportunities, and so on. But the love of the Lord is **not** one of these variables. It is steadfast, enduring, faithfully consistent.

We are called to seek and trust the Lord, and find our security in his love. The apostle Paul tells us that nothing in all creation can separate those in Christ from God's love (Romans 8:39). That's a solid promise, lay hold of it.

The king who wrote this Psalm is celebrating his victories and the blessings of riches, life, splendour and majesty. He recognised that all good things come from God. 'Blessings forever.' We too can be thankful to God and take note of his goodness in our own lives. But the king's security is not in the 'results', in the way things worked out. Rather, it is from the foundation of God's steadfast love.

If there were ever an example of someone secure in the Father's love, it was the Lord Jesus. Our king achieved eternal blessings for us; he now enjoys matchless splendour and majesty. But it was not through a crown of gold but rather via a crown of thorns. He trusted, secure in God's love, winning life forever for all who follow.

So now we sing of him, 'Be exalted, Lord', for **he** has done this for us.

May we in each day find our confidence, our true security and peace, not in circumstances and how things work out, but in the reality of God's steadfast love for us.

He makes me lie down

Psalm 23:2 *He makes me lie down in green pastures, he leads me beside quiet waters.*

Many love the twenty-third Psalm; it is a favourite at weddings and funerals and has inspired songs and hymns. It condenses such beauty, power, tenderness, hope and majesty about God and our relationship to him into just six verses. It's well known, you can read it in 30 seconds but its value lasts a lifetime.

Verse 2 can suggest that God forces us to take a break: 'He makes me lie down.' Like an overtired toddler being made to take a nap, or a worn out player called off the pitch by the coach to get a rest. But notice where this is happening: green pastures for the sheep (a place of feeding, flourishing, new strength) and quiet waters (a place of stillness, rest, refreshment, renewal).

The meaning is closer to 'He settles me down …' 'He 'settles me down' from the rush, the hurry, the hassle. The Lord who is our Shepherd comes to 'settle us' from the demands and strains of the day.

Where the sheep are worn out, hurting or anxious, he comes to bring the fresh goodness and strength of the 'green pastures'. He settles our minds and emotions as though 'beside quiet waters.'

How do you need him to settle you, to bring you that deep rest and fresh strength? He is able and delights to do so.

What might be stopping you from letting him 'lie you down' and 'lead' you to rest, to be renewed, to dwell in his presence? Pause, listen, recognise what he might offer, and ask for his blessing over you today. Recognise that he knows your needs; he would lead you into his good ways but is also our source of strength and renewal.

Learning to walk

Psalm 25:8-9

Good and upright is the LORD; therefore he instructs sinners in his ways. He guides the humble in what is right and teaches them his way.

Jesus grew up as the carpenter's son. Joseph was a craftsman, probably familiar in building and shaping with wood and stone, with nails and blocks. Jesus would have grown to understand how to work with these materials: hewing, planning, cutting, smoothing, joining. Different types of wood and stone would need a different approach, a particular way of handling their properties.

God knows the way he works too. His 'ways' are not just the commands he gives in scripture, the ways we are meant to live for the good, godly, wise life that honours him and his kingdom. His ways are also about the kind of God he is, how he works. His ways are the fabric of the kingdom that when you go with it proves a joyful, fruitful path even amidst challenges, rather than going against the grain of the kingdom and only getting splinters or producing rubble.

God is good and upright in all his ways. They are not merely morally good ways but completely the best ways to live. So he 'instructs sinners in his ways' – he tells us his commands, he offers us his wisdom and he reveals his character.

Every Old Testament episode and character is an example of this: they are not life lessons in what Moses should have done, or for us to marvel at Noah's engineering prowess, Samson's strength or Nehemiah's leadership abilities. They are to reveal the ways of the Lord – his patience, grace, mercy, justice, love of the lost, compassion on the outcast, attention to the needy, and so on.

The Lord guides us as we come to him in humility. He guides us in his ways – good ways to live well, ways that honour him and lead us into the fruitful fullness of his kingdom. Let's ask him to lead us and shape us today.

The voice of the Lord

Psalm 29:2-4

Ascribe to the LORD the glory due his name; worship the LORD in the splendor of his holiness. The voice of the LORD is over the waters; the God of glory thunders, the LORD thunders over the mighty waters. The voice of the LORD is powerful; the voice of the LORD is majestic.

David summons the whole choir to sing with one focus – to the LORD, to recognise and praise him alone in his glory, strength, might and majesty. I wonder what is the most powerful experience you have had that was man-made? Being on a very large aircraft as it 'miraculously' takes off? The bone-shaking noise of a stadium concert? The scale of a massive factory or power station?

These are all dwarfed by the power of nature – a hurricane, tsunami, volcanic eruption or earthquake make human powers seem very small indeed, even fragile.

Where does human power lie today, or strength? Political power and the rule of a kingdom, an empire or a state are significant. But kings, prime ministers, emirs and presidents will all pass on, resign or die. Military power struts the world stage, exerts pressure to threaten neighbours, brings violent destruction on others and is a false confidence for some. At a more personal level, we might trust in our physical strength and fitness, our money and financial security, our emotional resilience and resources.

The Psalmist rejoices and delights in where real, true, good power lies: the mighty, majestic Lord. His glory thunders, sometimes it whispers.

God speaks, and creation happens. God speaks, wars end. God speaks, human empires are humbled and slaves set free. God speaks, our fears are quietened, our peace restored, our faith grows. God speaks through his Son, and the dead rise, sins can be forgiven, eternal promises are made.

His words are powerful and good. They can humble the proud and lift up the weak and direct our lives. The Spirit of the Lord is still speaking, his glory is seen in how his word brings tender comfort, fresh courage, peace in the turmoil and eternal life. That's real power.

May we treasure his word today and let him speak words greater than any storm we may face. His word is for us, for our good, and it is powerful indeed.

You are my hiding place

Psalm 32:7 *You are my hiding place; you will protect me from trouble and surround me with songs of deliverance.*

In the Bible, we are encouraged to draw near to God in the happy days and the hard days, days where all is straightforward and goes to plan as well as days when nothing is simple and everything seems to fall apart. But especially in tough times, the Lord reminds us that he is a safe place, a refuge, our rest and help.

The Psalms return to this theme often and today's verse is a lovely and powerful image: God is our hiding place. David knew what it was to survive in times of danger and distress. He was familiar with the wilderness, being on the run, of personal betrayal or his own failures. In the desert he knew how to find a hiding place from rising, rushing floodwaters, from wild animals, from the prolonged heat of the sun and from enemies pursuing him.

Our difficulties might seem far removed from these (I hope you are not hiding from wild animals today!), even mundane, but the promise stands. In days of adversity, God himself is our hiding place. He is the One we can go to, be secure with, and find rest and security.

In any circumstance, God offers protection for his children. Our heavenly Father cares for us, protects our hearts and mind, and sings over us his songs of deliverance to quieten our spirit's anxiety, to change our perspective, to remind us of his presence.

Come hide in him when trouble strikes.

The Lord is close

Psalm 34:15-18

The eyes of the LORD are on the righteous and his ears are open to their cry. The face of the LORD is against those who do evil, to cut off the memory of them from the earth. The righteous cry out, and the LORD hears them; he delivers them from all their troubles. The LORD is close to the brokenhearted and saves those who are crushed in spirit.

The Lord is with his people, always.

He is amongst us, his Spirit roams over the world: '*the eyes of the LORD are on the righteous and his ears are open to their* cry'. Whether in offices, streets, schools or homes, the Spirit of the Lord goes with God's people, just as in the fire and cloud in which he went with Israel through wilderness and sea, by night or day, close by them.

He is present in power and yet also in great tenderness. Do we recognise his presence especially with those who are broken-hearted, weighed down by grief, crushed by hardship and trials? Do they look for him? The Lord is close to them, and to us.

Grief can rob us of strength and sleep, deprive us of energy to reach out to others, cloud our future as if joy can never return, but the Lord can and does save those who feel crushed in spirit. The Lord is near, we need not fear.

He is active to teach us his ways, the loving Father in heaven to his beloved children. From a fiery presence he spoke and commanded Moses. Do we submit our words and ways to him? The Lord is close, to teach and train us.

He is not silent or indifferent to evil either, to lies and falsehood. His face is set against them. They will not have the last word and will face his justice in the end.

The Lord is with us, the great I AM. May we find joy in seeking his face and leaning on him.

A firm place to stand

Psalm 40:1-3

I waited patiently for the LORD; he turned to me and heard my cry.
He lifted me out of the slimy pit, out of the mud and mire;
he set my feet on a rock and gave me a firm place to stand.
He put a new song in my mouth, a hymn of praise to our God.
Many will see and fear and put their trust in the LORD.

We naturally seek security in life. We aim for provision and protection: providing for ourselves, our family, for a home that is warm, safe, clean and a place to restore us – whether that's quiet or noisy! And we seek protection from harm, whether facing health concerns, living costs, an uncertain job future or even people who might wish to harm us. It is right to seek security, safety, wanting to live without fear and with peace.

We rightly seek peace of mind, to overcome worries or fears. In the workplace, we want to be valued, to do work that matters, to have a sense of purpose and achievement, to be listened to.

We also want to be secure with God, knowing he accepts us, even loves us. The good news is we can know this, that Christ's love is stronger than our fears, his death breaks the power of sin, the way to the Father is open for all who trust him.

Whatever our fears, God is able to lift us from treacherous ground - from a dark pit or where we don't know the next steps - and set us upon a rock. There is no more solid ground than resting our life on Christ Jesus.

From fears, shame, worry, the impact of others or that of our own failings, God is able and ready to set us securely on new ground, with a new song in our mouth, and we can rightly give him praise as he does so.

Keep calm and carry on

Psalm 46:1-3, 10

God is our refuge and strength, an ever-present help in trouble. Therefore we will not fear, though the earth give way and the mountains fall into the heart of the sea, though its waters roar and foam and the mountains quake with their surging. "Be still, and know that I am God; I will be exalted among the nations, I will be exalted in the earth."

"Keep Calm and Carry On" was the caption of a motivational poster produced by the UK Government's Ministry of Information in 1939 in preparation for WW2. George Orwell's novel, *1984*, made this department famous with his Ministry of Truth. It now appears in a myriad of adaptations on tea towels, album covers, T-shirts and political slogans.

I have a mug on my desk with the words 'Keep Calm and Know that I Am God', a mash-up of wartime motivation and biblical truth.

'Be still and know that I am God' comes from the one who speaks the truth without deception or false hopes. No empty promises or manipulation here. We can truly know the living God, and he offers us his presence, refuge, strength and peace at all times by faith but especially so in times of crisis.

Psalm 46 depicts the world crashing down around us in chaos and disorder. It is a threatening scenario of catastrophes: earthquakes and floods, of warfare and political collapse. These and other disasters and pressures are real to all of us at one level or another, a world full of potential for harm, distress, disruption, violence and even chaos.

The Lord knows. He speaks into this; he draws our attention to his city (verse 4), to a river as a sign of ever-flowing blessing and restoration. He speaks to us to remind us that he, the Lord Almighty, is with us, to see what he has done and to find our security and peace by resting in his rule over our lives.

We can persevere in faith, assured of his presence. With him, we can 'Keep calm and carry on'.

Deep clean

Psalm 51:1-3, 7, 10

Have mercy on me, O God, according to your unfailing love; according to your great compassion blot out my transgressions. Wash away all my iniquity and cleanse me from my sin. For I know my transgressions, and my sin is always before me. Cleanse me with hyssop, and I will be clean; wash me, and I will be whiter than snow. Create in me a pure heart, O God, and renew a steadfast spirit within me.

King David has behaved appallingly. He has committed a grievous sin and his conscience is scorched, his spirit weighed down, his bones crushed by this. This Psalm is an honest lament. Here is repentance that faces the horror of sin's darkness, stain and cost.

Three different terms are used to convey the breadth and depth of how David has broken his relationship with God:

Transgressions – the crossing of moral boundaries into places of harm and immorality.

Iniquity – the pollution of wrongdoing, the corruption of the soul, the stain on the mind.

Sin – moral disobedience, rebellion, wrongdoing.

So he asks for what every sinner needs in response: mercy, grace and loving kindness. We cannot be forgiven or restored unless God comes to us in these ways, rather than in the ways we deserve.

What he needs of God's actions is also clear: cleansing, full forgiveness and the removal of that which bars him from God's presence.

The heartbreaking reality of sin, expressed so honestly in Psalm 51, is a confession before a God of mercy. He accepts those who repent and believe, he delights in humility and faith. So David can look with hope for a renewed heart, new motivation and attitudes, as God also renews his spirit and wipes away sin's stain.

We all need this mercy and restoration. We can all come to a throne of amazing grace. When we realise how deeply we have fallen, how dark sin is, then salvation and the Saviour shine all the brighter.

My soul thirsts

Psalm 63:1 *O God, you are my God, earnestly I seek you; my soul thirsts for you, my body longs for you, in a dry and weary land where there is no water.*

As I write this, it's the hottest day of the year so far. My water bottle is being regularly drained and refilled. Fans have appeared in the church office (the rotating kind, not the keen followers). Stepping outside feels like a different country, as the heat and humidity hit. We love talking about the weather in the UK!

Psalm 63, a Psalm of David, includes a note in my Bible that says, 'written while he was in the Desert of Judah'. I was able to visit the Judean wilderness a few years ago on a trip to Israel. It was over 40°C, a dry and unrelenting heat. A fierce environment to be out in, not a comfortable place to live or work. In this Psalm, David was reminded of his physical thirst but speaks of a different deep thirst – a thirst of his soul.

Where can you and I turn for spiritual refreshment? Where will our soul find all that it needs, in a world that can leave our soul 'dry and weary', thirsty for relief, for rest, for peace, for courage under pressure?

The Psalm points the way to God, to his God and ours, the only true source but one that Jesus spoke of as sufficient and abundant; in him and flowing from his life in us, we need never be thirsty again (John 4:14).

May we know his refreshment, life and sustaining grace, whatever the weather.

Precious in God's sight

Psalm 72:11-14

All kings will bow down to him and all nations will serve him. For he will deliver the needy who cry out, the afflicted who have no one to help. He will take pity on the weak and the needy and save the needy from death. He will rescue them from oppression and violence, for precious is their blood in his sight.

A Psalm of Solomon, king of Israel, one familiar with incredible personal wealth and power, surrounded by privilege and comforts. But his subjects were not all in this position. There were, as there are in any town, city, country or kingdom, the 'haves' and the 'have nots'.

A consistent theme of the Bible in both Old and New Testament is God's concern for the oppressed, the poor, the outcast. For the least, the lost, the last in line. Widows, orphans and strangers get special mention, particular attention, greater protection in the eyes of the Law of God than others, because he sees and knows.

The Psalm celebrates the rule of a great king, and Solomon was familiar with the honours from surrounding nations and kings. His greatness was measured in gold, literally.

But the greatness of God's kingdom, of his rule, is not measured in cash, military power, fine buildings or possessing land (as earthly kingdoms tend to be rated). The kings bow before the Lord of all because he will deliver the needy, the afflicted, the weak, the oppressed. The kingdom of God is one of righteousness that treats all people well and deals with them rightly, of justice and mercy to those in need so they are no less favoured than the rich, powerful, strong or secure of this world.

God sees the victims of the injustice and oppression of this world. Their very lives are precious in his sight. His kingdom, for which we can pray and work, will count all lives precious, will pursue justice especially for those least able to find it, and seek peace for those lacking resources to maintain it. What a beautiful kingdom to aim for, for the sake of our beautiful King.

An undivided heart

Psalm 86:11 *Teach me your way, O LORD, and I will walk in your truth; give me an undivided heart, that I may fear your name.*

We live in a distracted world, a noisy world, with demands on our time not just in each day but for each waking moment, especially if – like me – you have a smartphone. Such devices, or specifically the apps, are designed to grab our attention, to distract with constant change, entertainment, news, and friends' updates. It's not accidental!

A flow of notifications, hits, likes, posts and pings can fill the day, and that's before we even get to the work-related stream of messages. The distraction and constant change can be low-demand entertainment of social media, or high demand work, but without care it can leave our minds restless, anxious, tired.

Long before social media, Jesus himself told the parable of the sower (Mark 4:19) and spoke of the realities of other distractions by worries, wealth and worldly pleasure. He said these have the capacity to stunt or stop our spiritual growth. We don't need gadgets for our life to wander or for our goals to drift from God's best.

Psalm 86 is a prayer for focus, for an 'undivided heart', where God's way, his truth, his name, hold the centre of attention. King David had an earthly throne, many legitimate needs and concerns, but knew that only our good God sits on the true throne, that his way is good for all our days and peace of mind comes from resting in him.

In this distracting, noisy world, perhaps in the busy day ahead for us, let's ask God to take the lead, to keep our hearts set on him amidst pressures or concerns, and bring the renewed peace of an 'undivided heart'.

Great is Your faithfulness

Psalm 89:1-2, 8, 14-15

I will sing of the LORD'S great love forever; with my mouth I will make your faithfulness known through all generations. I will declare that your love stands firm forever, that you established your faithfulness in heaven itself.

O LORD God Almighty, who is like you? You are mighty, O LORD, and your faithfulness surrounds you. Righteousness and justice are the foundation of your throne; love and faithfulness go before you. Blessed are those who have learned to acclaim you, who walk in the light of your presence, O LORD.

Psalm 89 is a song of praise to God's faithfulness. It surrounds him, it underpins him, his throne is grounded on it, it is to be declared and taught. In every possible way, David sings 'Great is Your faithfulness!'

We love people who keep their word; we struggle with those who don't. You trust people or companies who prove themselves reliable and truthful, who at least try to deliver on their commitments. Faithful friends are precious. God truly does keep his word – if he didn't he couldn't really be God. A God who is not faithful is no god at all, certainly not the God that we know. When we come to know him we find, again and again, that he is faithful.

He is faithful to creation, sustaining all things moment by moment. He was faithful to his Son, raising him from the dead. He is faithful in his love to all who seek him. He has been faithful to his global church, especially in times of persecution. He will be faithful to us even through death, leading us into eternal life.

God's faithfulness, especially in the Old Testament, is always tied to his promises, the covenant with his people, what he has said: God keeps his promises, God keeps his word.

Declaring that God is faithful is very personal – we are each called to a personal trust in God – but it is also to be public, not private. Faith is not to be hidden but sung, preached, talked of, shared with our family and friends.

God's faithfulness towards us should motivate us towards greater faithfulness towards him, a deeper and clearer trust. It should prompt our worship, as it did for the psalmist, who composed this tribute – to God's faithfulness.

We are dust

Psalm 103:13-16

As a father has compassion on his children, so the LORD has compassion on those who fear him; for he knows how we are formed, he remembers that we are dust. As for man, his days are like grass, he flourishes like a flower of the field; the wind blows over it and it is gone, and its place remembers it no more.

Have you ever tried to make a sandcastle? Sometimes the sand is too dry or fine to build with, but even wet sand crumbles when the tide comes. Lego is certainly more robust but not very practical for the beach! Drop the model though and it will probably break, or ignore the instructions and you might have finished it but have key bits left over! How about a gingerbread house? Great fun to build, usually a sticky and messy job, hard to get the walls to stay upright, but with the bonus that you can eat the results.

Some things are more promising as building materials than others. Some seem more robust or solid than others. However, I imagine none of us have ever tried building anything from dust.

Yet the Psalm says of God, 'he knows how we are formed, he remembers that we are dust.'

We are dust.

God sees us as we are: so weak and just like dust. Made by his power, the breath of life put in us by him, each life is a unique, precious creation of immeasurable worth and dignity. Yet, we are still dust: fragile, earthly, and to dust we shall return.

Our heavenly Father loves us, and no less so because we are not always robust, strong or promising 'building materials' for an impressive life. He doesn't measure us with the measuring values of this world. In our weakness, in our suffering, with our transitory and fallible natures, he looks on us with love as a Father cares for his small children (verse 13) with tenderness and kindness, with infinite compassion. His love for us passes all understanding.

We come from dust, will return to the dust, but in his hands we are also shaped by and heading for eternal glory and for resurrection renewal in his presence. He is building us for this even now.

May we know his compassion and the confidence of his purposes as you we trust ourselves to God today.

Still the storm

Psalm 107:28-30

Then they cried out to the LORD in their trouble, and he brought them out of their distress. He stilled the storm to a whisper; the waves of the sea were hushed. They were glad when it grew calm, and he guided them to their desired haven.

These words sound very familiar, don't they? Three of the Gospels – Matthew, Mark and Luke – tell the story of Jesus doing just this: stilling the storm to a whisper as his friends cry out in fear and distress. Waves are hushed, it grows calm, they get safely to shore. But these words from the Psalms come from 1000 years before Christ stepped into that boat. Why is that? Why the similarity?

It is a lesson for us of God's consistency; we might also call it his faithfulness. He doesn't change. What he did then (celebrated by the writer of the Psalms) he can do again – hear our cries, our prayers, as we 'cry out to the LORD in our trouble', and he can act for our good.

Jonah's fellow sailors weren't the first to see a raging sea grow calm and give thanks to the Lord (Jonah 1:15-16), and certainly not the last. The disciples in the storm, with Jesus in their boat, saw at first hand who had power to help.

Psalm 107 is just a reminder that God still has power to bring calm, to rescue and restore, to guide us home through our own storms. It's also a reminder that prayers reach him and to express our gratitude to him. May we learn to trust and to give thanks today in the midst of our storms. He can do it again.

Who is like the Lord?

Psalm 113

Praise the LORD. Praise the LORD, you his servants; praise the name of the LORD. Let the name of the LORD be praised, both now and forevermore. From the rising of the sun to the place where it sets, the name of the LORD is to be praised.

The LORD is exalted over all the nations, his glory above the heavens. Who is like the LORD our God, the One who sits enthroned on high, who stoops down to look on the heavens and the earth? He raises the poor from the dust and lifts the needy from the ash heap; he seats them with princes, with the princes of his people. He settles the childless woman in her home as a happy mother of children. Praise the LORD.

Everyone, everywhere can praise God – you don't need special status, you need faith. So we don't need bishops, priests, popes or pastors to do this for us. God invites us all, 'you his servants', to bring ourselves as we are before him in praise and prayer. No red tape, no small print. Come in humility, come knowing his great worth and it is all of grace that we can come, but come before him.

Everyone, everywhere can praise God and the Psalm reminds us that everywhere on earth, across the nations, from the rising of the sun to its setting, is where God should be praised. The whole earth is his, from Ampthill to Antarctica, from Juba to Jerusalem, from the shiniest city to the remotest community. We all live under his skies, rely on his creation, share our humanity's needs and potential, and he wants all to hear the gospel that invites people into his kingdom.

God can and should be praised by everyone everywhere. This is what we are made for, to be in relationship to this awesome, loving glorious Creator and Ruler.

For all his divine majesty and limitless power, the Psalm shows us the tenderness of the Lord, how he humbly descends to the lowest, the least, the poor and needy. God has stepped into the dirt and the darkness, supremely in his Son the Lord Jesus. This Lord is not aloof, indifferent or remote. Our God saves. He lifts the sinner to his presence, restores the guilty and sets them free, lifts us from death to be fully alive, lifts the poor and rich alike and gives them the greatest of status as daughters and sons of the living God.

Wherever we are, whoever we are, we were made to praise the Lord and find our joy, rest and life with him. Where else would we find these, for who is like the Lord our God?

Looking for mercy

Psalm 123:1-2

I lift up my eyes to you, to you whose throne is in heaven.
As the eyes of slaves look to the hand of their master,
as the eyes of a maid look to the hand of her mistress,
so our eyes look to the LORD our God, till he shows us his mercy.

The Psalms are perhaps over 3000 years old. They come from a different time, a society and culture very different to our own, but the image of looking to God for help is not hard to grasp.

The writer has to lift his or her eyes. God is above; his throne is in heaven, a reminder of his great authority and rule over this world. We look to the one with sovereign power to bring change, to offer relief, to show us his mercy in our need.

For a slave looking to their master's hand, the weak looks to the strong. This is for a directing hand – to show us the way, when we need wisdom to find our way through the mess, to resolve the difficult relationship or make progress at work or as a family.

The master's hand is a providing hand too; the slave is dependent on them. We can look for God's mercy to give us what we need, our daily bread, the energy to tackle something or courage to keep going or simply help from others when we need it.

The prayer puts us in the place of the maid too, looking to the hand of her mistress. God acts in both fatherly care and protection and motherly love and tenderness (not that earthly fathers and mothers own these qualities exclusively). The psalmist is experiencing contempt and ridicule from others, being mocked and scorned: where we are in similar circumstances for our faith, we look up and see the Lord who knows.

He looks on us, ready and willing to show mercy and grace in our time of need (Hebrews 4:16). We can come to God with real, faithful expectation that we can receive good things from his hand. He knows our needs and is willing to help. So look up.

Waiting on the Lord

Psalm 130:5 *I wait for the L<small>ORD</small>, my soul waits, and in his word I put my hope.*

As you read this, can I encourage you to take 10 minutes at some point in your day to 'wait for the L<small>ORD</small>'. Find somewhere quiet, still, undistracted, comfortable. Sit silently, set aside all activity, turn off devices and in prayer invite God's presence. Recognise his care and attention towards you. Recognise that you are precious in his sight and deeply loved. You don't need to tell him anything; you can just 'wait on him'. As the psalmist said: *'I wait for the L<small>ORD</small>, my soul waits'* – his very inmost being was seen and known by God.

Now ask what he might say, perhaps simply through this verse today.

'and in his word I put my hope.'

His word – the Bible, the written word of God – speaks of God's promises to us, of his unchanging character, mercy, love and power. It speaks of the direction he wants for us: growing in holiness, growing in confidence in him, setting aside sin, enjoying his presence, building our life on the best foundation of Jesus, the living Word. It can diagnose our daily needs.

May we know the Lord's great love and fresh peace as we turn to him, his presence as we wait on him, and his direction and reassurance as we reflect on his word.

Inescapable presence

Psalm 139:5 *You hem me in—behind and before; you have laid your hand upon me.*

When you watch a President or a Prime Minister in any kind of public appearance outdoors, it doesn't take long to become aware of their security team. The people in suits scanning the crowd, standing close by but not too close, looking very 'purposeful'.

They might surround the 'principal' in a cordon of a close protection team of just a few people, then a wider ring of vehicles and personnel set further back with access to a building, cars or an exit route, and further out still, and largely out of sight, are the various other layers of support, protection and control to keep the roads clear, ensure safety, maintain communication and so on. Hollywood films love to use all this to elevate the tension, build the drama.

If you are the person at the centre of this, it perhaps becomes second nature, perhaps a frustration too. President Barack Obama once joked about going swimming in the sea off a Hawaiian beach with his family, with only a Navy destroyer, a SEAL team, a helicopter and the Secret Service coming along for the day.

God does not offer us an armed protection team! He does offer something better: the security of our soul, the great assurance of HIS presence, so close as to be 'behind and before' us.

There is no situation we can step into or await that he doesn't go with us. We can give our fears, concerns, anxiety or hopes to God by faith, asking him to walk with us, knowing that he is not just close at hand but 'lays his hand upon us'. He is with us in his love, his favour on his children, his strength in our frailty, his grace when we sin and his peace in our storms.

So we walk on, as he walks with us, his hand is upon us.

False hopes and our true help

Psalm 146:1-4

Praise the LORD. Praise the LORD, O my soul. I will praise the LORD all my life; I will sing praise to my God as long as I live. Do not put your trust in princes, in mortal men, who cannot save. When their spirit departs, they return to the ground; on that very day their plans come to nothing. Blessed is he whose help is the God of Jacob, whose hope is in the LORD his God, the Maker of heaven and earth, the sea, and everything in them—the LORD, who remains faithful forever.

Psalm 146 is timeless. In every era, people are tempted to look on particular people to deliver a breakthrough for a cause. These could be formal political leaders such as prime ministers or presidents, or informal leaders like civil rights campaigners, justice advocates, celebrities, influencers, activists or billionaires. We can actively focus our hopes on such people. But they are not up to the task.

To put the weight of our trust on particular human beings to save the planet from climate change, cancer, racism or food poverty is a timeless temptation. The goals are good and worthy, however, the people can't deliver this, not alone. There are many superbly capable, highly motivated and indeed remarkably gifted such people. But often they will let us down, let down the cause, or succumb to the reality that they too are finite: we are all human, we all die and return to the ground, to dust.

But not the Lord. He is a hope who lasts, who remains in the fullness of his power and sustaining grace. He remains faithful forever. Make him your hope, your help, and you will find the blessing of God in the midst of every generation, regardless of who is elected or who leads.

This hope saves us from despair when leaders reject God and his ways, and saves us from false hope if we overvalue the leaders of Westminster, the media or the White House. They cannot deliver. Only God can save and he will pursue justice, righteousness and peace. He sustains creation, not the government of the day. He acts for the poor, the downtrodden, the hungry, the blind, those trapped in sin, and will confound the wicked in his time. He works through elected leaders, even the corrupt or incompetent, and through countless people without any apparent power or status.

Regardless of who occupies earthly seats of power, there is only one throne that counts and one place to put our sure and certain hope. Do not be anxious; be blessed.

Joyful promise

Psalm 150

Praise the LORD.
Praise God in his sanctuary; praise him in his mighty heavens.
Praise him for his acts of power; praise him for his surpassing greatness.
Praise him with the sounding of the trumpet, praise him with the harp and lyre, praise him with tambourine and dancing, praise him with the strings and flute, praise him with the clash of cymbals, praise him with resounding cymbals.
Let everything that has breath praise the LORD.
Praise the LORD.

Imagine being asked to compile a playlist of songs to reflect Christianity. What would you make the theme of the final song? Or you are putting together an art display of the world's 100 greatest paintings – what kind of work would you pick as the climax?

The book of Psalms begins with the call to choose well and find the path of life, of a fruitful and secure life with the Lord (Psalm 1). It ends, in Psalm 150, with great joy, the joy of the Lord. This is the climax: joy in God's presence, joy towards him and his creation, joy in praise for what he has done (his acts of power) and for his great glory (his surpassing greatness).

The Psalms take us through every possible aspect of the life of faith; they give us the vocabulary of praise and complaint, of grief and celebration, of anger and hope. They stretch our spiritual imagination and equip us to live more fully with God. The Psalms encourage us to pray more honestly perhaps and vent **to** him rather than **about** him. They also give us so many words of great gospel hope – of the Lord our shepherd, our refuge, our shield, our salvation, his word as a light for our path, of his faithful watching over us, his presence wherever we go, of the forgiveness of sins so we are 'whiter than snow'.

That journey of faith, the walk with God, is in his company but the life of faith holds on to the hope of being with him face to face. The righteous will live again, the door to eternal life is open for all who embrace God's promises in Christ Jesus. And what awaits us? JOY.

Joy with God, joy from God, joy about God, expressed in this Psalm with the whole orchestra and by everything with breath!

We are heading for great joy, and in God's goodness he offers us regular foretastes of that joy now, supremely, when we encounter him and the love, life and sacrifice of Jesus as gifts to us. We find joy as we see his signature in creation, the church, the cross and as we hear his voice in the Bible. We are made to enjoy his ongoing goodness in love, people, laughter, music, food, sunsets, babies, sport, silence and more. Today can be a foretaste of eternity.

Joy now, joy forever. An end to look forward to. A God well worth our praise.

4

WALKING IN GOD'S WAYS:
WISDOM FOR LIFE

Jesus spoke of God as his heavenly Father and as a very good Father (Matthew 7:11). He gives gifts to his children, gifts for our life to flourish and be blessed, gifts that we might know him and his love more fully and to enable us serve the good purposes he has in mind for us and his kingdom. God is generous, kind and wise.

His wisdom is part of his generous love towards us; he trains us in the way to live. This is not only a 'spiritual' training where our hearts and minds are shaped and renewed, trained in love and obedience and hope, marvellous though this is. His wisdom is also completely practical, it forms us as the people of God who have the Spirit of God within us, so that our lives model Jesus in this world. His wisdom shapes our speech and work, our parenting and spending, how we grieve and how we plan and all things in between.

This wisdom is seen throughout scripture as God calls and leads people; it is revealed in their experiences, faith and God's dealings with them even when they falter or fail. It is seen in stories, commands, songs and prayers. It is seen in person, wisdom supreme, in the life and teaching of Christ Jesus and through the cross.

Wisdom starts with knowing God: 'The fear of the LORD is the beginning of wisdom, and knowledge of the Holy One is understanding' (Proverbs 9:10).

In the fifteen reflections that follow, we trace some of the ways of God, his wisdom for our life – a good, beautiful, godly and secure life. This is what our heavenly Father calls us to in his love.

Deuteronomy 29:29	Humble trust
Proverbs 2:7-8	God's wisdom protects us
Proverbs 4:18	Believers are like the sunrise
Proverbs 8:30-31	Wisdom in person
Proverbs 10:13-14	Powerful of words
Proverbs 14:31	Remember the poor
Proverbs 16:1-3	Making wise plans
Proverbs 16:32	Character matters
Ecclesiastes 3:1,11-13	Everything good in its time
Isaiah 30:20-21	This is the way, walk in it
Isaiah 55:1	Come and eat
Isaiah 55:8-9	The Lord's ways and ours
Jeremiah 6:16	Stand at the crossroads
Daniel 2:20-22	He gives wisdom and knowledge
Hosea 14:9	The righteous walk in God's ways

Humble trust

The secret things belong to the LORD our God, but the things revealed belong to us and to our children forever, that we may follow all the words of this law. (Deuteronomy 29:29)

It has been said that as you start to study something, the more you know the more you realise what you don't know.

The eminent and brilliant physicist Enrico Fermi once said, "Before I came here I was confused about this subject … I am still confused. But on a higher level."

God does not withhold anything in order to deliberately confuse us, but even we know the merits of not explaining everything to everyone. Small children don't need to understand the issues on the M25, they just want to know "Are we nearly there yet?" Someone who is grieving does not need to know much beyond immediate concerns; they have enough burdens of the day. The sensitive concerns of a family, a church or a government policy do not need to be publicly aired for all to examine; there may be excellent reasons to keep things more private.

So how much more should the Sovereign Lord over all history and creation keep things beyond our view, for his own purposes and for our own well-being?

There is a wisdom of knowing and trusting that **God** knows all things. There is a wisdom of knowing and trusting that it is ok that **we** don't!

Yet what an honour that he <u>does</u> choose to reveal that which can help us live: his own good purposes of salvation, the way to eternal life, his wisdom for a good and flourishing life. These good things are not hidden but given as gifts to his children 'that we might follow all the words of this law.'

All God's good ways, his law, is given for our life. We only see in part his full plan, his wider working in history, the whisper of his true power. For now it is our calling to live in humble trust before an infinite and infinitely wise God, to accept that we are finite and fragile, but as beloved children of a good Father.

God's wisdom protects us

He holds victory in store for the upright, he is a shield to those whose walk is blameless, for he guards the course of the just and protects the way of his faithful ones. (Proverbs 2:7-8)

We all make many decisions each day, most of which are routine and don't carry any significance. Muesli or cornflakes? Blue jumper or green? Coffee now or later? Occasionally we will need to make decisions that are more 'weighty': those with real potential to resolve problems, strengthen friendships, develop our career, improve our health, have fun, enrich our family or make life simpler. Decisions are good things. They enable positive change.

Sooner or later we may also experience not getting decisions right and find ourselves working hard to change the outcome. Sometimes we lack that precious gift: wisdom.

The Book of Proverbs deals with this above all – God's wisdom, a practical and potent wisdom, not something abstract or detached from everyday life. God's wisdom is given here to help us to live, offering insights into work, money, how we can deal with conflict, handling the truth or lies, leadership, friendship, facing temptation, valuing integrity, and lots more! At its heart, wisdom is found in a life rooted in God, trusting his ways and words.

Today's verse is an encouragement to walk well with God and shows how this brings us under the protection of his shield. God's wisdom protects us, it guards the course of our life and leads to victory. That victory is the joyful fulfilment of life with God rather than walking through life without him. We get a taste of this victory along the way as God blesses our lives.

This does **not** mean that if we trust God everything will go well – with no illness or flat tyres, no work issues or exam disasters, permanently happy relationships and sunshine every day. Look at the lives of the prophets and apostles! The stuff of life is ups and downs – and surely God does protect us from many of the 'downs' by his grace.

The protection his wisdom offers is from sin and the damage it causes; protection from the impact of sin and choices that he knows won't help. He offers us his wisdom and direction when we are wrestling with decisions.

Will we walk with him today, living under his shield? A decision to make!

Believers are like the sunrise

The path of the righteous is like the first gleam of dawn,
shining ever brighter till the full light of day. (Proverbs 4:18)

December can be a month with some gloomy, dark mornings and the days getting shorter. Every year we seem surprised by this ("Dark at 4 o'clock?!") but we really shouldn't be! We look forward to the sunrise, enjoy bright days when we get them, and look forward to spring too!

This Proverb paints a lovely picture. It depicts the life of a Christian as being like the sunrise. The light breaks into our lives - the light of God's love and awareness of forgiveness when we first accept Jesus. When we first call on him in repentance and faith, God does his miraculous work of salvation in us and brings us to new life. The apostle Paul describes it in vivid terms; that we have been rescued from the 'dominion of darkness' and brought into the 'kingdom of the Son', the 'kingdom of light' (Colossians 1:12-13). From darkness to great and enduring light.

The path of the righteous, the life of the believer, is like the sunrise. Light breaks into the darkness. The Son is rising over our lives, bringing his light and love, with an ever-increasing awareness and experience of this as we walk with him and as we grow in faith.

His love isn't growing, our experience of it is. And this light shines on, through every season of our lives (even if the 'clouds' obscure it at times). His light, his presence, his love and mercy, his grace and power, are towards us and for us because we belong to Jesus. The Holy Spirit is at work in us, so we might enjoy the Son more and more.

Until one day when we will know the full light of day, a new day, standing before him. Then there will be no darkness at all.

So as we walk with him, may his light and love grow ever clearer and brighter in our lives, as faith, hope and love grow. And may his light spill out into his world from us, to point people to his way and the light of life himself.

Wisdom in person

Then I was the craftsman at his side. I was filled with delight day after day, rejoicing always in his presence, rejoicing in his whole world and delighting in mankind. (Proverbs 8:30-31)

God's own wisdom is seen most magnificently, most perfectly and personally in Jesus Christ. Wisdom walked among us: wisdom was seen in his life, his teaching, his saving death, and he's now at God's right hand, our wise and awesome high priest still displaying God's perfect and mighty wisdom.

In Proverbs chapter 8, wisdom is depicted as a person who was with God at Creation and active in creating all things. In Proverbs 8:22, this wisdom was with God before the world began.

Wisdom was 'the craftsman at his side'. We might wonder what the young Jesus of Nazareth made of this verse, being the son of a carpenter, growing up in the home of an earthly craftsman, learning a trade at his side.

These verses are a reminder of God's delight and care over the detail of his world. Creation is his masterpiece, embedded with his goodness and the abundance of beauty and variety reflecting the Lord himself. His verdict over all that was made was 'very good', and we were the pinnacle of that creation week.

God's plan was for his own Son to live a life of holy obedience and joy, to teach God's ways, and to die to save us from sin. In each of these areas we see wisdom in person and God's wisdom displayed.

As God rejoiced over his creation, so also being with him is to rejoice. He is a source of limitless joy. He looks on humanity with love, wanting all to know him by faith, and inviting us in each day to find our lasting joy and deepest rest with him. May his wisdom guide you to that joy and security, and to his wisdom in Christ.

Powerful words

Wise words come from the lips of people with understanding, but those lacking sense will be beaten with a rod.

Wise people treasure knowledge, but the babbling of a fool invites disaster. (Proverbs 10:13-14, NLT)

The Book of Proverbs is immensely practical, its relevance is so clear. The wisdom of God is so good, helpful, even simple. It can steer us towards the good ways to live and away from harm, disappointment and sin.

Proverbs has much to say on the value of wise words and the hazards of being a fool or listening to one. Having lots to say does not equate to more wisdom; words that come across as charming or exciting are not necessarily true, good or worthy of our attention.

Good words have **power**:

> *The words of the mouth are deep waters, but the fountain of wisdom is a rushing stream.* (Proverbs 18:4)

> *The tongue has the power of life and death* (Proverbs 18:21)

Words can refresh, stir up life and renew hope. Words can restore or destroy. Good words can bring joy, peace, courage, healing and growth.

> *A cheerful look brings joy to the heart, and good news gives health to the bones.* (Proverbs 15:30)

As we weigh our words, there is much of which we should be cautious (for we know ourselves) but we can also ask God to fill our mouths with good words, for how we engage both in person and online, so that we might bear good fruit and be the means of refreshment, blessing and encouragement to others.

Apt words are **precious**:

> *A person finds joy in giving an apt reply—and how good is a timely word!* (Proverbs 15:23)

> *Gold there is, and rubies in abundance, but lips that speak knowledge are a rare jewel.* (Proverbs 20:15)

> *The one who has knowledge uses words with restraint ... and whoever has understanding is even-tempered. Even fools are thought wise if they keep silent, and discerning if they hold their tongues.* (Proverbs 17:27-28)

Sometimes the best option is when our words are **few**. Good listening is a superpower. Being silent may be the best option.

Proverbs offers both guidance and warnings, our words really matter, and to seek God's wisdom is to ask him to train and shape us within, so that which comes from our mouths is good, true, faithful to him.

May we speak up when injustice is done, be silent when words are of no help, tell no lies, cherish what is good, and guard our hearts in all this.

Remember the poor

He who oppresses the poor shows contempt for their Maker, but whoever is kind to the needy honours God. (Proverbs 14:31)

There are about 2000 verses in the Bible about helping the poor. Two THOUSAND! Does this not say something profoundly clearly about God's heart, his priorities?

God has a concern for the *materially or financially* poor – those in practical need, those in deep poverty or in the long struggle to make ends meet. So we can rightly urge governments to act on behalf of those in need, both here and overseas, and consider our own giving, praying, lifestyle, consumer choices and so on.

The Lord also sees those who are *spiritually* poor, those lacking his Spirit as they have not asked, sought him, accepted him into their life. Others are *poor in their spirit*, they see themselves laid low or burdened by grief, pain, loss or the hardships of life, and God opposes those who would add to their burdens.

God is also aware of those who are attentive and caring towards the poor of all kinds. He delights when we show mercy and seek justice. This mindset of kindness and work for the sake of the poor honours the God who is our Maker. Every person is loved by God, unique and precious in his eyes.

Take time today to consider how you can see the world with God's eyes, and show kindness to those who are poor.

Making wise plans

To man belong the plans of the heart, but from the LORD comes the reply of the tongue.

All a man's ways seem innocent to him, but motives are weighed by the LORD.

Commit to the LORD whatever you do, and your plans will succeed.

(Proverbs 16:1-3)

We plan for the short term (What time shall we meet?) and the longer term (Can we afford that? Should we move house?) We might plan around relationships, work and career, money, hobbies or home improvements. Almost any kind of work requires plans – who to ask to do this or that, how to get resources from A to B, planning when to start a new project, and so on.

We recognise the value of plans that impact on people: education follows a curriculum (it's not random), builders rely on architects' designs, and a course of chemotherapy is part of a structured care package. A good plan in advance can release us from stress of deciding in the moment, it helps keep the fridge stocked or the team on target, or just gives us a bit of certainty so we can either enjoy the holiday or get on with the work. Plans are good things.

Some plans are beyond the ability of one person to fathom: the invasion of Europe on D-Day, June 1944; the Moon landing; how to tackle climate change. Some plans are obviously not adequate in hindsight: Brexit, the war in Afghanistan or… any children's party involving a bouncy castle!

Proverbs has much to say to us about this very common, even basic, activity of making plans, and specifically making wise plans. Why is that? Why would God speak to this?

At least one answer is this: planning is an expression for us of shaping our future, of what we might want to achieve or to be, even of who we become. And God cares about these things. God cares about our lives, how we serve, who we become. So Proverbs prompts each of us to ask: where is God in our plans?

It is not wrong to plan. In the Bible we read how God revealed his plans to Adam, Noah, Abraham and others. He required Moses to follow deliberate plans on a vast scale but also intricate in detail. Nehemiah was expected to make plans, so was Joshua. The apostle Paul shared his plans in his letters (including when they didn't work out). Planning isn't unspiritual at all and we do it all the time. *Not* to plan in some circumstances would be irresponsible, a failure of discipleship, even lacking in love for others.

The question Proverbs often prompts is this: as we make our plans, who is our source of <u>ultimate</u> confidence in? Are we putting our greatest confidence in ourselves?

May we learn to plan well, with love for God and others, and to hold the outcome lightly.

Character matters

Better a patient man than a warrior, a man who controls his temper than one who takes a city. (Proverbs 16:32)

Martin Luther King's famously shared this vision: *I have a dream that my four little children will one day live in a nation where they will not be judged by the colour of their skin but by the content of their character.*

Character matters. We know this in our own dealings at work, with friends, in church, in marriage and family. We should expect it in leaders especially. Where leaders fail in character, many are affected. We seek to grow children in their ways of seeking what is good, true, trustworthy and so on and to reflect these qualities in themselves, in their character.

God values godly character far more than earthly honours, status or skills. Character is of far greater importance in Christian life, service and ministry than competence: a degree of competence is important, but nowhere near as important as Christ-like character. This matters in everyday church life for every Christian, even though it matters far more for those who lead, and deep character flaws have been the tragic undoing of too many Christian leaders.

Proverbs reminds us of the wisdom of God. The example comes from Solomon's time when walled cities were the common form of defence against raiders, enemy tribes and hostile warlords. To take a city was to gain renown and glory as a leader and a warrior, to boost claims to keep power and probably a means of gaining wealth too. It brought prestige and power, honour and status. Yet God says that character matters more.

To be able to keep your temper in check, to patiently endure hardship or insult rather than simply react or pick a fight: these are better in God's eyes. God's ways may be hard but they are for our good and for those we serve or lead.

Remember Jesus Christ, patiently enduring, and ultimately winning far more than a city and honoured high over all. Godly character, walking God's ways, follows in his steps.

Everything good in its time

There is a time for everything, and a season for every activity under heaven.

He has made everything beautiful in its time. He has also set eternity in the hearts of men; yet they cannot fathom what God has done from beginning to end. I know that there is nothing better for men than to be happy and do good while they live. That everyone may eat and drink, and find satisfaction in all his toil—this is the gift of God.
(Ecclesiastes 3:1, 11-13)

Our world has been described as 'hyper-connected', as the Age of Distraction. We live through constant, rapid technological change, which can be exciting, confusing, and dizzying. We are surrounded by more information than we can possibly process or respond to, available more easily and abundantly than at any previous time in world history. The devices, software and messaging systems are all designed to encourage constant interaction and connection. It takes some self-control to take control, to switch off, to unplug, and to be at ease with not giving in to the constant noise and flow.

Ecclesiastes is strong medicine for our time, both much needed and very apt. It reminds us that we are not masters of our time, but creatures within time. We cannot extend a day by even a second. We are not just finite but also frail. We lack superhuman strength and capacity, but that's ok!

God's beautiful and restorative wisdom to a stressed-out, hurried and hassled world is this: there is a time and season for everything. He has made everything beautiful in its time.

What do you notice? Firstly, we are not made to live at a pace that demands everything all the time, everywhere. It is right and wise to live within limits. It is not just healthy but how things are meant to be – a time to weep, a time to laugh, a time to be silent, a time to speak. We have permission to live well, in different seasons of life, with a different pace. This is God's wisdom too.

Secondly, we are creatures who live in time but with eternity in view, in our hearts. Our daily lives, our diaries, our energy levels and our health remind us that we are time-bound. Each day brings demands, joys, routines and news of its own. But we are also made to know the God of eternity, Lord over our beginning and end and all days in between, and so we can invite him into our days and the everyday matters of each day.

Thirdly, he cares about the everyday stuff of life. It is good to recognise the good gifts of God in the simple things: eating, drinking, sleeping; walking the dog; serving the customer; washing the dishes; writing the report; phoning a friend. Life is a gift from God. We are wise to see this and be glad.

This is the way, walk in it

Whether you turn to the right or to the left, your ears will hear a voice behind you, saying, "This is the way; walk in it." (Isaiah 30:20-21)

'God does not offer us a map so much as a promise to guide us on the journey.' (Hannah Anderson)

The life of faith with God is one where he promises to be with us each day. Each day is a new day, full of unknowns. We begin the day with some ideas about what it will hold – the usual home routines, where we might go, heading to work, phoning a friend, checking in on family, picking up kids from school, meeting up with friends or a small group in the evening. Maybe it's a special day like a birthday or potentially a tough day with a medical appointment. We know what we might expect but can't know exactly what lies ahead.

We do know that the Lord has gone before us and is with us in every day.

The Bible encourages our hearts with God's company in many and varied ways. Today's words from Isaiah are another reminder of his activity and presence – he is our guide. The Spirit of God speaks. Israel were living through times of hardship and affliction, easily distracted by the problems around or the ways of the world or their own failings, and God tells them to listen up: "This is the way; walk in it." To walk with him, his way, in each day.

In whatever today brings, may you know his company but also give space to hear his voice, to give attention to his leading in the midst of many voices, and be assured that he is our good guide.

Come and eat

"Come, all you who are thirsty, come to the waters; and you who have no money, come, buy and eat! Come, buy wine and milk without money and without cost." (Isaiah 55:1)

It wasn't just the Rolling Stones who couldn't get satisfaction. U2 still hadn't found what they were looking for either. Songs, books and films often speak of our longings, our needs, our deep desires for what will truly satisfy.

When the people of God were wandering in the wilderness for forty years, they learned that God would supply their needs. Manna from heaven, water from the rock – the most fundamental physical needs didn't come from their ingenuity or Moses' great leadership skills but from God's goodness and generosity.

Here in Isaiah's words, we hear God's appeal for us to recognise that he can and would still meet our deepest *spiritual* needs too. Our appetites go beyond food or drink. Our soul's thirst is satisfied as we come to God, as we truly take in his words directed to us and recognise that they are for our good (verse 4): "Listen, listen to me!"

The Lord Jesus declared that it is truly good to hunger and thirst after God, after the righteousness of a life found in him and in walking his ways. The blessing and favour of God is found on those who we seek after these things and 'they will be filled' (Matthew 5:6).

God gives generously, freely and abundantly to all looking for satisfaction for the soul. As Jesus fed 5000, so he still offers ultimate satisfaction. Our life is meant to be oriented so that we seek after God. Come to him and find your deepest satisfaction.

The Lord's ways and ours

"For my thoughts are not your thoughts, neither are your ways my ways," declares the LORD. *"As the heavens are higher than the earth, so are my ways higher than your ways and my thoughts than your thoughts."* (Isaiah 55:8-9)

One of the greatest gifts of Christianity in terms of our view of the world and who we are, is this: we are NOT in charge.

This is completely 100% the opposite of what the world, especially via social media, wants us to believe, where we are being formed in the belief that we are the 'masters of the universe', you are the 'captain of your soul'. So, "go be yourself, make yourself, become all that you dream of being." It's exhausting, it's nonsense, it's a really bad idea, and it's impossible! It is the source of much disappointment and anxiety, the burden of shaping up to the world. It doesn't sit well with loving God and loving others, if it's all about 'me'.

The good news from God is that we are not made to be in charge. We can rest easy in being who God made us and is making us. We don't need to 'make ourselves' or 'find ourselves', but find God, to rest in the great freedom that he is in charge, that we are made to know him and his ways. In Christ we find our greatest joy, purpose, meaning and confidence. There is great peace – He is in charge, so we can bring our questions, hopes, ambitions, fears and tears to him. Always.

One of the greatest minds of Christian history, Augustine, wrote this: 'You have made us for yourself, O Lord, and our hearts are restless until they rest in You.' We are made to be filled and fulfilled in God.

So it is a comfort that God's thoughts are not our thoughts, that his 'ways are higher' than our ways. Whatever we hope for, strive after, question or struggle with, we can trust that he rules and reigns, he will show us the best way, and we can find our deep rest in relationship to him.

Stand at the crossroads

This is what the LORD says:
"Stand at the crossroads and look; ask for the ancient paths, ask where the good way is, and walk in it, and you will find rest for your souls."
But you said, "We will not walk in it."
(Jeremiah 6:16)

C. S. Lewis coined the phrase 'chronological snobbery'; the idea that anything new must be better than anything old, and anything old worse than anything new. We see it most obviously in advertising – your perfectly good appliance/phone/shampoo/toothpaste is simply not good enough because there is now a brand new one! We see it in politics: the policies of last year or the previous government are now 'terrible' and completely 'unsuited to the needs of today' – which might be true, in part, but are they really so bad and is the new one really any better?

Honesty, integrity, kindness, protecting the vulnerable, honouring the elderly, seeking peace not war – these are all very old ideas, ancient even, yet they have proven to be good for society when people choose to live this way, deliberately and consistently.

We can easily be drawn to what seems new, shiny and exciting. But that which has been tried and tested by experience, proven its value to society, nations or ourselves, should not be discarded so quickly. That's foolish.

Jeremiah's words are relevant in every age, for every person, for our spiritual direction and wellbeing. They apply to so many moments in life: 'ask for the ancient paths, ask where the good way is, and walk in it.'

God's wisdom is ancient but tried and tested, proven in the lives of his people and in history, made plain in scripture, demonstrated and commended in the life and teaching of the Lord Jesus and the prophets and apostles. But will we choose it? Will we choose holiness over personal desires? Will we choose service of others over comfort or status? Will we choose popularity with the world over honouring Jesus and his ways?

These are timeless questions. We make small decisions each day. But we must all face the key decision, the major crossroads: is our life heading in God's path, his good ways and wisdom, to eternal life, or are we walking on our own way to destruction?

He gives wisdom and knowledge

"Praise be to the name of God for ever and ever; wisdom and power are his. He changes times and seasons; he sets up kings and deposes them. He gives wisdom to the wise and knowledge to the discerning. He reveals deep and hidden things; he knows what lies in darkness, and light dwells with him." (Daniel 2:20-22)

If you could have anything, what would you ask for? A new home or car? Better health? A holiday? A different job? Superhuman powers?! King Solomon famously was asked by God what he would want and he chose **wisdom**.

We all need wisdom. We need it to navigate life, in countless decisions and reactions, weighing up what to do, how to live, what is important or not, how to seek the best outcomes especially when a situation is stressful, uncertain or pressured. Much of this we do without thinking (what to have for breakfast, how to respond to everyday conversation, how to do many tasks in our work). Most decisions are *not* weighty and take little effort; many of our interactions with other people don't need huge insight and care to respond well with kindness, truth and grace. God is good in this way!

But at other times, real wisdom *is* needed. We may not know what to do for the best, what to say (or not to say). That might be in work, in parenting, in church life, towards a friend or neighbour, in a conflict situation or when someone is hurting. It could be in seeking a new relationship or shaping an existing one, in overcoming personal failure or trying to make an idea work. It could be with a financial decision or a friendship. Wisdom is needed to grow in our faith and understanding of God. In countless ways, wisdom is a precious gift when we have it or when someone else shares it with us.

Daniel's wonderful prayer reminds us that **God gives wisdom**. He knows – he has wisdom, and power. He gives wisdom, knowledge, insight, understanding and discernment. He gives to the wise – those who seek after his wisdom are wise!

May you know wisdom from God today, and continue to seek after more. He knows all that you need.

The righteous walk in God's ways

Who is wise? He will realize these things. Who is discerning? He will understand them. The ways of the LORD are right; the righteous walk in them, but the rebellious stumble in them. (Hosea 14:9)

'You can tell a tree by its fruit' is an ancient proverb. You can tell a person's character by their actions. So Hosea's book ends with this verse, having considered especially what living faithfully in relationship with God looks like in a godless, unjust, often violent world (much like ours). What does it look like? What does God call us to do or be? It looks like those who are wise. But who is wise?

The wise in God's eyes are those who aim to walk in God's ways. 'The ways of the LORD are right; the righteous walk in them.'

See what great value God puts on walking in his good ways! He who calls us to acknowledge him in all our ways and will make our paths straight (Proverbs 3:6) wants us to walk in his ways.

So in whatever you do today, wherever you work, rest, serve or play, God delights for you to simply walk in his ways: ways of faith, hope and love; of justice and mercy; of holiness of mind and body; of compassion and kindness; promoting what is good and resisting evil; comforting the broken-hearted and showing welcome to the stranger.

Far more than earthly wealth, power, status or fame, these matter before God. They are the 'wise' life, the good life he desires. May we enjoy walking his ways with his company.

5

THE COMING KING

Like a golden thread that runs through a beautiful tapestry or precious jewels on a seamless royal robe, the Old Testament reveals promises, prayers and people through whom we see a glorious coming king. The story of the Messiah, of a redeemer and Lord sent from God, coming to restore and to judge, to lead and to bless his people, is there from beginning to end.

Abraham, Isaac and Jacob received stunning promises of countless descendants from their offspring. All peoples on earth will be blessed through Abraham's offspring (Genesis 12:3; Acts 3:25-26). Jesus Christ is the son of David, the son of Abraham (Matthew 1:1).

At the end of his life, Jacob blesses his sons and declares that the sceptre, symbol of royal rule, will come through Judah and the obedience of the nations will be his (Genesis 49:10). A king is coming.

Israel's greatest king, David, the shepherd-boy-giant-killer-worship-leader, recognises who is truly on the throne of history, the King above all kings, and who sets out the choices for them and for us all with eternal consequences:

> *Therefore, you kings, be wise; be warned, you rulers of the earth.*
> *Serve the LORD with fear and rejoice with trembling.*
> *Kiss the Son, lest he be angry and you be destroyed in your way,*
> *for his wrath can flare up in a moment.*
> *Blessed are all who take refuge in him.* (Psalm 2:10-12)

Isaiah will speak of his suffering as the Servant, stricken and crushed, pierced for us, yet bringing healing, peace and justification (Isaiah 52:13-53:12). A king like no other, who stoops so low to serve and to save, who is good news in person (Isaiah 61:1; Luke 4:18-21) and whose kingdom is an eternal kingdom and whose dominion endures (Daniel 4:3).

2 Samuel 7:11-13,16	A king and kingdom forever
Daniel 7:13-14	The Son of Man
Psalm 110:1-2	The King over the kingdom
Isaiah 2:4	He will judge the nations
Micah 5:4-5	He will be their peace
Isaiah 9:6	To us a child is born
Zechariah 14:9	Lord over the whole earth
Luke 1:31-33	Waiting for the Messiah
Luke 1:46-49	The Mighty One has done great things
Matthew 1:21	His name is Jesus
John 1:14	The Word made flesh
Luke 1:74-75	Set free to serve
Luke 2:8-11	Good news of great joy
Matthew 2:1-2, 11	Bow before him
Matthew 25:5-6	Watching and waiting for the bridegroom

A king and kingdom forever

*"The L*ORD *declares that he will make a house for you – a dynasty of kings! For when you die and are buried with your ancestors, I will raise up one of your descendants, your own offspring, and I will make his kingdom strong. He is the one who will build a house – a temple – for my name. And I will secure his royal throne forever. Your house and your kingdom will continue before me for all time, and your throne will be secure forever."* (2 Samuel 7:11-13,16, NLT)

Perhaps the most significant news in the entire Old Testament is found in these words. The Lord God declares to King David that he is not going to build a temple (a 'house') for God, as God has no real need of a house. He doesn't live in places made of stone, brick, steel or wood. He still doesn't, even though church buildings have great significance and can be beautiful.

No, David won't be building anything soon, but God would. David's son Solomon would build a temple, a grand and shiny affair, but God is going to build a far bigger, better, more glorious house for David. That house is a 'dynasty', David's inheritance, his greatest offspring will be born in the town of David 1000 years or so from this point. He will begin life in a manger, end it on a cross, but his throne and kingdom will last forever.

David died, Solomon died, their descendants died, but the kingdom lived on until one of David's 'offspring' died and rose again to live forever. Now he is King. Jesus Christ, Son of God, the appointed ruler of the kingdom, who sits over the house of God's people.

Today, by faith, you are part of his household, an unshakeable kingdom, and nothing can take you from it. You are a son or daughter of the King. By faith you belong in his house forever. Rejoice in that good news!

The Son of Man

In my vision at night I looked, and there before me was one like a son of man, coming with the clouds of heaven. He approached the Ancient of Days and was led into his presence. He was given authority, glory and sovereign power; all peoples, nations and men of every language worshiped him. His dominion is an everlasting dominion that will not pass away, and his kingdom is one that will never be destroyed.
(Daniel 7:13-14)

Daniel had been honoured by the king for his wisdom, insight and ability to understand dreams. He saw and perceived what God was doing or saying, whether through the writing on a wall or the trials of Nebuchadnezzar's disturbing visions. He was a reliable interpreter.

This vision in chapter 7 is for our benefit too, reliably shared for us to see. What was revealed to Daniel is that God would welcome into his very presence one 'like a son of man' – a human being, a title which the Lord Jesus often adopted for himself in the gospels. Yet this man comes with the clouds of heaven; it's a divine appearance.

This God-man is led into the presence of the Almighty, the LORD, the Ancient of Days and given divine authority, glory and sovereign power. Here is an honour, reward, commissioning or elevation unlike any other. It is incomparable to any prophet, priest, king or religious leader before or since. This son of man is worthy even of worship from all humanity.

This son of man, the true Son of Man, will rule forever. His kingdom is eternal, unbreakable, unshakeable. Other kingdoms: take note.

The one whom Daniel sees has now come. His glory and power were veiled on earth, laid in a manger, utterly hidden on a cruel cross, but fully evident now and forever. His authority is absolute, his kingdom established, and he invites us to find our secure home under his glorious rule.

The King over the Kingdom

The LORD says to my Lord: "Sit at my right hand until I make your enemies a footstool for your feet." The LORD will extend your mighty sceptre from Zion; you will rule in the midst of your enemies.

(Psalm 110:1-2)

One of the Psalms known as a royal Psalm, it depicts a coronation event. The LORD, God Almighty, appoints one to sit at his right hand, the position of authority and rule, of power and glory.

This appointed king is David's 'Lord', yet David is truly a king. So there is one greater than David on this throne, one greater than earthly kings or powers, invested with all God's own authority. God has set someone for all time as King over the kingdom, and his name is Jesus.

This coronation Psalm is picked up in the teaching of Jesus and his apostles (e.g. Matthew 22:44; 26:64; Acts 2:34-35; Romans 8:34). David saw more than he could fully comprehend, the eternal rule of the Son of God at the right hand of the Father.

This rule will subdue all enemies; he has no rival and will be victorious over all our enemies. His rule will forever bring peace, life, joy and the goodness of the kingdom to all its citizens. But first the king would come and be with us, as one of us. He would stand amidst our enemies, face the full onslaught of the evil one, bear the weight of our sins, be pierced for our transgressions, go to the cross in all its shame, and die as an atoning sacrifice in our place.

This is the King that David worshipped, that Peter preached, and all heaven now praises. We can join that praise today.

He will judge between the nations

He will judge between the nations and will settle disputes for many peoples. They will beat their swords into plowshares and their spears into pruning hooks. Nation will not take up sword against nation, nor will they train for war anymore. (Isaiah 2:4)

Outside the United Nations headquarters building there is a wall, a prominent site for demonstrations to gather. Inscribed in the wall are these words from the prophet Isaiah. It speaks of an end to all conflict and war, something we can barely imagine. Human history is littered with examples of violence and warfare; our news cycle can barely keep up. War cemeteries are sobering places to visit for the scale of loss they remind us of. Social media offers plenty of scope for disputes, anger and lashing out. Personal conflict is something we are all familiar with at some point – at home, in the family, at work and in church too. We may well struggle with it significantly and God sees and knows our hurts too.

The UN was created as an act of hope and Isaiah's words point towards a hopeful future, not through human resolve, however, but by divine intervention. "He will judge."

In Advent, we reflect on the coming King who was born in Bethlehem but is the Ruler over all. He will come again as the Victor, heaven's greatest champion, offering lasting and joyful peace with God forever as we put down our arms and surrender our lives to him. He's a perfect Judge, but also a Saviour to all who call on him.

Wars will end, conflict will be no more, enmity between us and God and between nations or friends can be overcome, because God would send his Son to win the greatest of conflicts, to overcome sin and death, to open the way to peace with God and finally into an eternal kingdom with God's *shalom*, the joyful wholeness and peace for God's people. He will do this, and he will stand over all the pains and wars and conflicts of this world, as both Judge and Saviour.

He will be their peace

He will stand and shepherd his flock in the strength of the LORD, in the majesty of the name of the LORD his God. And they will live securely, for then his greatness will reach to the ends of the earth. And he will be their peace. (Micah 5:4-5)

We have a mighty Shepherd. So we are a secure flock, the people under his care.

The Old Testament contains over 300 prophecies about the Messiah (three HUNDRED!). The people who lived before Christ came and the church since then have explored this rich backdrop to God's great act in sending Jesus – prophecies of a saviour from God, the anointed one sent by the Lord, to fulfil God's great promises. Advent reminds us to wait on him – Jesus the Christ – in repentance and faith, to trust him afresh and to recognise his light in a dark world.

Today's verses connect with a particularly famous prophecy. The Magi, the wise men from the East, arrived in the court of King Herod on their search for the newborn king (Matthew 2:1-8). Herod's own council of wise men refer him to the Old Testament and Micah's words: there is one coming. This will be a good King, the good Shepherd to all God's people and one with the Lord's own strength and majesty, offering real peace for our soul forever.

Many centuries before Jesus was born, Micah relayed the word of the Lord about one to stand and rule over God's flock. This shepherd would arise in the little town of Bethlehem but his rule would extend beyond the fields to the ends of the earth!

We can join with the joyful confidence of Micah and many prophetic voices like his, that the child in the manger came to display God's mighty and good rule. He is our security; in him we can say that all is well. And he is our peace, all our cares and hopes and fears find rest as we bring them to him.

This is who we can know, by faith, with us. We can know Jesus and experience living securely in him amidst any uncertainty, difficulty or dark times.

Thank you Lord, for sending your Son, our Shepherd, our peace.

To us a child is born

For to us a child is born, to us a son is given, and the government will be on his shoulders. And he will be called Wonderful Counsellor, Mighty God, Everlasting Father, Prince of Peace. (Isaiah 9:6)

I wonder what you can recall from a school report about your achievements or potential? Was it encouraging, odd, unkind? Or perhaps what sticks in the mind comes from a work appraisal, or the unhelpful remark of a team - mate after a losing match, or words spoken by a loved one in the heat of the moment that stung. Words can become labels we hang onto, some we treasure and appreciate as truly encouraging and others can feel like burdens we try to shrug off or would rather forget.

We are reminded through the prophet Isaiah to fix our gaze again on a son raised up by God, given by the Lord, to bring peace, to save, to deliver us from our enemies. The people of Israel would experience this in a king in their day – temporary military deliverance and security from their enemies. But Isaiah speaks of a greater child, a greater Son.

Here are some of the titles for the Lord Jesus Christ: wonderful Counsellor, mighty God, everlasting Father, Prince of peace. The labels the people of Israel would come to associate with a truly great king. These would recognise his profound wisdom and rule, his mighty power, how he reflect the presence and authority of God the Father, and how he comes to bring his peaceful rule. In Christ we see these to the greatest, most perfect extent.

When we see Jesus in the gospels, we can see his interactions with people, hear his words about the kingdom and the ways of this kingdom, words of his promises and love and invitation. Isaiah's words are beyond the reach of any mere earthly ruler but match our divine King.

One of the blessings of belonging to Jesus is that he continues to offer his wisdom and comfort, his power and love, his direction and peace, and he does so to all his disciples regardless of the labels we are given in this world. It is his voice, his judgement, that really matters. And the Prince of Peace says over his own, "You are mine, you are loved, you are called to follow me and rest in me."

This is the child, the son, given to us. Let his true words shape and encourage us today.

King over the whole earth

The LORD will be king over the whole earth. On that day there will be one LORD, and his name the only name. (Zechariah 14:9)

The season of Advent is particularly helpful as a time that encourages us to reflect, remember and worship the coming King. It is a time of 'watching and waiting'. Jesus Christ, Lord of all, would come into our world as an infant that first Christmas. He lived, died to defeat sin and evil, rose again as the conqueror of death, and ascended to glory where he now reigns and intercedes for us.

He will return. This same Jesus will come again, to judge and to save. Advent is a season to remind us of the King who has come and will come again. We are in the waiting time.

The prophet Zechariah was one of many who knew what it was to watch and wait. He knew what it was to be amongst God's people who had been exiled from their home, lost their way spiritually, lost their security militarily, lost their prosperity economically and in danger of losing their identity. Where was the Lord?

Many of the prophets pick up this theme of looking forward with confident expectation of the Lord's response, of divine intervention. Looking to that day when the King comes and his rule will be over the whole earth, and 'his name the only name'; as the restored, rescued, glorified people of God we will live under his protection, care and love forever.

How good it is to choose to live under his name now, to know we belong to King Jesus. May we know his holy love towards us, his courage to enable us and his gentle leadership over us today.

Waiting for the Messiah

"You will be with child and give birth to a son, and you are to give him the name Jesus. He will be great and will be called the Son of the Most High. The Lord God will give him the throne of his father David, and he will reign over the house of Jacob forever; his kingdom will never end." (Luke 1:31-33)

The world of Mary's day was waiting for God to speak, to move, to rescue, for the Messiah to arise amongst them. What would he be like? Would they recognise him? Would he be able to deliver on the hopes they held, perhaps even more than great prophets and kings of their history like Moses and David?

Into the silence, God spoke. He sent a mighty angel from his own heavenly presence who came into our world of space, time, dust, dirt, tears, people, work, families, home, plans, fears, doubt, laughter. God's words spoke not to a parliament or to a global audience of TikTok or YouTube followers but to a girl, Mary.

To Mary and to those who were waiting, the angel's words were astonishing. The Messiah was coming and he would be her child but also the Son of the Most High!

As for how much he would deliver on the promises, the Lord God would install this child, his Son, as King. He would have David's throne, the true and greatest king of Israel was coming – a greater king, a higher throne, an enduring kingdom, and his name is Jesus. His rule was beyond Mary's grasp or ours, but the invitation to enter his kingdom still stands.

The world was waiting, and Christ has already come and will come again. He is the king of God's kingdom forever and we can find our soul's rest and greatest joy living under his wonderful rule.

The Mighty One has done great things

And Mary said: "My soul glorifies the Lord and my spirit rejoices in God my Saviour, for he has been mindful of the humble state of his servant. From now on all generations will call me blessed, for the Mighty One has done great things for me – holy is his name."
(Luke 1:46-49)

How do you see yourself before God? What kind of 'status' would you choose to describe where you stand? Mary, the mother of Jesus, had a unique role in all of human history and in God's salvation plan. She was indeed 'blessed', with the remarkable dignity and honour of bearing the Christ-child, the very Son of God. But in other ways, we are like her.

Mary offers every believer a clear-sighted view of how we stand before God. Like Mary, we are in a humble position: lowly, weak and poor compared to Him, as servants of the Lord. Yet, like her, we are also blessed beyond our understanding! Look at Jesus, the holy One, and see the Father's gift for you! See how great God's love is, that He would give His one and only Son to save all those who believe, who acknowledge Christ as Saviour and Lord. Hear His promise: "I will be with you always."

Today we can say and we can sing with Mary, "the Mighty One has done great things for me – holy is his name!"

His name is Jesus

"She will give birth to a son, and you are to give him the name Jesus, because he will save his people from their sins." (Matthew 1:21)

When we come to Christmas, Christ is 'the reason for the season!'

We rejoice in the gift from heaven, that God sent his one and only Son into the world for us, to call us to believe and have life to the fullness, to rescue us from sin and death and from life without God's presence and joy. What amazing generosity and kindness!

The angel's words tell Joseph of this remarkable divine mission, of eternity breaking into history, that Mary's son will have the name Jesus. It means 'the Lord saves' and that is exactly his great purpose: 'he will save his people from their sins'.

The promises, expectations, longings, prayers and temporary acts of salvation in the Old Testament were all pointing here, to him. We could focus on many notable events in the life of Israel, such as the covenant promises of blessing the nations, the salvation from flood and Philistines and a fiery furnace, the rescuing of slaves, the defeat of enemies and destruction of idols, the new land as a good home, the visions of God's glory, the promises of a good shepherd and a new heart, of sins washed away and a fountain of life: they all lead to a this child.

The glorious Father who would not withhold his one and only Son would fulfil all these promises. Jesus, who lived as one of us and one with us would die as the one for us to bring you and me to new life and into the Father's welcome.

May we know his joy and true peace – at any time of the year – as we receive and give thanks for this greatest Gift.

The Word made flesh

The Word became flesh and made his dwelling among us. We have seen his glory, the glory of the One and Only, who came from the Father, full of grace and truth. (John 1:14)

These well-known words should never become familiar. They are astonishing. They make a claim that the eternal God entered time and space, that the invisible and immortal Almighty One took on human form and was no less God but also one like us. For many in our world today this is unbelievable, for some blasphemous, for others it seems absurd. For Christians, it is should be a source of wonder and worship.

The Word became flesh.

He came and made his home amongst us, dwelling as God's presence amongst humanity, more glorious and powerful than any temple.

The script of all history is written by him, yet in Christ the Author enters the story to reveal himself. So the apostle John can say, again astonishingly, 'We have seen his glory' – he has SEEN the Word, not just heard **of** him or **from** him.

Jesus Christ, the Son of God, revealed God to us in human likeness, so John could say he has seen 'the glory of the One and Only' – the one and only God.

Let us never lose the wonder that Christ came as one of us, fully human, a vulnerable baby born into obscurity, extraordinary danger and the ordinary everyday trials of life. He came from the Father, full of grace and truth, that we might know our heavenly Father and receive his grace and truth for ourselves.

Set free to serve

[The Lord swore an oath to our father Abraham] "to rescue us from the hand of our enemies, and to enable us to serve him without fear in holiness and righteousness before him all our days." (Luke 1:74-75)

Zechariah was 'well advanced in years' (Luke 1:7) or, as other versions put it less diplomatically, 'very old'. He was an elderly man, full of faith, upright in God's eyes, and had a terrifying encounter with the angel Gabriel (Luke 1:11-20).

Months later the words of the angel are fulfilled; the elderly priest's wife Elizabeth gives birth to a son, John, who will become John the Baptist. The astonishing work of God, a miraculous gift of a child, is part of God's great plan not just for this couple but for the world.

Zechariah's heartfelt praise draws us to catch something of what God is doing and will do as the child prepares the way for the coming king, the Saviour. God is sending a rescuer.

The rescue will be from our enemies, and this is not the Romans or any earthly power – although those kingdoms will all fail – but rescue from the evil one, from sin's grip and penalty, from the fear of death and from a destiny in hell. God alone has power to rescue us from these and Zechariah saw rescue was coming.

Freedom from such enemies and oppression in our time restores a people or country to be able to flourish, live without fear and in new hope. We see this wherever wars cease and justice is restored. How much more does God's rescue in Jesus set us free, to serve God without fear for He is not against us but for us, and to live renewed lives 'in holiness and righteousness before him all our days.'

We are saved from sin and saved for a new life, a life with God of godly freedom, to live well before him without fear.

Good news of great joy

And there were shepherds living out in the fields nearby, keeping watch over their flocks at night. An angel of the Lord appeared to them, and the glory of the Lord shone around them, and they were terrified. But the angel said to them, "Do not be afraid. I bring you good news of great joy that will be for all the people. Today in the town of David a Saviour has been born to you; he is Christ the Lord."
(Luke 2:8-11)

The coming of the Saviour into the world was anticipated by the prophets and announced by the angel. A glorious, awesome heavenly being flooded the fields with light and brought the shepherds' usual business to a standstill. The shepherds were terrified; the reaction of the sheep is not recorded.

The words of the angel are recorded, however, and through the fearful appearance come these words that speak through the ages: "I bring you good news of great joy for all the people." What the shepherds receive is for them but also for many far and wide, for the sleeping citizens of Bethlehem, for the cosmopolitan Jews and Gentiles of Jerusalem, for the Roman oppressors and the untouchables on the street. This is good news for the nations of the world, for those billions throughout history since who have heard and believed.

This good news was not merely a message but a cosmic event, a divine act of rescue and grace, a revelation of God: "Today in the town of David a Saviour has been born to you; he is Christ the Lord."

The wait was over. The hopes of Israel for a better David, a Messiah, a saving One, had come, born among us.

May this good news flood our souls with joy too. May we know that Christ was sent for us, and we need not fear but know his welcome as we open our lives to the only Saviour and Lord over all.

Bow before him

After Jesus was born in Bethlehem in Judea, during the time of King Herod, Magi from the east came to Jerusalem and asked, "Where is the one who has been born king of the Jews? We saw his star in the east and have come to worship him."

On coming to the house, they saw the child with his mother Mary, and they bowed down and worshipped him. Then they opened their treasures and presented him with gifts of gold and of incense and of myrrh. (Matthew 2:1-2, 11)

Some of the most famous presents delivered in all of history. The stars of many a school nativity play, following the silver star, are carefully delivering their treasures wrapped in sparkly paper whilst crowns slip and dressing gowns need adjustment. It's often endearing and amusing. The reality was coloured by altogether starker and stronger tones of danger, divine guidance, fulfilment of ancient prophecy and wholehearted worship.

The wise men have travelled far - into a foreign country, with a degree of personal risk and at considerable expense. What would we endure to truly find Christ Jesus? Their gifts are not tokens but costly; 'treasures' is not hype in this case. They cross paths with the pseudo-king of the region, Herod, but still seek the true king of the Jews.

The signs in the skies led them here, the heavens declaring the glory of God in a particular time and place. Herod's courtiers confirm that the scriptures are also speaking of this; a ruler will come from Bethlehem. The search party reaches its goal as they see the child and bow and worship him.

Here is the wisdom for which the Magi are known: not the discerning of star charts, the evasion of Herod's dangerous plot, the choice of gifts fit for a king, but supremely that they see, bow down and worship. This is the response of true wisdom, the right and clear-sighted response to the Son of God, the long-awaited and much promised king of the Jews. May we bow our hearts and live lives that worship him still.

Watching and waiting for the bridegroom

The bridegroom was a long time in coming, and they all became drowsy and fell asleep. "At midnight the cry rang out: 'Here's the bridegroom! Come out to meet him!'" (Matthew 25:5-6)

Advent means 'coming', the season of waiting and watching reminds us that we live in the in- between time, between two great days – the day the Lord Jesus returned to his Father in heaven and the day when he will return from there with glory and great power to bring salvation and judgement. For now, we wait and watch.

Today's reading comes from a parable taught by Jesus where he speaks of watching and waiting for the bridegroom. In his day, the bridegroom would come to the house of the bride to take her to the wedding. They would then gather to celebrate and feast together with friends and family. His arrival would be so highly anticipated, the 'bridesmaids' keeping a lookout for signs of his arrival. A time of watchful joy for those ready to welcome him, and, of course, most of all for the bride!

In this parable, Jesus identifies himself as the Bridegroom (and John the Baptist does, and Jesus elsewhere). His people – believers, the church – are the bride. We await our joyful, happy, glorious meeting with him when he comes.

So let us be awake and alert, living in the light, living holy lives, ready to meet the Bridegroom and one day to hear his own summons as others shout, *'Here's the bridegroom! Come out to meet him!'*

.

6

JESUS THE GREAT 'I AM'

Who is Jesus?

He's the one who came from heaven (John chapter 1) and who turns water into wine (John chapter 2). The very first miracle is to enable a party to continue for a bride and groom and their guests. John calls miracles 'signs': they point to and reveal this Jesus.

That first sign, the 'rescue' of a wedding and the jars full of superb wine, tells us that Jesus brings joy and hints at his own role as the Bridegroom for the church. It's a sign that we can expect to experience something of greater joy in his presence. Is this part of our experience of Jesus already, the joy-giver?

In this section we explore the person of Christ Jesus and begin with 9 reflections where he speaks directly of who he is: his divine identity or mission. He wants us to know who he is. Each revelation also speaks to how we can know a transforming experience of Jesus in our life.

Notice, for example, how Jesus says that he provides the water of life, the bread of life and light for the world. In the wilderness wanderings, Moses led the people of God. What were their essential needs? Water, food, protection and direction.

God supplied water from the rock, food (manna) from heaven, and to protect and lead them he provided a pillar of fire. The God who spoke from a burning bush (another fire) and met them at a mountain ringed with thunder, lightning and fire, is himself the great light.

So in all three of these images and allusions Jesus is not just declaring who he is, speaking of his divine power and identity, but also presenting himself as greater than Moses, providing what God provides, not just for Israel, for one nation, for one season, but to all, for all time, as they look to him. Bread and water for life, light for the whole world.

As in Moses's day, our experience of God is also to be transforming one, meeting our fundamental needs. It shapes our heart and mind. God is able to restore and heal our deepest wounds, to overcome our inner darkness, to strengthen the hungriest and weakest soul, and fill us with joy.

Experiencing God is to encounter Christ, by the presence and power of the Holy Spirit: both supernatural and mysterious on the one hand, yet intended for everyday life of 'ordinary' believers. It is also clearly too good to keep for ourselves.

John 8:58	The eternal Son of God
John 4:13-14	Living water
John 6:32-35	The bread of life
John 8:12, 1:4	The light of the world
John 10:7-10	The gate
John 10:11,14-15	The good shepherd
John 11:25-26	The resurrection and the life
John 14:6-7	The way, the truth and the life
John 15:1-2, 4-5	The true vine

Pause, reflect, pray, receive

Matthew 11:28-30	Jesus our source of rest
Mark 2:19	The joy of the bridegroom
Luke 4:32	His amazing teaching
Luke 9:34-35	Listen to him
John 6:20	No fear
Hebrews 1:1-3	The supreme Son
Revelation 4:8-9	The song of heaven

The eternal Son of God

"I tell you the truth," Jesus answered, *"before Abraham was born, I am!"* (John 8:58)

Some of the words of Jesus which we find in the gospel accounts are quite staggering. In John's Gospel, there is a collection of sayings known as the 'I am' sayings which we will explore in the following pages. Jesus speaks of who he is; he reveals particular aspects of his identity, his mission, his nature and the impact on our lives. Each of these statements are stunning, far-reaching, echo the promises and actions of God in the Old Testament, and speak into our experience of Jesus and our faith in him today.

In John chapter 8, Jesus finds himself once again in conflict with the Jewish leaders who question him over his ethnicity ("You are a Samaritan") and even whether he is demon-possessed, implying in this instance that he is actually insane. Jesus refutes these and further claims that anyone who follows him will be spared or delivered from death! (John 8:51)

This only seems to confirm for his opponents that Jesus is mad, demon-possessed, for even Abraham and the prophets died, so who does this Jesus think he is? Does he have the secret of eternal youth or eternal life?

To which Jesus replies with a series of breath-taking claims: that the God they speak of he knows as Father, and that Abraham looked forward to the coming of the Messiah – of Jesus and his saving mission. The onlookers are bewildered. How can Jesus claim he has seen Abraham, who lived over a millennia earlier?

"I tell you the truth, … before Abraham was born, I am!"

They hear this plainly as a claim to deity. Jesus is the eternal I AM, the God-Man, the divine Son of the Father. They are ready to stone him for such blasphemy, but he speaks the truth.

Jesus speaks the truth plainly still. His words might humble, shock, encourage or amaze us. He has come as God in the flesh as Jesus of Nazareth, to walk amongst us and reveal the kingdom of God, to show and tell of the way to the Father. He is also the eternal Son of God, the great 'I am' and yet in Jesus he is also God with us.

As you seek to listen to and meet Christ through these reflections, ask him to root your life afresh in this awesome, majestic, glorious and humble Lord of all, who is full of grace and truth.

Living water

Jesus answered, "Everyone who drinks this water will be thirsty again, but whoever drinks the water I give him will never thirst. Indeed, the water I give him will become in him a spring of water welling up to eternal life." (John 4:13-14)

There are some jobs which must bring great satisfaction in particular ways. Every job should offer some satisfaction, whether it is working as postal workers, architects, decorators, nurses, engineers, pilots, window cleaners, IT support, accountants or indeed any role. But each one will have a different version of being fulfilled. I can imagine that being in advertising it must be immensely rewarding to see your ideas appear on TV adverts, online, on billboards or at cinemas. It's often about how clear, attractive, simple and compelling they can make their 'offer', and a creative setting.

By a well, in a hot country, in the middle of the day, Jesus offered a drink of water that would end all thirst for ever. "A spring of water welling up to eternal life." It could not have been a better setting, a better offer, a more universal human need, or a clearer appeal.

We all thirst – we have deep and real needs and not just for water. Jesus offers to meet our deepest spiritual thirst, to bring new and transforming life, to renew, refresh and sustain us. Ultimate satisfaction from him alone. Complete fulfilment.

Our experience of Jesus, of knowing God, can be that deep inward renewal and is by the Holy Spirit. Just as water is the symbol of life, renewal and washing clean, so the Spirit washes us from sin's stain and penalty, applying the power of forgiveness won by Christ on the cross. It's ongoing and deep spiritual refreshment that he offers, not a one off superficial encounter.

Living water from a spring or a fountain is an image of the Spirit of God at work. The Old Testament prophets point to this image of his cleansing power (e.g. Zechariah 13:1). Ezekiel speaks of water flowing endlessly from God's temple with a relentless power to bring life, growth, healing and restoration to a people in exile, desperate for hope and renewal (Ezekiel 47:1-12).

Jesus says who he is: living water. He is our source of life. We can know his salvation, forgiveness and healing. Refreshment and renewal, for our deepest needs, hurts, wounds, doubts and from the stain of sin – new life flows from him.

The bread of life

Jesus said to them, "I tell you the truth, it is not Moses who has given you the bread from heaven, but it is my Father who gives you the true bread from heaven. For the bread of God is he who comes down from heaven and gives life to the world."

"Sir," they said, "from now on give us this bread."

Then Jesus declared, "I am the bread of life. He who comes to me will never go hungry, and he who believes in me will never be thirsty."

(John 6:32-35)

We can read in John chapter 6 how, having fed the 5000 (and that's just the men, so it could well have been *far more* hungry people), Jesus is once again the focus of the crowds but also withdraws by himself (John 6:15). On returning to public view, he openly announces that if they thought *that* bread was good, important, perhaps impressive, they need to realise that *he* is **the bread of life**.

Moses oversaw the feeding of a vast multitude in the wilderness with bread from heaven, with manna. Jesus is showing that *he* is the bread from heaven, the bread of life, to sustain and satisfy our souls and not just our stomach.

As water washes clean and brings life, bread in every culture today fills stomachs. Granary, white, bloomer, sourdough, naan, chapatti, baguette, rolls, pizza bases, sliced brown, bagels, rolex or Vollkornbrot. Bread is a staple. Are we not taught to pray, 'Give us this day our daily bread'?

Now Jesus is for us that central spiritual source of food, sustenance and deep satisfaction.

How do we know God? As we come to Christ and are satisfied in our soul's needs. The desert tribes were fed for a generation, the crowd on by the Sea of Galilee for an afternoon, a day. We can be fed for life, by Jesus the bread of life.

This can be our experience of knowing God, knowing Jesus Christ, our ongoing sustaining life from God.

The light of the world

"I am the light of the world." (John 8:12)

In him was life, and that life was the light of men. (John 1:4)

Jesus declares who he is: "I am the light of the world." The source of God's life, direction, revelation and hope for all, available to all. What a picture that is of all that Jesus can offer!

As you read this, it may or may not be a sunny day where you are, but there will be light! Take a moment simply to look up, to notice the light in the sky, to see how far it spreads and how it brings out colour and shape. It reveals what you can't see in the dark. In the light, plants grow, life emerges – even in winter. The sun's light warms the earth.

As we let the light of Christ into our lives – as we seek him in prayer, open his Word and let it speak to us, as we spend time amongst his people, as we ask him to equip us at work or in our families to live for him – so we find he guides us by his Spirit, he brings new growth, he grows our love and confidence. He would dispel darkness of sin or fear. His light, his life, is shining from the Son.

Have you ever been to a music festival with maybe tens of thousands if not 100,000+ people. You can imagine it anyway: a massive crowd – celebrating, singing, dancing, with food and music. That is what the festivals for the Jews were like in ancient Jerusalem (just without the security fences, mobile phones, portaloos and speaker system). They were a big deal though, with a big crowd.

Jesus was in town for the Feast of Tabernacles (John 7:1-2), a national religious festival for the Jewish people centred on Jerusalem. A huge party and worship event. Time to celebrate and declare God's goodness again, remembering their past history and God's amazing grace in the desert, when they lived in tents (tabernacles). And God did too! Yahweh, the Lord, made his home amongst them, showing his presence in the Tent of Meeting – the tabernacle, a mobile temple.

In the tent, they were instructed to light the lampstands, flaming torches, and keep them lit. The continual light was a symbol of God's blessing and presence.

At this feast, they would celebrate as the priests came dancing and singing bearing torches to light golden menorahs – elaborate candlesticks – celebrating God's light, his presence amongst them in the desert. A light for the Jews, for the temple, and now for Jerusalem.

What does Jesus say? *I am the light of the world*.

A universal light: for the world, not just now for the Jews, no longer limited to a temple or one city. A light for all who receive him. The only light: no other source of light and life compares to him. Salvation, spiritual life, complete forgiveness, hope in the face of death – these only come from this light, the Lord Jesus Christ.

May we choose to let the light of the Son shine into our life, and walk by faith in his light.

The gate

Jesus said again, "I tell you the truth, I am the gate for the sheep. All who ever came before me were thieves and robbers, but the sheep did not listen to them. I am the gate; whoever enters through me will be saved. He will come in and go out, and find pasture. The thief comes only to steal and kill and destroy; I have come that they may have life, and have it to the full." (John 10:7-10)

In John chapter 10, we find one of the statements of Jesus which is most familiar and comforting to Christians, and yet one which is far from clear to someone who is not a Christian or churchgoer: Jesus is a *shepherd*? Prior to that, we get a saying that many Christians miss, many preachers miss too, and is perhaps even less clear in revealing his identity: Jesus says, 'I am the gate.' (John 10:7,9)

I don't know if you have a garden gate or a gate to any space at home. Maybe a stairgate to stop children advancing boldly up or stealthily down the stairs. Is Jesus keeping people in, or keeping them out? What would that even mean?

He speaks of his people as being like sheep, brought into a safe place, and protected there like the shepherds of his day. They would pen the sheep into an area with boundaries – a cave, a cliff or some rocks perhaps at one edge – and thorn bushes dragged or grown around the other sides, with an opening for sheep to enter and leave by. That opening was the gate. The shepherd would open it, close it, or the shepherd themselves would be the gate. Both gate and gatekeeper.

How do we experience Jesus as the gate? As the one who leads us into his fold, into his safety and security; a place where there is no threat, no distress, no harm or shame, no loneliness, and no burdens on our heart from him. He leads us *into* spiritual life with him watching over us, keeping us safe.

A gate also kept wolves at bay. He guards our well-being and stands against evil and threats. Jesus would do that for us as the gate. Jesus leads us into his presence and stands in our defence and for our safekeeping, as the gate.

The gate leads in but also leads *out*, it's the gateway to pasture for the sheep, to feeding. He leads us out through this gate into life with him and into places of feeding and flourishing. He is with us, so we have life, life like no other, the fullness of life with Jesus.

He's our protector, provider and the gateway into life from God.

The good shepherd

"I am the good shepherd. The good shepherd lays down his life for the sheep. ... I am the good shepherd; I know my sheep and my sheep know me—just as the Father knows me and I know the Father—and I lay down my life for the sheep." (John 10:11, 14-15)

What makes something 'good'? It might be a good meal because it was tasty, hot and nutritious. Or a good match if it was well played (which is a variable experience if you follow the English national sports teams). Or a good journey if you didn't get stuck in traffic and there were no random roadworks and no mishaps. Other things are 'good' if they deliver on quality or performance – your car, supermarket, phone company or central heating.

Jesus says he is a 'good' shepherd, in fact *the* good shepherd (singularly good). And the measure or standard of goodness he highlights is that he would lay down his life for the sheep, for the 'flock of God's pasture' (Psalm 95:7).

He would not withhold even his own life for the sake of his sheep. That is an extreme, ultimate, total mark of his goodness. A no-limit goodness. Not mere occasional kindness but total commitment for the greatest good of our salvation, our adoption into God's family, our present hope and our eternal joy.

Is God good? Look at the cross. See how he loved us. See what God has done. See the love of the Son who still watches over his own, the flock of under God's care.

He promises us his company. Moses, Joshua or David were each told that God cared for his people (and he called them shepherds over the people). Now Jesus is the greatest shepherd, and with us in person.

This is what the good shepherd does. He walks with the sheep. He calls to them and directs, to lead the way. Our role is not to dictate to the shepherd that we have better ideas, that his timing is lousy, or that he doesn't understand. We fail to grasp that Jesus is the good shepherd when we react like this. We enjoy his care as we follow.

He is not simply good in terms of 'competent to lead', but wholly good in that he loves us, completely, and wants us to know the love of God over our lives. Where other 'shepherds' might lead our lives with a lack of care, with false ideas, and with their own status, popularity or power in mind, we can submit our lives with great confidence to the very good shepherd of God's people who has proven his worth by laying all aside for the sake of saving us.

The resurrection and the life

Jesus said to her, "I am the resurrection and the life. He who believes in me will live, even though he dies; and whoever lives and believes in me will never die. Do you believe this?" (John 11:25-26)

Being a Christian, knowing God through the Lord Jesus Christ, does not cancel out grief or loss nor avoid such times. God doesn't offer us a spiritual vaccine or a divine airbag to cushion every impact. However, he does offer to be with us in these experiences, to transform them, and to show us his kindness, power or compassion in new ways.

We don't need to *live* in the valley of the shadow of death of Psalm 23, we don't make our permanent home there, but we will *walk through it* at times. He says that even there we need not fear for he walks with us. We get a glimpse into something of that experience of Jesus with us in our darker times in John chapter 11.

Lazarus, a dear friend of Jesus has died. His sisters, Mary and Martha, are grieving. Jesus is summoned and arrives later than they had hoped, but clearly on his own terms, his own timescale. Our grief, each grief, has its own timescale. We can't rush or force it.

He arrives, doesn't criticise them for grieving, and he weeps himself. The God we *know*, the one we can *experience* alongside us, is not aloof and remote from human loss and concern.

What do we see of Jesus by the grave of Lazarus? We see his own grief, but also anger and divine rage against death, against the sheer wrongness of it and against the enemy he would later face, endure, and defeat. He reacts to an offence against God's good creation, a cosmic crime, but also a personal loss. Here he declares: *I am the resurrection and the life.*

In the presence of death, Jesus stakes his claim to offer life. It is still gloriously true. He offers us real, concrete hope in the face of death so we need not fear. Death never has the last word for those in Christ. This can be our experience of him. But it does not suggest weeping is wrong nor magically wipe away all sorrow. This side of eternity, we live in a vale of tears, but God is here too.

As Lazarus would rise that day, so Jesus would rise on the third day, forever alive. His grave remains empty. He will return, and bring all God's people to himself, the living and the dead, to a full, whole and glorious new life. Let us take our grief to Jesus and receive hope and comfort from the Lord over life and death.

The way, the truth and the life

"I am the way, the truth and the life. No one can come to the Father except through me. If you had really known me, you would know who my Father is. From now on, you do know him and have seen him!"
(John 14:6-7, NLT)

Have you been to a wedding recently? Or seen one perhaps? We certainly had some interesting experiences of weddings in our church during the COVID-19 lockdown restrictions and it led to some novel wedding planning moments. Can we have 100 guests? Or 70? Or 30? Or 10?! Singing or no singing?

They were all incredibly joyful days, as they should be, and each couple planned around the restrictions well. At the end of a wedding day, if you get to see the parents of the bride or groom, there is usually a mix of great joy, relief that the day went well, strangeness that one of their offspring is now married and perhaps changed their surname, and a need to lie down!

What if, at the end of the wedding, the father of the groom said, 'You can all come back to my place, and I will provide a home for you all!' That would seem extravagant and strange in our culture, and might mean he'd had a bit too much of the fizzy drink at the top table. But in the ancient world of Jesus' day, the Father of the groom would provide for his son and his son's bride, and extend the family house to give them a home.

In John chapter 14, Jesus tells his disciples that he is leaving them, going away, but they are not to be troubled, worried or fearful. What? Why?! How will he deal with their fears?

Jesus is speaking as if his Father will provide a home, a room, for all who know him. As if he – Jesus – is the Bridegroom offering this for his bride. And who is the bride of Jesus? The church! In God's eyes, we are beautifully dressed, prepared for him, to be united with Christ by faith now and to be with him forever.

Jesus tells his friends that his Father – our heavenly Father – has room for them. We have a home with God. As we listen to Jesus and trust him, we are not strangers but children of God, accepted and loved. The very Bridegroom of heaven, the Son of the loving Father, has gone ahead to prepare room for his bride.

Our experience of Jesus is meant to be that we know we belong, we are loved, that we have a place with our Father awaiting us. And

Jesus is **the way** through life, the way through death, all the way home, and all the way to his Father and our Father. Not just the way to his 'home' but to really know the Father's love.

He is **the truth** amidst all the worlds lies, false hopes, life-sapping idols and self-centred delusions. He is the one to unite our life with, he is the truth of God.

And in him is **life**. He is life, the life of God for the world. To know him is to have life.

The wedding party awaits all who choose this way, this truth, this life, which is Jesus.

The true vine

"I am the true vine, and my Father is the gardener. He cuts off every branch in me that bears no fruit, while every branch that does bear fruit he prunes so that it will be even more fruitful. ... Remain in me, and I will remain in you. No branch can bear fruit by itself; it must remain in the vine. Neither can you bear fruit unless you remain in me.

I am the vine; you are the branches. If anyone remains in me and I in them, they will bear much fruit; apart from me you can do nothing."

(John 15:1-2, 4-5)

How does this speak to our experience of God? It suggests a strong sense of belonging: 'Remain in me'. 'Abide' is the sense of it. Jesus illustrates connection, intimacy and the promise of growth.

Jesus isn't calling us to a knowledge of God that is a fleeting awareness, or casual acquaintance. I sometimes call myself a fan of English cricket, but often find the actual experience when I get closer to reality and follow the matches can been deeply frustrating!

I'm also a fan of Liverpool Football Club, which is happily an altogether more positive association in my mind. But I haven't been to a match in decades, haven't ever been to Anfield, and couldn't tell you the whole line-up of the first team. It's hardly an intimate relationship.

But I could talk all day about the churches I've been part of and served in: in Ampthill, Ruislip, Leeds and Bath. Why could I tell so many stories and be enthusiastic, drawing such encouragement from them still, even be moved to tears by some of these memories? Because of the deep connections, the intimacy of life, the mutual love between people, the sharing of joys and sorrows, and more. And because there is Jesus in the midst of his church – sustaining, leading, feeding, and saving. He is the focus of our life and worship.

Jesus calls us in these words to recognise how central he is to our mutual life. The branches don't just exist somewhere in the general vicinity of the vine, they are connected. They abide, they remain.

Jesus is the means of our collective life and growth, and a place of belonging with Father, Son and Holy Spirit. We experience God as we choose to draw our life from him. We don't need to draw it from ourselves, from our sense of being busy for God, certainly not from the world. He is the vine, the true vine, central to the life of God's people, and we can be the fruitful, much loved, growing disciples.

Pause, reflect, pray, receive

As you read through this chapter focused on the Lord Jesus Christ, take some time to stop and look back at what God is saying through these few words of Jesus in the preceding reflections.

The apostle John shows us, like a trail of breadcrumbs for us to follow, that we can know Jesus for who HE says he is. Not simply statements about his status as God (although that is unmistakable), and not simply a future eternal hope we can hold onto (although that is abundantly clear too), but what he says of **our present experience of Christ**.

As Jesus says, we can know God, truly, by knowing God the Son. He leads us to the Father. It is his Holy Spirit poured out on us. So we can experience:

- Jesus as the water of life for renewal and forgiveness;

- Jesus as our bread to sustain and strengthen us, to feed our soul;

- Jesus as our light to guide, awaken, protect and remind us of his presence;

- Jesus as our gate, as the gatekeeper, leading us into salvation security and out into the good pasture of life with him;

- Jesus our shepherd, who loves us to the end, leads us so well, and cares for us completely;

- Jesus the resurrection and the risen one, who knows our grief but also overcomes our fear and walks with us through dark places;

- Jesus the way, the truth and the life – the Son of the Father, the bridegroom waiting for his church, in whom we have a forever home, a belonging; and

- Jesus the vine, an unfailing source of life, of God's love and new life flowing to us, joining us to him, equipping us for all that God wants for fruitfulness growth, service, and mission.

How MUCH he loves us!

How GOOD is Jesus Christ. See what God has done.

Thanks be to God for his indescribable gift! (2 Corinthians 9:15)

I pray that you might be encouraged in heart in your own experience of Jesus, that you can know God in your everyday life, not because of who you are and what you do, but because of who he is and what he has done and is doing.

Some response questions for you to consider:

What have I most appreciated of Christ's company in the past year?

Is there any aspect of Jesus which he speaks of here in John's Gospel that I need to receive more fully?

Who has encouraged me in my walk with Christ in the past few years? How might I encourage them?

In which part of my life do I want to know Christ more fully? e.g. Work, home, family, marriage, friendships, Christian service?

How am I nurturing my own growth in Christ?

Jesus our source of rest

"Come to me, all you who are weary and burdened, and I will give you rest. Take my yoke upon you and learn from me, for I am gentle and humble in heart, and you will find rest for your souls. For my yoke is easy and my burden is light." (Matthew 11:28-30)

When Moses was appointed as the leader of God's people, he was unnerved by the enormity of responsibility. It weighed heavily on him. He asked the LORD who would be sent as a companion, to support and encourage and strengthen him for the task.

The LORD replied, "My Presence will go with you, and I will give you rest." (Exodus 33:14)

The promise of God was of his own 'face', his Presence. The LORD himself would be present in power by his Spirit and with angelic protection. Moses then asked for an encounter with God's glory (Exodus 33:18). Notice the assurance of what God's presence would bring to Moses and Israel: 'I will give you rest.'

In the words of Jesus to his disciples, then and now, we hear the same promise: "Come to me, all you who are weary and burdened, and I will give you rest."

Jesus cared for the physical well-being of his friends when they were tired and hungry. He knew human needs and burdens too. But he offers us rest for our soul, rest from the striving to find acceptance before God, rest from spiritual performance or guilt. He offers us a new heart alive to God, forgiveness of sins and a clear conscience, and peace that God is for us so we have rest in his presence.

God's own presence stood before the disciples, clothed in humanity but in the fullness of God himself. The glory of the Lord is found in this Jesus too, who alone offers our soul the great rest of God's peace both in this world and in our eternal future. The promise made to Moses is fulfilled in greater, clearer terms by Jesus who still beckons us to come to him for our rest.

The joy of the bridegroom

Jesus answered, "How can the guests of the bridegroom fast while he is with them? They cannot, so long as they have him with them."
(Mark 2:19)

You can't get far in reading the gospels and seeing the impact of Jesus without realising that he prompts **joy**. This is a key characteristic of the Christian life still – the life of Jesus within us prompts joy, a lively sense of thanksgiving and well-being and soul-strengthening-good-to-be-with-Jesus joy!

His first miracle was a clue to this: providing copious amounts of high quality wine at a wedding party. Not just a good thing to do, not just a popular contribution, but a joyful gift and a sign of who he is. The ultimate joy-giver.

Today's verse isn't at a wedding but Jesus speaks of himself as the bridegroom. He is the ultimate bridegroom for the wedding to top all weddings, for it is the wedding to his own bride – the church, to all believers who own his name 'Christ-ian'. Those 'in Christ'.

At the end of all time, Christ will return and call to himself all his own, those living and those who have died, and be united to them as a bridegroom to his beautiful bride. A Christian marriage is a mini-model of this great reality. What joy a wedding includes now, what joy there will be then at the great wedding feast!

As Jesus spoke with his friends, they could not fail to be joyful, to rejoice at having him amongst them. It was not the time to *fast* but to *feast*. And by his Spirit, we have him with us now and his joy can be our strength and comfort.

May the joy of Jesus be ours today, for he is with us and would offer us great joy.

His amazing teaching

They were amazed at his teaching, because his message had authority.
(Luke 4:32)

Jesus was a carpenter's son (Joseph was a *'teknon'* (the Greek term); a builder, carpenter, stonemason, probably not just a carpenter.) Jesus was not the son of a rabbi or from a position of influence, which is the background most people would have expected of their religious leaders.

Jesus was even from Nazareth, considered a rural backwater, not glorious Jerusalem – the city of kings and home of the temple.

In the assessment of the crowds, he didn't *seem* like someone who ought to be impressing them, but they could not take their eyes off him, nor fail to find that his words grabbed their attention and stuck in the mind. And it was said that he had performed miracles. This was the kind of talk around this Jesus as he began publicly to preach and share the message of God's kingdom.

Today's verse from Luke comes from that very early point, as Jesus begins to be noticed and heard on the stage of public appearances. Religious teachers would be trained in how to teach and preach, typically referring to a long line of traditions and other well-known teachers as their sources of authority. Not Jesus, he simply taught. He spoke and said 'Truly, I say to you ...' His own message had authority, an obvious and weighty significance, a sense of ultimate truth, from himself!

This was what 'amazed' them. The message, the teaching, was not just memorable, or interesting, or even exciting (and inviting people into God's kingdom was all those). It came with authority and the authority rested in Jesus himself.

As you come to the Bible, the Old or New Testament, recognise that behind it stands the authority of God, fulfilled and focused on God the Son, who speaks to us truly. He is the guarantee that God's words are good, true and for our life. And they were right, he really is amazing.

Listen to him

While he was speaking, a cloud appeared and enveloped them, and they were afraid as they entered the cloud. A voice came from the cloud, saying, "This is my Son, whom I have chosen; listen to him."

(Luke 9:34-35)

Everywhere Jesus went people remarked on his wisdom and authority. His words had weight. His lessons on life were immensely perceptive and memorable. His insights connected with the deepest human needs, our fears and hopes, our temptations and worries, our spiritual hunger and thirst. No wonder crowds were drawn to him.

It is from Jesus that we learn of the Good Samaritan, the Prodigal Son, and the Lost Sheep – memorable stories of depth and power. It is Jesus who spoke of his word like good seed, the kingdom growing in our hearts as we receive and don't reject the word (Mark 4). The apostle John spoke of him as being the Word, the living word of God, as the word made flesh.

Everything about Jesus tells us to listen to him and in Luke's account of the transfiguration Jesus we have a compelling instruction to do so. The voice of God speaks over his Son, his beloved and chosen Son: "Listen to him."

Jesus himself taught that to build your life on his words is to build it on solid foundations, as if on rock rather than shifting sand. Such a life resists spiritual storms and stands firm to the end before God (Matthew 7:24-27). This outcome relies on hearing his words and putting them into practice: that is, to listen to him.

To go to him is to find that he has the words of eternal life, so, as the apostle Peter asked, if not to Jesus then "Lord, to whom shall we go?" (John 6:68) Who else is sufficient to lead our lives, to bring us to the Father? Our heavenly Father sends us to the Son, to respond to Christ in obedience and submission: "Listen to him."

When we do, we find we have surrendered to a Master who is gentle and humble in heart, who leads us into rest for our soul, and that his ways are good. The truth from him is no straitjacket from the best life, the truth will set us free. May we listen to him – truly, carefully, humbly, daily and deeply.

No fear

But he said to them, "It is I; don't be afraid." (John 6:20)

A lake can be a place of great beauty. The Lake District is one of the most popular areas for tourism in the UK and the lakes are the jewels in a dramatic landscape of mountains and valleys. As the water reflects the sky and surrounding terrain so each lake can display very varied 'character' depending on the light, the weather, the season and your perspective. Being on the lake brings quite a different sense to merely gazing from the shore.

In John chapter 6, Jesus is on the lake. His disciples are also on the lake, with one significant key difference: they are in a boat.

It is dark as they cross the lake and it is a significant distance to cover, it is 8 miles across the Sea of Galilee at the widest point. The wind is rising, the waves growing more rough, progress is getting slow. This is no tourist trip to admire the lake. It would be unsettling and demanding, even for experienced fishermen.

They then have an extraordinary experience: in the middle of the lake, in the dark and on the rough water, someone is coming towards them. Jesus is walking on the water. 'They saw him and were terrified.'

Immediately Jesus speaks and it is both a revelation of who he is and words to still their fears: 'It is I; don't be afraid.' Literally, 'I, I am, do not fear.'

To have fear in such a situation would be entirely natural. To recognize the divine power of Jesus over the forces of nature is enough to inspire awe and holy dread before him. Jesus demonstrates the same power as that of the Living God over this world:

> *He alone stretches out the heavens and treads on the waves of the sea. (Job 9:8)*

Jesus would come to us today and want us to know him truly ('It is I'), without diminishing his glory and power, yet he also wants to still our hearts ('don't be afraid.') Knowing his presence with us changes everything.

Like the disciples, he can take us safe to shore. So with Jesus we need have no fear, awesome though he is.

The supreme Son

In the past God spoke to our forefathers through the prophets at many times and in various ways, but in these last days he has spoken to us by his Son, whom he appointed heir of all things, and through whom he made the universe. The Son is the radiance of God's glory and the exact representation of his being, sustaining all things by his powerful word.
(Hebrews 1:1-3)

When a new film is approaching its release date, the trailer is launched: typically a short, 2-minute collection of brief soundbites, snippets of action, hints to the main plotline, shots of the main characters and hopefully no 'spoilers'. The best trailers leave you wanting more and wondering what is to come (and the worst leave you knowing exactly what the film is about and how it ends). But even the best trailer is no comparison to the full feature, to the real thing.

The Book of Hebrews begins by saying that we have already seen the trailer. Those who sought after God, the living God of Moses, Yahweh, heard his voice. God's word came to them 'in the past' to various people, through many prophets, in various ways. It was wonderful yet fragmented and occasional, not the fullest picture. God spoke through fire, lightning, parted seas, manna from heaven, humbled enemies, dreams and visions from heaven, through angels and animals, with signs on the earth and in the sky, and by inspired prophetic words. The 'trailer' was incredible, beautiful, wide-ranging and full of anticipation.

But that was just the trailer, now behold the real thing: 'In these last days he has spoken to us by his Son.' It literally reads 'by Son' – a whole new category of revelation, incomparably greater and fuller and clearer than the prophets. In Jesus we meet and hear God's word in person, the supreme word of God. All scripture points to him.

He is supreme in his ***revelation***. He is also supreme in his honour and dignity: God appointed him heir of all things. He inherits the cosmos. All creation will honour him and bow before him.

Jesus is supreme in ***power***, for God created all things through him (John 1:3; Colossians 1:16). Every part of creation bears his touch, comes from his hand, and is still sustained by his powerful word – his ongoing active fulfilment of God's purposes.

So it follows that Jesus is the one from whom the bright ***glory*** of God shines out. He radiates the holiness, beauty, love, power, wisdom and more of God Almighty. He is the 'exact representation', the perfect vision of God; when we see Jesus we see God in person, his very character and perfect ways.

The trailer was a sight to behold, stunning in its impact, yet the main event is supreme beyond our comprehension. There is none like Jesus.

The song of heaven

And when he had taken it, the four living creatures and the twenty-four elders fell down before the Lamb. Each one had a harp and they were holding golden bowls full of incense, which are the prayers of the saints. And they sang a new song:

"You are worthy to take the scroll and to open its seals, because you were slain, and with your blood you purchased men for God from every tribe and language and people and nation." (Revelation 4:8-9)

For all eternity, Jesus will be the focus of heaven's worship. This is what the choir will sing, and we are invited to join in.

He is the object of praise and thanks for his great worth, glory and greatness. This worthiness has been demonstrated to all the powers and authorities in all creation, seen and unseen, to all humanity and to the angels and demons. He is unquestionably worthy of praise without limit.

The reason for his praise, the measure of his worth, is 'because he was slain'. The Lamb of God, the Holy One, was sacrificed for sin to rescue sinners and to satisfy holy justice. He went into death so that we might not be held captive by death. He endured wrath so that we might receive mercy. He paid the price that we could not pay.

So we are bought at a price, at great cost, and by a living faith in Christ we now belong to him.

Heaven sings and the salvation party is so large, so widespread, encompassing people from every tribe, language, people and nation. Not all people are there, only those in Christ, but people from all walks of life, from all corners of the globe, rescued from every possible kind of sin and in our earthly life have been sent into every possible area of good work in Christ's name.

In the busyness or demands of each day, take time to reflect on the wonder of Jesus, on his greatness and beauty, and that he died so that you might join in the ultimate choir with great joy. He has made the way open into eternal life for all who trust in him and heaven is filled with singing already.

May our lives echo this song as we prepare to join the party.

7

THE LORD'S PRAYER

The Lord's Prayer is a gift of great value indeed, from Christ to his disciples. When they asked how to pray, the Lord Jesus gave them this prayer. It is simple but not simplistic. It is short yet covers such a broad range of rich themes, taking our gaze from heaven to earth and back again.

The Lord Jesus did not teach them *what* to pray but *how*, so other forms of words are allowed and encouraged of course, as Jesus himself demonstrated and as the Bible records. The Lord's Prayer is a model for our approach to prayer.

The three-fold opening lines call us to come before God, to bring him praise and adoration, beginning with petitions and prayers for God's honour, glory and kingdom purposes. It then moves to three prayers for ourselves: for our physical needs and well-being, for our forgiveness which is key to our relationship with God and others and for our guidance and protection in spiritual life and in moral challenges. The conventional closing line of the prayer is not found in the accounts of Matthew or Luke but is a fitting conclusion of praise, a doxology, returning our focus onto our God and Father.

As you read and reflect, may the Lord again enrich your life with him through prayer.

John 20:17	Our Father in heaven
Isaiah 57:15	Hallowed be Your name
Mark 1:15	May Your kingdom come
Luke 9:23	May Your will be done
Habakkuk 2:14	On earth as it is in heaven
Matthew 6:8	Give us today our daily bread
Colossians 3:13	Forgive us our sins
Proverbs 2:7	Lead us not into temptation
Ephesians 6:13	Deliver us from evil
1 Chronicles 29:11	Yours is the kingdom, the power and the glory, Amen

Our Father in heaven

Jesus said, "Do not hold on to me, for I have not yet returned to the Father. Go instead to my brothers and tell them, 'I am returning to my Father and your Father, to my God and your God.'" (John 20:17)

When Jesus taught his disciples to pray, he said: 'This is how you should pray, "Our Father in heaven …" '(Matthew 6:9). He spoke of his Father as "My God and your God" – one and the same. In prayer we get to address God, to approach him and Jesus calls us to do so regularly, confidently, personally and to come before our heavenly Father.

It would have been unheard of and scandalous for first century Jews to address God as "Father", yet Jesus teaches us to do so. He is the true Son of the Father and he invites us, collectively, to pray with our fellow disciples to God as **our** heavenly Father.

Prayer is personal. It is not directed to a vague unnamed force nor to fate and it is not merely hedging our bets that it will help. We don't pray to improve ourselves or to summon up good feelings at the start of the day. Prayer is a means of grace for Christians. God is 'our' Father, not Father to all, and we intentionally seek him as we pray.

In prayer we bring ourselves before the living God who is a divine person and resides in the glorious kingdom of heaven but whose eyes are set on his children on earth. He is transcendent, unseen, yet we can come before him as the Son ushers his disciples into his Father's presence.

Today, may we know that we can bring all things to our heavenly Father. Jesus has opened the way and leads us into the Father's presence with a "Welcome". The Holy Spirit carries our prayers and enables us to pray, even when words fail us. And our Father hears.

Let us bring ourselves before our unseen yet ever-present heavenly Father, and know that he delights to hear the prayers of his humble and faithful children.

Hallowed be Your name

For this is what the high and lofty One says – he who lives forever, whose name is holy: "I live in a high and holy place, but also with him who is contrite and lowly in spirit, to revive the spirit of the lowly and to revive the heart of the contrite." (Isaiah 57:15)

In the Lord's Prayer, Jesus teaches his disciples everywhere how to pray. Here is a model of prayer, one to shape our praying. Today as we pray we might bow our heads, perhaps we feel 'lowly in spirit', but let's look up by faith to our Father in heaven who welcomes us.

Let us recognise that he is God in a 'high and holy place'. He's always ready to lift our heads and revive our hearts. He's all-powerful yet gentle towards us.

Our Father is holy, everything about him is pure and holy and therefore wholly good. His 'name' means all he is and stands for. It represents his character and reputation, his glory and honour. May his name receive all that is due to him.

All he does and says is true, right and good. He is above and beyond our imagination but, in Christ Jesus, God lived amongst us as one of us, to show us the Father and to save us. This holy One took on human nature so he knows our needs and struggles. Jesus is wonderfully ready to walk with us through each day. He is humble and gentle in heart towards us, and gently leads us and teaches us to live holy lives, 'hallowed' lives.

As we pray, 'Hallowed be Your name', we rely on our 'high and holy' God to revive us as we come in humility, trust and repentance. We can pray that our wonderful and holy God would be known in our world, his name be held up as holy, and that many would seek him and find him for themselves.

May Your kingdom come

"The time has come," he said. "The kingdom of God is near. Repent and believe the good news!" (Mark 1:15)

Abraham *Kuyper was a Prime Minister of Holland, a journalist and a theologian (quite the CV!). He once said,* 'There is not a *square inch* in the whole domain of our human existence over which Christ, who is Sovereign over all, does not cry, Mine!'

When Jesus said, "The time has come," it was the King in person inviting people into the kingdom, his kingdom. "Repent and believe!" Good news came in person.

The kingdoms of this world, every empire and company, every fad and fashion, will change and fade. There is one kingdom that is eternal, unshakeable, always good and spreading over the world: the kingdom of God. Entry is free but difficult; in fact it is impossible to enter without God's gracious action. We must be born again, born from above, by the Holy Spirit as we repent and believe (John 3:3).

The gate is narrow, the way is hard, but the King beckons us in to his most excellent kingdom and the fullness of life with him. The gatekeeper, Christ Jesus, has declared the way "open" through him! He has made the way for all who will follow. The King invites all to enter and seeks out the lost to find their way home. All are invited, but only by grace can we enter, only by faith will we be saved.

As we go into our day, we can know that the King of the kingdom goes before us, and by faith we can trust him to help us as we seek his kingdom through our prayers, our good work, our interactions with others and as we serve.

May Your will be done

Then he said to them all: "If anyone would come after me, he must deny himself and take up his cross daily and follow me." (Luke 9:23)

When we pray the Lord's Prayer, we say to our heavenly Father, "May your will be done." The Lord Jesus encourages us to pray that God's own purposes and plans would be accomplished in our lives and in the wider world, recognising our needs and wants too.

This part of the prayer reminds us that his concerns should be our concern, and not overlooked with "MY will be done." That excludes what he may desire for us or in our world, even as he cares for our needs. When we pray into God's purposes and in line with his word, we find that we are changed, perhaps challenged, and often encouraged or comforted. We don't lose out by focusing on God!

This selfless focus, however, is not natural for us! We naturally look to ourselves or gravitate to our own concerns. Prayer changes us; it changes our perspective. It brings us before God and reminds us that he is good, his kingdom is great, and that he desires us to pray and act. We want his will to be done.

Jesus taught this prayer to his disciples. In the final hours before his death, in the garden of Gethsemane, Jesus was facing the prospect of the cross, of abandonment and humiliation. The horror of bearing sin and shame in our place was before him; the divine punishment which would fall on him rather than us. In that dark and painful place, he prayed "Not my will but yours be done" (Luke 22:42). He saw the goodness of seeking the Father's will, always.

As we follow Jesus today, as we 'take up our cross', let us surrender our needs and plans, our challenges and concerns, into our Father's strong hands. Like Jesus, let's humbly trust, "May Your will be done."

On earth as it is in heaven

For the earth will be filled with the knowledge of the glory of the LORD, as the waters cover the sea. (Habakkuk 2:14)

When we pray for God's kingdom to come and his will to be done '*On earth as it is in heaven*' this is a BIG prayer! It spans the world and it calls for a deep and glorious transformation. We don't just want little signs of God's kingdom here and there, just in our home or workplace; we want to see the kingdom of God everywhere and touching everyone with God's own love, rescue, healing, kindness, justice, mercy and goodness. That is a prayer filled with hope and one to pray boldly.

When we look at the news, such an answer to prayer seems so unlikely. We see refugee crises, wars, the gross inequality of rich and poor, the absence of integrity in many leaders, food poverty in the UK and famine around the world, racism, the grim nature of much of that appears online and so on. Where is the sense in our day of heaven's presence, of God's glorious ways on earth? Yet Jesus tells us to pray like this.

The prayer reminds us that we look up to a God with whom all things are possible, and he is able to work in us and through us. It reminds us that his kingdom started small but is growing, irresistibly. Prayer connects us with his power and his purposes. Prayer enters a spiritual battle fought in God's mighty strength.

We can bring the kingdom's presence into our world through how we live, what we do, what we speak up for and against, and through God's character shaping our choices and speech. Let us not overlook prayer though.

We also have hope: one day the whole earth will be renewed, and God's people with it, and 'The earth will be filled with the knowledge of the glory of the LORD'. That day is coming.

Come, Lord Jesus.

Give us today our daily bread

"... your Father knows exactly what you need even before you ask him!" (Matthew 6:8, NLT)

Are you hungry? Perhaps you are reading this before or during breakfast. Food is one of our basic requirements, an essential human need. We don't get through much of the day without it. If we pause and take stock of our health, well-being and circumstances, we recognise that we each have a diverse range of needs including physical, emotional and spiritual needs. We are complex beings, 'fearfully and wonderfully made', and life presents many and varied challenges.

God knows what we really *need*; he is our Maker after all. Surely, he understands our needs in ways that are fuller and clearer than we can. He is able to give us wisdom to discern our needs, to assess what we need to restore our well-being or support our family or make progress in a career, overcoming a problem or deepening a relationship. This includes what we need to grow in our faith.

When Jesus encourages us to pray "Give us this day our daily bread", he is reminding us how wonderfully practical God's care is. The Creator of the universe invites us to pray for what we need today.

Bread was the staple food of Jesus' day, as it still is for many societies of the world. Jesus isn't just saying we can pray for our supply of carbohydrates, he encourages us to bring before our heavenly Father God our true needs, of body, mind or spirit, as part of his good purposes for us. For our Father already knows; he delights to hear us, and he is so good. He doesn't need long prayers or long words; he delights for us to lean on him.

May his word feed us, and may the Lord meet our deepest needs even today.

Forgive us our sins

Bear with each other and forgive whatever grievances you may have against one another. Forgive as the Lord forgave you.

(Colossians 3:13)

It used to be that bills demanding payment came in the post. Increasingly ours come by email, which is better for the environment but to be honest I can easily glaze over with 'official' emails and not check the payments going out. I once had a gas bill that was £800 higher than it should have been, and I was very glad I noticed!

Paying attention to our financial debts or obligations can be done by reading the letters, emails or bank statements. It's hopefully not that complicated. Paying attention to what we owe other people in other ways takes more care; it requires thoughtfulness and reflection, and we don't receive notifications by email.

The Lord calls us to 'Bear with each other' and to 'Forgive one another'. We have a duty of care, a debt of love and compassion, to be patient with the needs or faults of others, as God's people, reflecting God's love and his forgiveness towards us.

Forgiveness is costly. It requires setting aside the urge to get even, to lash out, to grumble or become bitter. However, as we bear with one another and forgive others, we are able to leave space for God to soften our hearts and those of others, to bring repentance or restoration, and to help us let go of hurt or anger. Forgiveness can be hard indeed but the Lord God has forgiven us, he bore the great cost of our wrongdoing and rebellion. Forgiveness can also show God's ways in a world in great need of kindness, reconciliation and grace.

As you go through today, the Lord's Prayer calls us to look to God for our forgiveness and be confident that he forgives, but also to forgive others, deliberately and carefully. May you know the joy of both – of debts paid and debts set aside, 'As the Lord forgave you'.

Lead us not into temptation

He holds victory in store for the upright, he is a shield to those whose walk is blameless. (Proverbs 2:7)

We live in a time where our security and protection are common concerns. We protect our homes and cars with alarms and locks. We protect our money and identity details behind passwords. We've been through a pandemic where we all learned so much about the protection of ourselves and others with masks, distance, hand-washing, PPE, vaccines and so on.

The Bible makes it abundantly plain that following Jesus does **not** automatically protect us from harm – we will experience the hurts and trials of life too. But God speaks equally clearly that he is our Shield. He protects us from spiritual harm and danger. He is with us in all troubles and temptation. Our soul, our spiritual life, is safe when we trust ourselves into his hands and follow his lead.

When we face spiritual battles for trying to do the right thing, or especially in speaking of the good news of Jesus, we will experience spiritual opposition. The many promises of God's protection, presence and guidance for his people are a wonderful source of assurance.

When we pray the Lord's Prayer and ask 'Lead us not into temptation', we put ourselves into God's hands, looking for that protection and his direction. 'Lead us' and do so away from spiritual harm, away from that which would destroy, discourage or point us away from God's good ways. 'Lead us' not into temptation – the short-term gain or pleasure of that which is sinful and selfish – but 'Lead us' towards what is true, right, just, kind, noble and loving. This is the way of 'the upright'.

He is our Shield and our Defender, may we know his care and wisdom today.

Deliver us from evil

Therefore put on the full armour of God, so that when the day of evil comes, you may be able to stand your ground, and after you have done everything, to stand. (Ephesians 6:13)

Jesus teaches us in the Lord's Prayer to pray "Father, deliver us from the evil one" (Matthew 6:13). He knows we face an enemy, the devil. Jesus faced him throughout his earthly ministry and defeated him fully at the cross, but the evil one is still at work. His days are numbered, his power is diminished, his end is certain, but he remains active for now against God's kingdom and God's people. Yet God is for us and with us! And we are called to pray.

Our God, the mighty Lord of Hosts, provides for us armour to wear that we might stand against evil or in the midst of it. We might feel overwhelmed in a personal situation where wrongdoing, injustice or outright evil is present. We might feel shocked and helpless by events in the wider world, terrible crimes perhaps, or by sinful behaviour in the church which grieves God. In such times, God's promise is still true: he will enable his faithful followers to stand their ground.

We're given the confident promises of God and his powerful gospel of salvation. God offers us strength, protection, peace, deliverance and more in the fight. The experience of his people in the Old and New Testaments demonstrates God's strength in our weakness time and again; they could stand, so can we.

As the apostle James said, 'Humble yourselves before God. Resist the devil, and he will flee from you.' Fresh strength and resolve come from God.

Prayer opens our hearts and minds to receive from God. May God grant us protection and peace. May we have wisdom in the good fight for when to speak and when to be silent, when to strive and when to rest. May he hear our prayers for our world in places where we see evil at work. Come, Lord Jesus, and deliver us.

Yours is the kingdom, the power and the glory, Amen

"Yours, O LORD, is the greatness and the power
and the glory and the majesty and the splendour,
for everything in heaven and earth is yours.
Yours, O LORD, is the kingdom;
you are exalted as head over all."

(1 Chronicles 29:11)

When we pray the Lord's Prayer, traditionally it ends with "For the kingdom, the power and the glory are yours, for ever and ever, Amen." These words don't appear in the Gospel versions in Matthew 6 or Luke 11 but they certainly are very fitting. They draw from many Old Testament prayers, such as our verse today, where praise of the Lord spills out to recount the breadth and depth of his rule and splendour.

God rules. All the glory of the nations is as nothing compared to his glory.

In prayer, we come before the Lord God who rules and reigns, who outlasts all empires, outranks all Presidents or Prime Ministers, who sees everyone from the least to the greatest and who sustains planets, nations, people and all life. The whole cosmos is held in his hands, sustained moment by moment by him in his radiant glory (Hebrews 1:1).

How thankful we can be that this God is supreme not just in power and glory but also in love, mercy and justice. That's the Ruler we need!

Give thanks today for God's goodness and greatness. Let's pray for his kingdom and glory to be seen across the world – from Ampthill to Afghanistan – for the name of Jesus and the ways of his kingdom to be embraced and honoured, and for our everyday lives to bring glory to our Father in heaven.

8

THE CRUCIFIED AND RISEN SAVIOUR

The centre-piece of the Christian faith and the heart of the Bible's storyline is where all four gospel accounts devote so much attention. The focus is on events which occur over just a few days, even hours, and within a tight geographical space: the entrance to Jerusalem, an upper room, Gethsemane, a rushed trial by night, the prisoner before the religious leaders and Pontius Pilate, Calvary and the man on the cross, and an empty tomb.

From death to life, from shame to glory. From hopes apparently dashed and scattered disciples to the growing global family of God's people, a family by faith whose hope rests on our crucified and risen Saviour, their songs already sung in heaven itself in praise of the Lamb who was slain.

The passion of the Christ, the way to the cross and from the tomb, dominates the story for each of the four gospel accounts. The message of the cross and resurrection are also the heart of the apostles' preaching, even their boasting, in the Book of Acts and the rest of the New Testament. These events don't simply explain our faith; they underpin it as the grounds for our faith, hope and love.

The following 16 reflections draw on only a few occasions where these are the focus, to draw us again to Christ Jesus and remind us why he is the one to whom all God's children will direct their praise forever.

Seven 'words' of Jesus from the cross:

Matthew 27:45-46	Forsaken
Luke 23:33-34	Father, forgive them
Luke 23:42-43	Today you will be with me
John 19:26-27	Here is your son, here is your mother
John 19:28	I am thirsty
John 19:29-30	It is finished
Luke 23:44-46	Father, into your hands I commit my spirit

Leviticus 16:30	Our scapegoat
Isaiah 50:7	Set his face like flint
Isaiah 53:5	He bore our transgressions
John 19:5	Behold the man!
1 Corinthians 1:18	The wisdom of the cross
Hebrews 2:14-15	To destroy the power of the evil one
Mark 16:6	Risen!
Acts 17:31	God's witness
Romans 4:25	The heart of Christianity

Forsaken

From the sixth hour until the ninth hour darkness came over all the land. About the ninth hour Jesus cried out in a loud voice, "Eloi, Eloi, lama sabachthani?"—which means, "My God, my God, why have you forsaken me?" (Matthew 27:45-46)

The first of seven 'words' from Jesus, seven sayings from the cross.

At the cross even the created world went dark; the physical world reflected the spiritual conflict.

Darkness in the middle of the day, a sign to everyone present of God's judgement. A fearsome sign. A warning that this day brought them near to a greater darkness still. Did anyone remember the plagues on Egypt in the days of Moses and the judgement of God then, with darkness over the whole land? That judgement did not end well for Pharaoh. Would the crowd and the soldiers of Jerusalem wonder who this was on the cross, and what they had done?

Jesus cries out. A desperate but clear cry that his friends catch as they watch their beloved leader and friend dying. For the first and only time, Jesus senses distance from God. The divine Son of God is also Jesus of Nazareth in his human frame, in his humanity now he feels deeply the darkness, judgement and an acute sense of abandonment by the Almighty. The Son cannot be separated from the Father, ever, but in his human nature he feels what we might: God turning his back on sin and on the one who now bears our sins.

Yet, even here in darkness, there is hope. For the words Jesus uses come from Psalm 22. The Psalm depicts the suffering of the innocent one, crying out for rescue, feeling abandoned. But take a moment to read that Psalm. See the parallels with Jesus' final hours. And see how it ends!

The innocent One trusted God and was vindicated. Generations will be told of him and his righteousness will be proclaimed 'for he has done it.'

The cry of Jesus is heartfelt and agonising, yet he holds on to hope. The abandoned One will be vindicated, his death proclaimed, for God the Father saw and honoured him. He has done it for us.

Father, forgive them

When they came to the place called the Skull, there they crucified him, along with the criminals—one on his right, the other on his left. Jesus said, "Father, forgive them, for they do not know what they are doing."
(Luke 23:33-34)

The second of seven 'words' from Jesus, seven sayings from the cross.

Jesus is between two criminals. If they were crucified, these men were unlikely to be guilty of minor offences. Revolutionaries possibly, or murderers, or enemies of the state. And Jesus is quite literally in their company, 'numbered with the transgressors' (Isaiah 53:12), counted amongst them. He is being unjustly punished and most violently and cruelly. Crucifixion was extraordinarily sadistic, painful and humiliating.

In this horrific situation, the words of Jesus here are completely remarkable. They are utterly, completely selfless. They show a love for God (turning to God as his beloved Father) and a love for his enemies. The very greatest commandment (Leviticus 19:18; Matthew 22:39) is being upheld and demonstrated when obedience, honour and such love were under the greatest possible strain. Here is the love of Jesus to sinners; not just sinners in general but specifically those killing him.

Here *from the cross* Jesus offers grace and forgiveness to those personally active in putting him to death, but the words echo through history to all sinners in all places. From the cross, through the cross alone, Jesus offers grace and forgiveness as he cries out to the Father to forgive those who do not recognise what they are doing: killing the Author of life, crucifying the King of Kings, the One who would save them.

We do not truly realise what we have done, not because we never recognise wrongdoing but because we can't measure the depth of our offence: what it means to sin against the Holy One or for Jesus to bear our sins in our place. We can't *fully* know what we have done. Nor can we fully know how great his sacrifice was or comprehend his great love for us.

He longs to forgive all those who look to him in humble faith and in heartfelt repentance.

What a merciful, faithful, loving Saviour.

Today you will be with me

Then he said, "Jesus, remember me when you come into your kingdom."

Jesus answered him, "I tell you the truth, today you will be with me in paradise." (Luke 23:42-43)

The third of seven 'words' from Jesus, seven sayings from the cross.

Easter brings our hearts and minds to focus on the most important cluster of events in human history – the meal with bread and wine and betrayal in the upper room, the prayers of the Son of God for his friends and for all disciples who will follow, the fearful prayer battle in Gethsemane, the trial of the Judge of this world before Pontius Pilate, the death of the Author of life himself on a cruel cross, the empty grave of the risen Jesus, the tears and fears and joy firstly of the women and then the men.

In the midst of this, today's words are from Jesus to a man with no name, only a criminal history and a cross. We have no idea of his background, age, education, community standing, religious knowledge, ethnicity, marital status, friendship groups, ambitions, wealth or any number of other aspects of his life. We do know his life is nearly over.

From one victim to another, Jesus offers what only Jesus can offer: entrance to God's kingdom. And the criteria? Simply this: the man recognises his need and asks Jesus for mercy. That's it, and that's it for us too.

The words of Jesus are unequivocal, 'you will be with me.' The man will enjoy forever the company of Jesus in new, healed, whole, joyful eternal life. No nails, no pain, no guilt, no death. Fully alive and at home with God.

Here in his own suffering we see the generous love and compassion of Jesus. It is not just **by** the cross he saves this man, but also literally **from** the cross. From there he would offer anyone new life at such cost to himself.

He offers us this hope of his company still, even today. Every day we can know his mercy.

Here is your son, here is your mother

When Jesus saw his mother there, and the disciple whom he loved standing nearby, he said to his mother, "Dear woman, here is your son," and to the disciple, "Here is your mother." From that time on, this disciple took her into his home. (John 19:26-27)

The fourth of seven 'words' from Jesus, seven sayings from the cross.

These are not words to strangers – to a crowd, to the crucified man, to the soldiers – these are words to those he loved most on this earth. A reminder that he was flesh and blood. He loved his mother, brothers and sisters of his actual family, even as his spiritual family now numbers billions of people.

As he suffers, Jesus recognises his mother, Mary. How unimaginably terrible for her to see him suffering and bleeding, to hear the scandalous insults being hurled at him. What searing pains she bore there. How the Lord Jesus would know this and more, knowing all our hearts and our sorrows.

He recognises too his beloved friend, the apostle John, the one with whom he had shared precious times of joy, struggle and prayer. He sees his dear grieving friend, who had witnessed miracles and revelation, who had shared in times of rest and celebration.

Jesus commends those he loves into the care of one another, with John entrusted with the care of Mary.

Here we see something of the tender care of Christ Jesus. He would enfold us with his love, and calls us to love one another deeply, as he loved his own.

I am thirsty

Later, knowing that all was now completed, and so that the Scripture would be fulfilled, Jesus said, "I am thirsty." (John 19:28)

The fifth of seven 'words' from Jesus, seven sayings from the cross.

The final request of Jesus is for a drink, but this comes after he has done all that he needed to do. The mission is accomplished, the work is done, '*all was now completed.*' That had been his focus and it is complete, his earthly life nearly spent.

Now in these words – "I am thirsty" – we are reminded of the physical cost of crucifixion. The impact of the beatings and flogging, the blood loss, the trauma, of dehydration and pain would leave Jesus with a desperate thirst. He is dependent on the mercy of others at this point, even as they will find he alone brings mercy from God to the world, on sinful humanity.

His words also bring to mind some words from Psalm 69:21, 'They put gall in my food and gave me vinegar for my thirst.' A thousand years earlier, king David's Psalm spoke of an innocent godly man suffering, and now Jesus fulfils this prophecy of the ultimate innocent One, the Messiah.

Jesus endured all this for us. The one who alone can satisfy our spiritual thirst and alone is the source of true mercy, looked to others. Here his humanity is in plain view. May we look to him for mercy today.

It is finished

A jar of wine vinegar was there, so they soaked a sponge in it, put the sponge on a stalk of the hyssop plant, and lifted it to Jesus' lips. When he had received the drink, Jesus said, "It is finished." With that, he bowed his head and gave up his spirit. (John 19:29-30)

The sixth of seven 'words' from Jesus, seven sayings from the cross.

This is just one word in Greek (*tetelestai*). It would appear on invoices that were paid in full, on the completion of a building. *It is finished.* Done. Nothing more is required, nothing more can be added.

This is a cry of final achievement, indeed of victory after all the spiritual battles faced by Christ Jesus.

The work his Father had sent him to do was done. He had called people to himself as the way, the truth and the life. He had proclaimed the call to repent and believe, to enter God's good kingdom, to find and receive eternal life in God alone and through himself, Jesus. He had called on all to renounce sin, to find healing and forgiveness, to know God's mercy on anyone and everyone who asks for it. He had paved the way into God's welcome and new life. He had offered the compassion of God from himself, the good Shepherd, to lead and care for the sheep. He had contended with evil, overcome the devil, pointed all to God's holy word and ways, loved his family and friends to the very end, taught and lived the gospel.

Now, on a cross, he had completed the final battle and the final work: sin was paid for, in full. All the charges had fallen on him, taken from us. So now there's nothing to add to our salvation, indeed we ought not to try, only receive it gladly by true faith in him.

'It is finished.' Thank you, Lord.

Father, into your hands I commit my spirit

It was now about the sixth hour, and darkness came over the whole land until the ninth hour, for the sun stopped shining. And the curtain of the temple was torn in two. Jesus called out with a loud voice, "Father, into your hands I commit my spirit." When he had said this, he breathed his last. (Luke 23:44-46)

The seventh and final of seven 'words' from Jesus, seven sayings from the cross.

From the middle of the day to mid-afternoon the sun stopped shining, darkness dominated. This would have been an ominous, fearful experience for the whole city, onlookers wondering what was happening.

The signs in the sky were a reflection of what was happening at the execution site, Skull Hill or Calvary, just outside the city walls. The looming darkness was a sign of God's judgement on sin. The cross of Christ was the place where the innocent One bore our sins in our place, and endured that utter darkness of stepping into the place of the guilty. The Light of the world experiencing God's holy wrath, our due guilt and shame, and gave his life as a ransom for many.

The work is done, sin is paid for, evil is conquered. The way into the holy presence of God is now wide open for all who will follow this Saviour in faith … and the thick, ornate temple curtain is torn open by divine power. Then, Jesus dies.

Jesus willingly gave his life. He could have come down from the cross alive by his own divine power, but he chose to set aside his power, to set aside his life, to trust himself finally as always into the hands of his Father.

As the words of Psalm 31 read:

'For you are my rock and my fortress; and for your name's sake you lead me and guide me; you take me out of the net they have hidden for me, for you are my refuge. Into your hand I commit my spirit; you have redeemed me, O LORD, faithful God.'

The faithful Son trusted the faithful Father, giving up his life, his spirit, for us. Standing at the foot of the cross, we remember and worship our good God.

Our scapegoat

"... because on this day atonement will be made for you, to cleanse you. Then, before the LORD, you will be clean from all your sins."
(Leviticus 16:30)

Brushed your teeth yet? Had a shower perhaps? In every culture and empire, washing, bathing or getting clean have been central to life. The heart of ancient cities was often built around their water supply. Many religions include washing as a sacred ritual, symbolising getting clean spiritually.

This verse in Leviticus is part of an instruction to God's people, the Israelites, for how the Lord would 'cleanse' them. Only this time it is not water but blood that is poured out. The uncleanness of the soul is so great we can't wash it off nor can we offer our efforts towards the performance of a good life to sort it out. It needs something greater, more powerful, truly holy.

A sacrifice of blood symbolised a life offered before the Lord. In Leviticus that life was an animal: a scapegoat symbolically carried the sins of the people away into the desert, another goat was killed and its blood sprinkled as an act to purify the people.

Today we need no such ritual. There is one who has offered his life, spilt his blood, who was cast out from God's presence for us bearing our sins so that we need not be cast out and need not perish in sin. He is the Lord Jesus Christ.

As we reflect on his sacrifice, trust him again with your sins and be assured of your forgiveness. His blood was poured out, full atonement was made that we might be 'at one', accepted and cleansed. What a gift from God.

Set his face like flint

Because the Sovereign LORD helps me, I will not be disgraced. Therefore have I set my face like flint, and I know I will not be put to shame. (Isaiah 50:7)

Jesus is determined to finish what he started. He is resolved, implacably set, on bringing all his own into his Father's eternal home. He has plans and purposes for you which cannot be frustrated. Once you belong to him by faith, he will not let go of either you or his steadfast work to keep you in his secure embrace. We are held to the very end of this life and then beyond.

The determination of Jesus is seen throughout the gospels. He did not give up in the face of lethal opposition, enduring the cynicism and apathy of some, the envy and insults of others. He steadfastly trusted his heavenly Father and followed the way marked out for him.

This verse today from the prophet Isaiah is one that we see reflected in the life and attitude of the Lord Jesus (Luke 9:51), heading to Jerusalem, to crucifixion, resolutely facing death; knowing he would not be disgraced or put to shame in the eyes of the only One who counts: God Himself.

Hebrews 12:2 reminds us that he endured the cross 'for the joy before him', the joy of saving many and completing his greatest work, the joy of divine victory and God's purposes fulfilled. He could be so determined for he trusted a good Father and saw beyond human wickedness and sin.

The Lord Jesus is determined, resolved, set on you knowing the joy of the Lord, on growing in grace, and following him to the end. May you know his company and encouragement as you seek to follow him.

He bore our transgressions

But he was pierced for our transgressions, he was crushed for our iniquities; the punishment that brought us peace was upon him, and by his wounds we are healed. (Isaiah 53:5)

In our mind's eye, we can each stand at the foot of the cross and reflect on what it meant for the Lord Jesus to give his life for us. There we see the terrible cost of our sin, the penalty on it, what Isaiah calls 'the punishment' on 'our transgressions ... our iniquities.'

In our world of the perpetually fast-moving news cycle, here is a depiction of what Jesus did without spin, lacking any shiny gloss, with a steady focus on that event on which history turns and our eternity rests.

A place of suffering, of sacrifice. Jesus in our place. The Messiah is crushed as he goes there for us, he is wounded – fatally. Yet for us, our sin is taken, borne, paid for and forgiven. His death for our life.

Today, take a moment to ponder and dwell on that day. Be still, silent and meditate on Calvary. See the depth that Christ would go to for you. There is no sin he cannot cover, for his sacrifice is the greatest possible, enough for all sin. There is no wound to our soul for which his wounds cannot bring healing – the full forgiveness, a fresh start, amazing grace towards us.

And he would bring us peace – peace from God, the peace of a clean heart of the forgiven. The peace of acceptance and security from God. That's a peace that the world cannot offer, it only comes through Christ as we accept our need of this great salvation.

'Hallelujah, what a Saviour.'

Behold the man!

When Jesus came out wearing the crown of thorns and the purple robe, Pilate said to them, "Here is the man!" (John 19:5)

In Trafalgar Square there is a fourth plinth on which appears a variety of contemporary art installations. A giant blue cockerel, an ice cream cone, a horse skeleton and an Assyrian gate-guardian have all taken the spot. Once it was deliberately empty. How ... arty?

Eye-catching, perhaps weird, always thought-provoking and a conversation starter, which is part of the power of art.

In 1999 there was a statue called 'Ecce Homo', from the Latin version of the Bible, the Vulgate, meaning 'Behold the man'. These are the words of Pontius Pilate presenting Christ Jesus to the mob. Bloodied and beaten, Jesus faced his imminent judgement.

This statue showed Jesus, in the words of the artist, Mark Wallinger, as a human being so that people could reflect on his humanity, and act as a reminder of political prisoners and victims of oppression and torture. His hands are bound behind his back; he wears a crown of barbed wire. He is an unassuming figure, not bristling with any obvious power or anger.

Yet Pilate said to the crowd (John 19), "Behold the man!" Behold him. Look at him. Fix your attention on him.

And when we do, we recognise a truly, fully human being, in the flesh. He walked the earth. He knew suffering and loss, friendship and laughter, the joy of a party and of knowing God the Father. He was familiar with the pain of bereavement and the grief of this world. Look at him and know that he is with us.

The only other time this phrase occurs in the Bible is when the Lord God himself points to Saul and says to Samuel, "Behold the man" (1 Samuel 9:17). God points out the first king of Israel.

Behold the man – Jesus Christ, the true king. King over all God's people not just Israel, king over all humanity, the Lion of the tribe of Judah, the Lamb of God. Our true Ruler, King, Lord. Fully human, one like us yet without sin. One for us, who died to save us. One with us, always.

The wisdom of the cross

For the message of the cross is foolishness to those who are perishing, but to us who are being saved it is the power of God.
(1 Corinthians 1:18)

The cross of Christ has been called the great dividing line. It stands over all of humanity and all of history. Everyone and everything is in its shadow. Every person makes a choice where they stand in relation to it. Even ignoring it is a conscious choice, a decision.

The New Testament is rich with lessons on what Jesus achieved on the cross (our rescue, clearing the charges, paying the debt, setting us free, uniting us to Jesus) but these only apply to us when we see and believe that he did it, that the cross truly <u>was</u> the place of his sacrificial death for us, of mercy on sinners like us, of God's power to save us.

For some, they stand on one side of a line that says, sings and shouts, 'Amen, thank you Lord!' In humility and repentance, they see the cross at the heart of God's saving purpose and trust the crucified Christ for forgiveness. Faith, joy, hope and love spring up in their hearts. New life is theirs, ours!

For others, on the other side of the line, they are no more or less worthy of salvation, not necessarily 'better people', not necessarily less kind or wise or educated. But they see the cross as irrelevant, offensive and bizarre. For some it is only a myth, a noble legend. For them, 'the message of the cross is foolishness' and they are 'those who are perishing.' This is a tragedy but is seen in every generation.

May we never cease to point to the cross, to call everyone to find hope in Christ, no matter how foolish they find it, for grace is available to all. Let us give thanks for the cross today and pray for those who need to stand under it with gratitude and trust.

To destroy the power of the evil one

Since the children have flesh and blood, he too shared in their humanity so that by his death he might destroy him who holds the power of death—that is, the devil—and free those who all their lives were held in slavery by their fear of death. (Hebrews 2:14-15)

When we read the four gospels and the various people who met Jesus, we find the great variety of reactions to him: adoration, wonder, amazement, love, gratitude, tenderness … hatred, confusion, cynicism, apathy, mockery and violence. These are often provoked by what they think he can do for them, or what he has already done – healing, rescue, miraculous food or drink, acts of power, words of wisdom or confrontation, a blessing or a warning.

The climax of the story, the last week of Jesus' life before Calvary, slows down the pace and picks up the details of events and conversations. The story is worth reading for yourself: pick up a Bible, read the final chapters of Matthew, Mark, Luke or John.

See what Jesus does and says. Notice the variety of reactions: the bewilderment of his friends, the plotting of the priests, the fear of Pilate, the anger of the crowd, the wonder of the centurion, the amazement of the women at the empty tomb.

Jesus was 'flesh and blood', fully human, just like us only without sin. So he felt all these human reactions, he wasn't indifferent or unaware. But he also saw something we cannot see so clearly and would endure something so we won't have to endure it: he went to war with the devil.

We rightly give little attention to the evil one; it is unhealthy and undesirable to do so. The focus of today's verse is not him, but the greatness of Jesus and the victory of Jesus. Amidst all the very human interactions, emotions, words and plans of others in that week, Jesus also knew he was at war. His enemy held people in slavery, in fear of death, in the grip of evil. And Jesus was going to destroy him.

So in our hearts, we can bow down before the cross, before Christ crucified, who endured insults and violence and pain, knowing that there he won an unseen victory. He fought the great battle, defeating our enemy and his. The devil is now stripped of his power and Christ reigns. In the end, that enemy will be utterly destroyed.

Rest in that assurance, that Christ has won, death has been conquered, and evil will not have the final word.

Risen!

"Don't be alarmed," he said. "You are looking for Jesus the Nazarene, who was crucified. He has risen! He is not here. See the place where they laid him." (Mark 16:6)

That first Easter morning, a Sunday over 2000 years ago, as dawn broke, the friends of Jesus were in a state of confusion, fear, bewilderment ... or joy. Some had rushed to the graveyard and amongst this realm of the dead they had stood by the empty tomb. The body of Jesus wasn't there. The stone had been rolled away.

Other disciples were hiding in fear. Some were doubting, and understandably so. People don't normally rise from the dead.

But the words to the first eyewitnesses confirm what we believe: our faith is not built on what we have done, but on what God has done. The cross is empty, sin has been dealt with. The grave is empty, death has been conquered. So we need not bear the penalty of sin, we need not fear death, and new life is ours. For Jesus has risen!

This risen Jesus is alive forever and now intercedes for us, praying for his own before our heavenly Father. Nothing can separate us from God's love in him. He wants all people to come to him and find life in his kingdom, born again by God's power and grace. He wants us to walk fully in the light and reject the darkness, to know him in his love and power, and live for him. When we do, we can share in that same Easter joy. He has risen and so will we!

God's witness

"For he has set a day when he will judge the world with justice by the man he has appointed. He has given proof of this to all men by raising him from the dead." (Acts 17:31)

In a world with much injustice, we can groan at the bad news, or feel helpless and hopeless to change it – either on the global scale or in the smaller injustices we might face.

Here is good news: God knows and sees. And he has already set a day in court for all the injustice of this world.

More good news: not simply will there be an end, but the Judge has also been appointed and is ready. He has been appointed by God. His status, the right to be Judge, has been shown by God's unique act of power in raising him from the dead. Our Judge is our Saviour and Friend, the Lord Jesus Christ. He will do what is right, all his ways are just. He will wipe all sin away and hold all evil and wrongdoing to account.

Although we too are among those who have wronged others and wronged God, this remarkable Judge has already noted all this, taken the charges on himself, paid the full penalty, declared us forgiven and set us free!

So may we live in the hope of our final salvation and assurance of amazing grace even now. May we seek after justice now, and point others to the one who offers full and free forgiveness. We know he can do it, because God raised him from the dead!

The heart of Christianity

He was delivered over to death for our sins and was raised to life for our justification. (Romans 4:25)

As a church we run an event called Big Questions looking at five common obstacles or objections to Christianity. These can seem like roadblocks in some people's lives to taking any kind of spiritual topic seriously. One such question we explore is this: 'Fake news: is Christianity a fairy tale?' We look at this big question because many do believe that Christianity is based on a myth, that none of it is true, that none of the stories happened and therefore it's irrelevant to life today.

This is not a view that any serious scholar could hold for long without ridicule, but it persists because it seems an easy way to dismiss Christian faith – that it's a nice story but basically just a moral fable about trying to live a better life, or a psychological crutch for the weak.

The Bible tells us plainly that Jesus of Nazareth lived, walked the earth, performed miracles, spoke the world's greatest ever wisdom, claimed to speak for God as God, claimed we all need a Saviour – him, and was crucified under the rule of Pontius Pilate. Three days later he rose from the dead.

He spoke of his death and resurrection as works of saving power for all who trust him, as signs of his identity as the Son of God, and as the gateway to eternal life for all who follow him in true faith.

Here is our confidence: not in a fairy tale or legend, not in a rule book or our own faltering efforts to live better lives, but in the stunning good news of Christ Jesus, Lord and Saviour, who died for our sins and was raised for our justification. He alone can make us right with God.

Here is the heart of Christianity, not merely a true story but a person who stands over history, invites us into God's love and new life. May he be our confidence and joy as we build our lives on this sure foundation.

9

THE GOOD NEWS OF THE GOSPEL

Christianity is a good news story. It is not merely a set of facts, as if it is data to learn, nor is it a set of rules to follow – although its impact is felt in every part of our lives. It is not a programme of good ideas but rather, it's a declaration of good news, and this good news is to all and for all.

The gospel is the proclamation or announcement of God's kingdom, of his great work of salvation for us, of the gift of new and eternal life and all these are centred on the Son of God, Jesus Christ. The gospel is very good news. It confirms that the promises of God are true and a Saviour has come, so we can be saved from sin and brought into God's family; we can receive new life from him and enjoy it with him.

Like holding up a finely cut diamond to the light, the reflections and refractions of the beauty of this gospel are endless as it is observed from different perspectives. The following 18 reflections are only a small selection of the wonder, glory, riches and scope of this gospel, as the apostles recount this good news that they have seen and heard.

May we see, hear, rejoice and believe as we each receive God's word – his gospel broadcast – as good news addressed to us.

Matthew 16:18	I will build my church
Mark 1:14-15	The kingdom of God is near
Mark 2:14	"Follow me"
Mark 4:26-27	The ever-growing kingdom
Luke 1:4	Confident disciples
John 17:26	The deep love of God
Romans 8:31	If God is for us ...
1 Corinthians 3:16	God's Spirit in you
1 Corinthians 6:11	Washed, sanctified, justified
2 Corinthians 8:9	The great exchange
Galatians 2:20	Crucified with Christ
Ephesians 3:8	God's unsearchable riches
Philippians 3:20	Citizens of heaven
Hebrews 6:10	He will not forget your work
Hebrews 11:1	Life now, life to come
2 Peter 3:14	Peace with him
1 John 3:19-20	Greater than our hearts
1 John 4:15-16	God is love

I will build my church

"And I tell you that you are Peter, and on this rock I will build my church, and the gates of Hades will not overcome it." (Matthew 16:18)

Throughout his public ministry, as recorded in the gospels, Jesus drew large crowds. People sought after this prophet and teacher from Nazareth with his miracles, his amazingly insightful and challenging teaching, his message of God's salvation and a kingdom to enter, his provocative stance towards religious power in favour of the marginalised and the outcasts, and his own personal character of godliness, kindness, courage and love. It was no surprise that his presence attracted great interest, whether from devotion, curiosity or hostility.

However, when Jesus made this promise it must have sounded bewildering: 'I will build my church.' The 'church' refers to a body of people, a new community, those who belong together by faith. Jesus was promising that he would build 'my' church – a people centred on him. This is a claim to be the Messiah, the Christ, that is God's anointed Servant sent to save and bring people to God.

The good news is centred on Jesus and goes out to the whole world, to every nation and culture. It is wholly inclusive – addressed to everyone – and clearly exclusive – the call is to come to Christ alone for salvation, and come willing to lay down our whole life in glad surrender to his Lordship. His burden on us is light, his leadership gentle and humble in heart towards us, but the surrender is to be complete: to take up our cross, to 'lose' ourselves that we might gain Christ (Luke 9:23-25). As we do, the kingdom grows one person at a time, but we find ourselves part of a great host – the church.

The promise of Jesus here is that he will build his church; he will call people to himself and bind them together, and that the powers of hell, death and evil will not overcome or withstand its presence. The church will never be overcome, despite persecution and opposition without, and human frailty, sin and division within. The true, universal church of Christ is being built –irresistibly – by the Lord of the church himself.

May we be faithful, hopeful, joyful and bold as his people.

The kingdom of God is near

After John was put in prison, Jesus went into Galilee, proclaiming the good news of God. "The time has come," he said. "The kingdom of God is near. Repent and believe the good news!" (Mark 1:14-15)

Mark's Gospel traces the story of Jesus with quite a pace. It reveals who he is, why he came, how we are to respond, and more. The gospel is always bigger than we can imagine; it encompasses eternity, every corner of our lives, indeed all of God's purposes. That's BIG.

In today's verses we are told that Jesus came with good news. He was 'proclaiming' this good news – broadcasting or announcing it. The stunning and momentous news of God's kingdom.

He said '*the time has come*' – it was time because **he** had come. **He** was the way into the kingdom, the king of the kingdom, the one and only way into the welcome and presence of the living God. It was time for people to respond to the good news, and it was good news in person.

It is still that time. It is the day to respond, today and every day while it is still this age, before the end. How will you embrace his good news for you today? How will you find hope, confidence, peace, forgiveness from Jesus Christ whose good news is still declared to be for us?

The kingdom is near. It is not out of reach, because the king came and reached out for us. We can be found, held, embraced, forgiven because of him. His appeal is that we 'repent and believe', and go on doing that – go on rejecting sin and life without him and continue trusting and finding our life in him.

Today, may this very good news be the headlines that bring you joy, and remind you that your king is not just *near* you but by faith he is even *with* you.

"Follow me"

As he walked along, he saw Levi son of Alphaeus sitting at the tax collector's booth. "Follow me," Jesus told him, and Levi got up and followed him. (Mark 2:14)

In today's world, Christians still talk of hearing from God. This experience isn't just for people we read of in the Bible or for some kind of 'super saint' – God can and does speak to anyone.

Christians might hear him most readily through the Bible: God speaks, it is all the word of God, all from Christ to us – not only the literal 'words of Jesus' from his own lips which we find in the gospels. We hear from God as the Bible is read or preached or prayed or sung – this is the content of our gathered worship!

At other times we would say we hear from God when our spirit or our conscience is prompted to do something, to reach out to someone, to give time or money, to pray, or to stop doing something unhelpful. The Spirit of God speaks.

In the wisdom of a friend we might discern it was not just them speaking to us but the wisdom of God's own ways – his kindness, encouragement or direction. He can also speak through the circumstances of our lives and as we reflect on the path of history.

Today's verse is a reminder that God can speak and completely interrupt our plans and even turn our lives upside down. Levi was literally minding his business, the unpopular but lucrative business of tax collecting, until Jesus spoke. "Follow me" … and Levi's day and life changed.

Jesus still calls to us, plainly and directly and without any exceptions, "Follow me", and we should expect our lives to be disrupted, to change, but now with life in his company, with his friendship, following his lead.

May you hear his word to you and be encouraged that he invites you to follow.

The ever-growing kingdom

He also said, "This is what the kingdom of God is like. A man scatters seed on the ground. Night and day, whether he sleeps or gets up, the seed sprouts and grows, though he does not know how."

(Mark 4:26-27)

Jesus told many parables about the kingdom of God and a consistent theme of his was this: **growth**. The kingdom of God is growing. It is unstoppable. How could it not be?! Who or what in all of creation could possibly be greater than God? Therefore, there is <u>nothing</u> that can frustrate his purposes and plans, and <u>nothing</u> can resist the growth of his kingdom.

In this parable in Mark chapter 4, Jesus uses the picture of seed sown into the ground – a favourite, familiar image that anyone could understand, both then and now. We know that seeds produce growth (of flowers, crops, weeds, trees, etc.). That much is obvious to us. What is <u>not</u> obvious is how. I don't mean the science of plant growth, but how this is simply what seeds do – how on earth this happens all over the world, this 'everyday miracle' of growth?

He is also making the simple point that it does not finally depend on **us** to make seeds grow: *'whether he sleeps or gets up, the seed sprouts and grows'*. So, too, with the kingdom of God. The kingdom is coming; it is growing, whether we work or pray or not. However, the questions for each of us are these: Do we want to be part of it? Do we want to enjoy God's joy, encouragement and blessing in working in his kingdom-building? Wherever we live godly lives and do good work, there is the kingdom too.

The irresistible, ever-growing kingdom of God doesn't seem spectacular or obvious everywhere, but God stands behind it and causes it to flourish. The King of the kingdom stepped out of the tomb and is ruling the world and watching over God's good purposes. May you know the joy of being in this kingdom and your part in serving him today.

Confident disciples

... so that you may know the certainty of the things you have been taught. (Luke 1:4)

If you are on a car journey trying to find somewhere, it can be really helpful to have a confident fellow navigator, and less helpful if it's pure guesswork! A bit of confidence or certainty can be a good thing.

Some decisions leave plenty of scope for varied opinions, e.g. choosing a birthday present, deciding what to eat or watch this evening, when to catch up with a friend. Other decisions or actions need a higher level of certainty: Does my car take petrol or diesel? Have I paid this bill already or not? Did I feed the pets/children?

Or perhaps you have a medical meeting about some symptoms – who of us wouldn't want a clear diagnosis, pinning down the problem with a high level of clarity about the likely outcome and best treatment? We may *want* this but hopefully we also recognise the challenges for the doctor or nurse – some symptoms could be from many and varied ailments, patients vary, treatments have different impacts. So 'certainty' is a rare quality in these situations.

What of faith questions?

The Lord does not offer us an answer to every question we might have. Some things remain secret to the Lord (Deut. 29:29), kept to himself for his own good reasons. Other things may be beyond our understanding (Isaiah 55:9). Faith grows through seeking, learning, understanding and experiencing but also as we learn to trust.

However in some areas of faith, the Lord surely wants us to be certain. He wants us to have confident faith. He has told us, revealed to us, those things that we are to grasp, believe and be sure of, so that we can grow in our faith and assurance. They are in his word.

So Luke's Gospel begins, 'I have carefully investigated everything ... to write an orderly account for you *... so that you may know the certainty of the things you have been taught.'* What are '*the things*'?

They are what follows – in Luke's Gospel and Acts – his two-volume good news story. 'The things' of the Lord Jesus Christ: his person, message, mission, commands and example. His saving death, resurrection to new life, return to the Father. His Holy Spirit given, his church alive and the world changed by his powerful Word and Spirit. We can have certainty. On these things true faith is built. Questions remain, but we have enough for confident faith.

The deep love of God

"I have made you known to them, and will continue to make you known in order that the love you have for me may be in them and that I myself may be in them." (John 17:26)

One of the most gifted and influential evangelists, pastors, apologists for Christianity and writers of accessible theology over the past 50 years was Tim Keller (1950-2023). He planted a church in New York City in the 1990s, starting with just his own family of five and a few friends. It grew to encompass multiple churches in that most secular of cities, several with congregations numbered in thousands, and a broad range of ministries working amongst the arts, business, the poor, church planting and more. He founded an organisation which trains pastors and equips ministry to cities, which has a network currently spanning 60 cities globally. He wrote more than 30 books. In all this he remained renowned for his self-effacing humility, his kindness, his graciousness towards those who held different views, and his great love for Jesus and the gospel.

He died in May 2023, three years after a diagnosis of pancreatic cancer. The day before he died he said, "I'm thankful for my family, that loves me. I'm thankful for the time God has given me, but I'm ready to see Jesus. I can't wait to see Jesus. Send me home."

He knew the deep, deep joy of knowing Jesus. He also knew that he was deeply secure in God's love. This was not because of what Tim had done for Jesus – the writing, speaking, pastoring, mentoring – but because of what Jesus had done for Tim.

The quite incredible promise of Jesus is that we can know the same love that the Father has for his Son, the Lord Jesus Christ, in our hearts and lives. This was the prayer of Jesus for all believers in that upper room. This is central to the good news of the gospel. To be saved is to know that we are deeply loved by God, with the same love that gave Jesus such security, such joy, such purpose and confidence.

Tim Keller once wrote, 'The gospel says you are simultaneously more sinful and flawed than you ever dared believe, yet more loved and accepted than you ever dared hope.'

That love of God pursues us; his heart is set upon us. His desire is for us to find our life, forgiveness, hope and joy from Jesus. Bringing our whole life to Christ in real repentance and faith, a joyful surrender to our Lord, we too can live in that great love and so we can also die with that great hope. Then we too can be sure: we will see Jesus.

If God is for us ...

What, then, shall we say in response to this? If God is for us, who can be against us? (Romans 8:31)

Romans 8:28-39 is a golden chain of promises; one great privilege after another. You might wish to read the whole text. But just the one verse is a powerful promise in itself:

If God is for us, who can be against us?

The apostle Paul wrote this from a prison cell, in chains for declaring Christ as King and a new kingdom under his rule. Yet still he had no doubt that God was for him, and that gave him great joy, real peace, a deep sense of God's love, lasting courage and hope in the face of an uncertain future, even facing death. His letters overflow with joyful confidence, despite most of them being written behind bars!

If God is for us, all his promises are for us. Opposition, self-doubt, hardship, our past, our unreliable feelings ... they can take a back seat, thank you very much.

If we are in Christ because we have put our faith in him, then we can say with confidence that before God and for all eternity:

I am free from condemnation. My sin no longer counts against me, for Christ died to cancel the debt, to become sin for us (vv. 33-34; 2 Corinthians 5:21). The evil one might wish us to think our sin still stands, digging up the past, but **God** is for us. He didn't even spare his Son. So ... what does it matter who is against us?

I am chosen (v. 33). God set his eye upon those he saves, as those now bound to Christ through faith. We belong to him. Our ultimate value is not defined by the world, by performance, by appearance or wealth, but by our heavenly Father's welcome and adoption into his family and by the Son's righteousness given to us. God is truly for us.

I am prayed for by Jesus! The Son of God intercedes for us (v. 34), so our lives might still have truly tough days, crazy moments, dark or even horrible experiences, but we have a great high priest standing for us. 'Strength for today and bright hope for tomorrow.'

I am loved. The love of Christ, the love of God in Christ, is the most indomitable power in creation (vv. 35-39). Nothing and no one can possibly separate us from his love. There is our great joy and security.

So: who is for you? God. The Almighty. Your heavenly Father. Who can be against you?

God's Spirit in you

Don't you know that you yourselves are God's temple and that God's Spirit lives in you? (1 Corinthians 3:16)

The apostle Paul wrote to a church in a confused world, a world filled with immorality, pride, self-promotion and insecurity. Not so different from our world. And he wrote to the church, who were affected by their world as we are.

Both then and now, we need the truth, encouragement and challenge of these words – those who follow Christ are holy: 'you yourselves are God's temple'. Our body, our physical material self, is holy and precious, as the temple was in the Old Testament. The body we have is not a plaything but a gift to be honoured, valued, treated with dignity and love. Jesus himself told us not to worry about our bodies for he cares for them (Matthew 6:25-26), which shows his concern for our physical frame not just our spiritual life.

This has practical implications for the importance of healthcare, and for how we care for the very young, the infirm, the physically vulnerable, and those living with disabilities or illness. It should shape how we treat our own body and lifestyle decisions; the body is a gift from God (which I can't pretend I immediately call to mind when it aches). Our bodies are holy in his eyes.

This verse gives us the reason to see ourselves, our bodily selves, as precious in God's eyes: 'God's Spirit lives in you.' This is **why** the body is holy. Each human being is made deliberately in God's image, so all human life is precious and our bodies are not kits to play with but gifts to honour. God's Holy Spirit takes up residence in every Christian. He lives in you. He cares for you. And our illness, weakness or appearance are no measure of the immeasurable value of his love towards us and our holiness in his eyes. He lives in you.

Washed, sanctified, justified

And that is what some of you were. But you were washed, you were sanctified, you were justified in the name of the Lord Jesus Christ and by the Spirit of our God. (1 Corinthians 6:11)

January is a month that can offer the range of the whole range of weather (possibly the favourite topic of conversation in UK if you happen to be with complete strangers). It can offer the deep freeze experience, the full-on downpour, dense fog, snow, drizzle, brilliant sunshine, and all of the above in the same day! It is also a month for muddy boots, grimy cars, and, for dog walkers, the same grubby news for paws.

I don't imagine dog-walking was a big thing in ancient Corinth, but Paul looks at his friends in his mind's eye as he writes to them and remembers that they – like us – were decidedly unclean, stained as they were by sin, rebellion, transgression and the darkness within.

Jesus outlined clearly the unclean state of our hearts and why we need a fresh start (Mark 7:20-23). But Paul can now say, with great joy, that God's grace cleans us thoroughly! "You were washed, sanctified, justified in the name of the Lord Jesus Christ and by the Spirit of our God."

Every time we baptise someone, the symbolism of this great act reminds us of God's powerful inner renewal. The visual drama of going into water, as if we are washed on the outside, points to the sacred, inner, deep cleansing we receive as a gift of grace.

God's Spirit has power to clean and forgive us. His work in Jesus is the evidence that he wants to do this, so may we ask for that sensitivity to his Spirit for where we need that renewal and change, and trust him with all our needs again today. We can be confident in God's power and purposes to set us right – justified – and to purify our lives.

The great exchange

For you know the grace of our Lord Jesus Christ, that though he was rich, yet for your sakes he became poor, so that you through his poverty might become rich. (2 Corinthians 8:9)

This has been called the Great Exchange.

Jesus went where we deserved to be, so we can go where we could never deserve to be.

Jesus offered his life completely, even to the point of death, death on a cross of all places, that we might have life, even eternal life, and not live in fear of death.

Jesus, the most beloved Son of God Most High, went to the place of the despised, bearing sin to the extent that he felt abandoned by the Father, siding with the lost.

Jesus who from eternity belonged in heaven – the glorious abode of light and love, abundant in the fullest sense of life and joy – exchanged that for the lowest of the low places. He was rejected and humiliated, beaten and insulted. He stood in our place of shame and guilt as he took our sins upon himself, and went to death, down into darkness.

A truly great exchange indeed; great in scope, great for who achieved it, and great for its benefits for us.

The riches of Christ are given to us: eternal life, the friendship of God, peace in our hearts and peace with God, cleansed conscience, no guilt or shame before the Lord, and freedom to live with God's favour and for his glory rather than as his enemies and seeking our own status. All this is to be rich indeed, regardless of our measure of earthly wealth or our poverty.

This is, says the apostle Paul, the heart of the reason why we 'know the grace of our Lord Jesus Christ.' We know this, what he has done, this amazing grace. So may you know the greatness of his grace still; realise that he has done this for you, and that God extends these great riches to you through Jesus Christ.

Crucified with Christ

I have been crucified with Christ and I no longer live, but Christ lives in me. The life I live in the body, I live by faith in the Son of God, who loved me and gave himself for me. (Galatians 2:20)

How does God look on you today? 'Does God accept me?' is one of the biggest life questions we can ever ask ourselves.

Our default earthly response is to think about our **performance:** what kind of person we are in our own eyes or how others might perceive us. We might think about our job, our home, our academic or professional achievements, our 'standing' in church or the community, the kind of car we drive, our athletic ability, or the family we might have raised.

We might instead think of spiritual performance: am I praying enough, feeling like a good Christian, living a good life, trying hard to please God? These can be good things! We try to please or impress others, God or ourselves.

This is the kind of problem that the apostle Paul was confronting the Galatian Christians with – measuring their standing before God by *earthly* measures. It's not a new phenomenon, it's as old as time.

The only measure that counts if we are to be accepted by God is this: does Christ live in me?

Do I recognise and rely on his saving death? Can I say that 'I have been crucified with Christ' – that in his death, he carried my sins and opened the way for me into the Father's welcome and embrace? That is what his death achieved. It was as though we were on that cross: by faith, we have been crucified with Christ.

If we truly see him and trust him to rescue and lead, as Saviour and Lord, and turn away from pursuing sin and proving our own self before God, we begin to grasp this: it's not *our* performance, it is *his* that counts. Jesus has already lived the life and died the death which fully brings God's greatest blessing on all who follow him. God looks on his Son with complete joy, delight and acceptance.

If we have been crucified with him, and Christ lives in us, the Father looks on us and sees us in Christ. The joy, delight and acceptance of God fall on **us**.

So, how does God look on you today? As the Father looks on the Son – with great joy and eternal love, for Christ died for you and by faith you are in Christ. Amen!

God's unsearchable riches

Although I am less than the least of all God's people, this grace was given me: to preach to the Gentiles the unsearchable riches of Christ.
(Ephesians 3:8)

There is always more of Jesus than we know already. Why settle for what we have now when he is so good, so glorious, and longs for us to know him more fully?

How deep could you swim in the sea – 2 metres? 3? How deep might a regular submarine dive safely? 400m, possibly. 500m at a stretch. The Challenger Deep in the Pacific Ocean is a whopping 10,935m (35,976ft) deep, almost 7 miles. A swimming experience splashing about above that leaves quite a lot more of the depths to explore!

Christ's riches are deep indeed. There is always more of Jesus to know – more of his wisdom, love and kindness to receive, and more of his truth to grasp and by which to live. The riches of Christ are unsearchable, inexhaustible and immeasurable. We can't fully fathom how great and glorious his true status is, how good he is towards us, and how comprehensive and wonderful is his saving, healing power.

His riches extend to covering the forgiveness of sins for all who trust in him. He then lavishes the love of the Father on God's children. He prays for us, continually before God's throne. He lifts up the lowly and humble of this world to the status of heirs of God's kingdom. He holds the church and guards the sheep of God's pasture in his unending care. These are just some of the riches we enjoy in him.

We can't exhaust the riches of Jesus so it should continue to surprise, delight, challenge and comfort us as we choose to follow him in each day. He is never 'routine'. Each day is a new day with him. He deserves to grow in our imagination and adoration. He is able to be alongside us, however deep we feel we have fallen, and – like Paul – grant us new grace.

There is always more from Jesus than we might imagine, may we not neglect to seek after his presence and direction.

Citizens of heaven

But our citizenship is in heaven. And we eagerly await a Saviour from there, the Lord Jesus Christ. (Philippians 3:20)

Have you ever felt you don't belong somewhere? Maybe in a new job, or at a party, or in a country? It can be discouraging, upsetting or lonely. I've spent time in jobs that I didn't enjoy, been to parties where I haven't known anyone, and lived overseas where I felt a bit lost! It is a natural and good human desire to want to belong, to feel at home, to find security, and to have a sense of welcome and peace of mind. What a blessing friends, family and church can be – people and places where we feel welcome and a sense of belonging.

Today's verse reminds us that in a real sense every Christian is a stranger, a resident alien, in a foreign land. We don't fully belong in this world, because we already have the rights and responsibilities of another world. We belong in God's kingdom, we're citizens under his divine rule, enjoying his protection and care, paying attention to his words and ways, and expecting one day to be fully present there.

Sometimes this will mean we feel out of sorts with the ways of this world. But that's ok – we know the One to whom we belong. Our Father is in heaven and his kingdom is real, growing and good. His Spirit is with us now.

So for now, we can seek to live faithfully and with hope. We can rest in his security and love, eagerly awaiting the day that our Saviour comes from there to here! We can enjoy the assurance that we always belong to him wherever we go, and his love is unchanging whenever we feel disconnected from others.

When heaven arrives on earth, we will truly belong, but we can enjoy being its citizens already.

He will not forget your work

God is not unjust; he will not forget your work and the love you have shown him as you have helped his people and continue to help them.

(Hebrews 6:10)

If you ever pass through a city at night, in the very early hours of the morning, you will probably notice that there is little traffic and there are few pedestrians. But those people you do see will be cleaning the roads or the buildings, emptying the bins, providing deliveries of supplies to shops, servicing or repairing infrastructure. There may also be those who cover night shifts – medical staff, members of the emergency services and security guards.

Such roles involve many hours spent working and are largely unseen by most of the population – those who live or work in the city, the tourists or shoppers of school kids – but they perform such valuable, even essential, work. We would notice if they didn't turn up.

God sees all the workers. Whatever your work, whatever the hours or pay or profile, God sees. There is great dignity in any work done well, work done as a means to honour God with our skills, hands, time and effort. He notices.

Today's verse reminds us of another unseen work: whatever we do for him especially as an act of Christian service for 'his people' – fellow Christians – is seen by God and he will not forget. God holds eternal rewards in store. Every prayer offered, every kind word, every note or message of encouragement, every financial gift, every rota you've been on, every act of service, every bit of time given for the sake of others and his church: God is not unjust, he will not forget.

No one else might see, know or appreciate it. I hope they do, but they may not. We don't do it for the earthly fanfare although a word of thanks can go a long way. But the One who looks on you with eternal love and holds eternal joy as a reward. He sees, he will not forget, and he knows when we serve because we love him.

Life now, life to come

Now faith is being sure of what we hope for and certain of what we do not see. (Hebrews 11:1)

One of the most inspirational and brave men to stand up to the tyranny, lies and evil of Nazi Germany was Dietrich Bonhoeffer. He returned to Germany in 1931, knowing the risks, convinced that he should be with his Christian brothers and sisters. He faithfully preached the gospel, pastored the church and encouraged fellow pastors. His forceful and unyielding stance led to his imprisonment. He was taken from his cell on 9th April 1945, just weeks before the camp was liberated, and executed by hanging. As he left the cell, his last words to his friends were these: 'This the end – for me, the beginning of life.'

Bonhoeffer was sure of realities beyond the gallows and the guards, beyond the grave even. His faith extended beyond earthly trials to a heavenly country, with a confidence that was striking

Today's verse is a reminder that there certainly is 'more' more to come, more from God, more of life in *this* life and the next to experience his presence and goodness.

Hebrews 11, as a chapter, points us from this world to the next, looking with the eyes of faith, through the lenses of God's promises. Because **he** has made the promises, **we** can be sure, we can have hope. Biblical hope, Christian hope, is not woolly wishful thinking that it will probably be alright; it is a bold confidence that God is true and good, that his word stands so his promises don't fail, and that we can know God both in this life and in the life to come. Although we do not see what lies ahead, we know the One who leads us and has gone before us. This has been the hope for all Christian martyrs, a sure and certain hope.

In each day, we can experience God's goodness, presence, mercy and joy. We can see his power and beauty in creation. We can experience his grace at work in the world. We can hear of his triumph over sin and death through the gospel story. God grants us these as a foretaste of the life to come. Are we made for still more? Absolutely.

Peace with him

So then, dear friends, since you are looking forward to this, make every effort to be found spotless, blameless and at peace with him. (2 Peter 3:14)

What is the most precious or valuable thing you have in your home, I wonder? Apart from people and pets! If you had to dash from your home, what would you grab first?

Some photos perhaps? A particular object that was a gift or a reminder of a loved one? Your laptop or games console?! Keys, phone, wallet and passport would probably be a good idea.

We each have things we count as precious for various reasons – even as irreplaceable. Some things are beyond price; the monetary value may be little but we would miss them dearly.

The promises of God are full of good gifts from our heavenly Father that are beyond price. You literally can't buy them and nothing on earth compares to them. Here is one such gift: **peace**.

The verse today points us to a gift, a promise from God to all who trust in the Son of God and find life in him. They – we – have **peace with God**. Peace in our hearts that he accepts us, that he loves us and he has wiped away our sins. The deep peace of this forgiveness is a peace of mind and heart that the past is dealt with and our future is secured. God's peace also comes to our worries and fears, as we trust that he holds us in the storms of life, in suffering or hardship, and in times of loss or pain.

The confident future for every Christian is to be finally welcomed home, 'blameless and at peace with him' – without any stain from our sins or any impact of the brokenness of this fallen world. As those gloriously alive, whole, renewed and holy in the presence of Jesus, we will be accepted without shame and with great joy.

This is not a 'peace' that is merely a quiet or restful experience – good as that can be in this life. It is the peace known in abundant, radiant new lives fully held in God's love, as a part of his stunning new creation, accepted into his forever kingdom. That is an inkling of the peace with God that we look forward to, and a peace that overflows into our lives now.

May God's Spirit grant you his peace today and an awareness where he wants to give you peace in places of anxiety, shame, uncertainty or tears. Grace and peace come from our Father and the Lord Jesus Christ.

God is greater than our hearts

This then is how we know that we belong to the truth, and how we set our hearts at rest in his presence whenever our hearts condemn us. For God is greater than our hearts, and he knows everything.

(1 John 3:19-20)

Our 'heart' in the Bible's terms is not the blood-pumping organ in our chest that we learn about at school (aorta, vena cava, tricuspid valve, etc.). (Anyone recalling gruesome biology lessons at this point?) The Bible also doesn't think of the heart as merely a bundle of emotions; a 'happy heart' or a 'peaceful heart' is a happy or peaceful *person*, not just fleeting feelings.

In the Bible, the heart is the innermost core of our character and being, it represents our values and true person. It is where we sense fear and love, security and joy. It is what we protect and what moves us to act. Our heart is where we sense our standing before God and what he sees, based on his words and promises, and our actions in response. We believe 'with our heart' (Romans 10:9).

But our heart is unreliable, isn't it? It tells us one thing when God sees another. The heart can point to our failings and wrong words; it can remind us of the people we let down. It can spotlight the criticisms we face and yet also twist, magnify, rewrite history or make them weigh heavier than they ever should. Here then is good news: 'God is greater than our hearts, and he knows everything.'

There is the pathway to a peaceful, happy heart. To 'how we set our hearts at rest in his presence.' We lift our eyes to the Lord.

We can bring our whole self – our heart – before him, in humility and trust, finding forgiveness, grace, strength and peace again, for he knows us, truly, and loves us.

God is greater than your heart. Let him rule your heart and rule over you again today.

God is love

If anyone acknowledges that Jesus is the Son of God, God lives in him and he in God. And so we know and rely on the love God has for us. God is love. Whoever lives in love lives in God, and God in him.

(1 John 4:15-16)

The very nature of God towards us is love. His love is unyielding and unbreakable, yet we experience it with his incredible compassion, tenderness and kindness towards us. He loves his children completely; he wants the very best for us. His desires for us are nothing short of completely good in every way and backed by this strong, eternal love.

His love doesn't run out or fade from day to day. It is not a feeling. He is not 'in love' with us. He IS love. Love is his settled, constant disposition to always love us, even when we ignore him, reject his ways, trample his good plans or just get it wrong. We need to repent and come home to enjoy his welcome and joy, but his love has not dimmed at all. Prodigal sons and daughters might feel lost, sinners and rebels might be wandering away from home, but the Father still loves them completely.

As today's verses remind us, it is in Jesus that we see God's love in person and in action. He gave his life for us, a love-gift from God. And when we acknowledge Jesus over our lives as God's Son, 'God lives in us and we in him' – and we are then secure in his love forever.

May we know that security and joy. May we not rely for our joy and significance on our reputation in the world or our performance before others or to our own expectations, but on the pure, steadfast love God has for us..

10

PRAYERS OF GOD'S PEOPLE

Prayer is hard work. Prayer requires effort, faith, intention and, to some extent, competence. We grow spiritually and deepen our discipleship as we pray.

Prayer is also opposed; to pray is to engage in a spiritual battle with an enemy who would rather we do anything except pray.

To pray is also to draw near to God in perhaps the most simple, extraordinary and transforming means of grace that the Lord provides. It can be the means of breathing fresh hope into our anxious hearts, of stilling our fears, of awakening a dry or lukewarm faith and of clarifying what matters when confusion could dominate. Prayer can bring us a new awareness of what God is saying to us, often as we pray over his word and what he has clearly said already. In doing so we can receive comfort, wisdom, courage, peace and more.

The Bible shows us our loving God who invites our prayers and enables us to pray, and his delight to answer – supremely through our great high priest, the Lord Jesus Christ, who is full of grace and mercy. We also find, in the pages of scripture, such a wealth of prayers and a hugely diverse range of circumstances in which people pray. The Book of Psalms offers us a collection of prayers reflecting every aspect of the life of faith.

The following ten reflections bring us alongside a selection of praying people, and one prayer given to us by the Lord for us to pray over one another.

Prayer will remain hard work but it is a privilege, an extraordinary gift, a powerful weapon, and an opportunity for us in every day to draw near to our heavenly Father. We can pray for ourselves, for those in need, for the world and for the kingdom. Lord, help us to pray!

Exodus 32:31-33	Standing in the gap
Numbers 6:22-27	How to bless people
Ruth 1:8	Seeking the Lord's kindness
1 Chronicles 29:11-14	But who am I?
Nehemiah 1:11	Praying for God's favour
Jeremiah 29:7	Seek the peace of the city
Daniel 9:20-22	Between two worlds
Jonah 2:6-7	Praying from the depths
Matthew 9:27-30	Have mercy!
Ephesians 3:17-18	Grasping the love of Christ

Standing in the gap

So Moses went back to the LORD and said, "Oh, what a great sin these people have committed! They have made themselves gods of gold. But now, please forgive their sin—but if not, then blot me out of the book you have written."

The LORD replied to Moses, "Whoever has sinned against me I will blot out of my book." (Exodus 32:31-33)

The whole story of Moses is remarkable from beginning to end. No wonder it is picked up throughout the Bible as a model example of God's rescuing power, his mercy, his deliverance from death and slavery, and how he calls a people to himself. It is also full of incident, including a burning bush, plagues, the sea divided and held at bay, fiery clouds, divine commandments etched in stone, water from a rock, a bronze serpent and, sadly, a golden calf.

In the midst of memorable and miraculous events, no less striking is the relationship that Moses has with the Lord. God speaks to Moses. He meets with him. He commands and comforts, shines his glory upon him, and listens to his complaints and questions. There is an intimacy between God and this elderly shepherd.

The prayer of Moses in Exodus 32 is bold, honest and brave. He does not hold back. Moses does not sugarcoat the sins of his people in their crass behaviour and foolish rebellion. He knows that in making the golden calf, the people have committed a great sin, an offence against the Lord who has rescued, led, fed and protected them.

What we hear in this prayer though is not merely honesty, but also how Moses puts himself between God and these rebels. Moses stands in the gap. His prayer is for them, even in their clear rejection of God. Moses prays out of selfless concern for others, even offering himself to fall under God's justified wrath.

Jesus is the ultimate intercessor. He stood in the gap for all, dying in our place, bearing our sins and receiving the penalty. He also intercedes for us, taking our needs before the Father, knowing who we are but having given his life to save us. From the cross he prayed "Father, forgive" (Luke 23:34).

Our privilege is to pray for those who cannot pray for themselves, perhaps in their distress where words are too hard for them to find, or for those who are persecuted harshly, or for others who don't yet know the Lord and will not look to God in prayer. We can stand in the gap.

How to bless people

The L*ORD* *said to Moses, "Tell Aaron and his sons, 'This is how you are
to bless the Israelites. Say to them:*
  "The L*ORD* *bless you and keep you;*
  the L*ORD* *make his face shine upon you and be gracious to you;*
  the L*ORD* *turn his face toward you and give you peace."*
"So they will put my name on the Israelites, and I will bless them."
(Numbers 6:22-27)

The amazing aspect of this prayer from the Book of Numbers, is that
although it was to be spoken by the priests over the people (so it is
truly a prayer for God's people), the one who provides the prayer is
God himself.

It is God's intention to bless his people. His unwavering purposes
include showing them his favour, to make his face or presence shine
on them and show them grace. His plan is for them to know his
loving attention and intentions, and to receive and enjoy peace. This
is always his desire. When we experience this, when we truly grasp
just a fraction of God's goodness and kindness and enjoy that in our
lives, then we know what it is to be blessed.

As the Lord gave this to Aaron and his sons for their priestly role, we
may confidently adopt this same prayer to pray over one another as
God's people – whether in their company in the context of worship,
or privately as they come to mind.

Three times the prayer invokes the divine name, the LORD, Yahweh,
the Almighty. The repetition emphasises who we turn to in prayer
and how assured we can be that he will indeed shine his light and
bring his intimate presence into our lives.

The prayer is for God's people but the pronouns are in the singular:
seeking the blessing on individuals, by which the whole of God's
people are blessed.

The people of Israel had known God's rescue, guidance, provision,
protection and his commands. We can enjoy these too. But God's
desire is for us to enjoy his presence, to live with the assurance of his
blessing and ongoing favour, to know that we are securely kept by
him, and to experience the deep and rich peace in our hearts and
minds through knowing him and seeking to walk faithfully in his
company.

God has blessed us. He wants to bless us. We can pray this same
blessing for one another.

Seeking the Lord's kindness

But on the way, Naomi said to her two daughters-in-law, "Go back to your mother's homes. And may the LORD reward you for your kindness to your husbands and to me." (Ruth 1:8, NLT)

The Book of Ruth is a short story that touches on aspects of grief, loss, hope, despair, faith, trust, courage, honour, love, vulnerability and more. Quite a lot in just four chapters! It's a beautiful, rich and powerful story.

It focuses on a small family and the tragedies and then restoration that they experience, but it is not just about them. It is a story of God's kindness, of his promises, of what relying on him can look like. It shows faith in action and the heaviness of heart and loss of hope in faith's absence.

The story includes Naomi in her despair and elation, and Boaz with his display of integrity and compassion. Ruth herself is at the centre of this in giving out care, comfort and reassurance. She is the recipient of such kindness, grace and honour. God is so active in the events, even as the faith of Ruth and others shine out.

But in the opening chapter, the outcome is uncertain. Loss and hopelessness dominate in a foreign country. The future looks fragile and difficult.

The way in which our own lives will 'work out' in this life is often uncertain, even if – by faith – the end is certain, and what comes next is very good indeed. Tears and trouble are part of this life and a mature faith finds God's presence there too. Such faith grows as it leans on God and hears his words speaking into our hurts and questions, rather than turning away from him.

Into their uncertain future, Naomi's prayer over her two daughters-in-law is one we can pray for ourselves, over our loved ones, or for those we work with or count as neighbours or friends: 'May the LORD show kindness to you.'

Let us pray for others to experience the kindness of the Lord, his amazing grace, and for them to recognise it and be drawn to the Lord for themselves. For he is good and kind, all the time, in all our circumstances.

But who am I?

"Yours, O LORD, is the greatness, the power, the glory, the victory, and the majesty. Everything in the heavens and on earth is yours, O LORD, and this is your kingdom. We adore you as the one who is over all things. Wealth and honour come from you alone, for you rule over everything. Power and might are in your hand, and at your discretion people are made great and given strength. O our God, we thank you and praise your glorious name! But who am I, and who are my people, that we could give anything to you? Everything we have has come from you, and we give you only what you first gave us!"
(1 Chronicles 29:11-14, NLT)

Who are we to pray? Who are you and I to approach God in prayer at all, never mind ask for anything?

To pray to the living God, to the Lord Almighty, who by faith we can call our heavenly Father, is an extraordinary privilege. We might also recognise something of the extraordinary surprise of God's grace.

Grace is amazing on so many levels. It should surprise and move us as we reflect on the wonder of God's forgiveness of sins – our sins. He would rescue and restore all those who come to him in genuine repentance and who in faith look to Jesus and set their hope on him.

His grace is a powerful and wonderful gift, freely offered to us but paid for at great cost by Christ on the cross. It should surprise us that he would do this for us, the righteous One demonstrating God's love to the least and the lost.

We might also catch a note of wonder in King David's prayer that God is *our* God, that we are now in a new relationship, held in his steadfast love; we are those to whom he makes wonderful promises, and we are recipients of so many blessings. We are not merely consumers or spectators but loved and known and blessed. Amazing grace – everything in heaven and earth is his and from this he bestows so many good things on his people.

There is a similar note of the consistent surprise of God's people who find themselves caught up in this grace, this giving from God, and it is heard in prayer, in worship and in scripture. The apostle Paul considered himself to be the least of all the apostles, undeserving of the title, but confessed 'by the grace of God, I am what I am' (1 Corinthians 15:9-10).

To pray is a privilege, but it is a natural response to come with gratitude and wonder to the God of all grace.

Praying for God's favour

"O Lord, please hear my prayer! Listen to the prayers of those of us who delight in honouring you. Please grant us success today by making the king favourable to me. Put it into his heart to be kind to me."
(Nehemiah 1:11, NLT)

Who might be a blessing to you today, perhaps a help or encouragement, maybe offering a source of wise advice or practical resources? It could be a neighbour, a company, a work colleague, your boss or a friend. It could be an 'anonymous' blessing to you through a book, a song, a piece of art, a company offering good service or a stranger on the street.

Nehemiah was a Jew and trusted the Lord. He was employed in the court of a foreign king. The king held absolute power over the land and people, a rule built on wars, violence and probably corruption. At least, it looks like absolute power – in reality, there was a higher throne, a greater Power, and Nehemiah looked to the true Lord over all. His prayer tells us whom he truly serves.

The outcome of Nehemiah's prayer was that God did indeed turn the heart of the king and granted this servant the royal help he needed. Nehemiah prayed and help came from via a godless ruler. He would have all the resources needed to rebuild Jerusalem's walls.

Grace and favour can come to us from unexpected quarters, in deliberate acts of kindness and good works or signs to us of God's favour towards us in even the slightest encouragement or ray of sunshine. We are surrounded by people whom God can use to achieve his purposes, in the good gifts that God generously shares to those who know him and those who don't.

How has God shown you his favour? What good things do you enjoy, what opportunities and blessings have come your way? How might we use these, as servants of the living God, that others might also know God's kindness?

Seek the peace of the city

"Also, seek the peace and prosperity of the city to which I have carried you into exile. Pray to the LORD for it, because if it prospers, you too will prosper." (Jeremiah 29:7)

In the time of Jeremiah, the people of Judah had been deported to Babylon. Jerusalem was just a memory and a longing, and Babylon felt alien, unsettling, even hostile. They were leaning towards sorrow and hopelessness. But these words, through the prophet, reminded them that there is nowhere they could be that God could not bless them, even in exile amongst the Babylonian idols and under a foreign power.

We are not in Babylon but it can feel like an alien world. We are surrounded by seductive idols and powers that do not all honour or recognise God's kingdom, his purposes for us or Jesus Christ as Lord of all. But God has placed us in our particular towns and villages, in workplaces and communities, amongst these neighbours and friends, in our offices and teams and schools.

It is here that God calls us to seek the 'peace' of this place – his 'shalom' as the Hebrew says. This peace is his flourishing and well-being amongst people and in all of creation. It is a reflection of his character of kindness and mercy, of his delight in truth and goodness. His peace is seen where his ways of justice and love are pursued and delighted in, where people are honoured regardless of colour, background, ability, age or gender. His peace is not a bland notion of mere 'peace and quiet' but a vibrant, rich, life-in-all-its-fullness goal of God's will being done on earth as it is in heaven.

As we seek these blessings where God has placed us, we can 'pray to the Lord' for our town, home or workplace for example, that it's flourishing will be a blessing to us too. This is not for the growth of wealth and better shops, or more houses, although God's blessing might bring these too, but growth of his peace and for people to enjoy **him**.

Where God has 'carried you' and placed us, may we pray and seek his peace.

Between two worlds

I went on praying and confessing my sin and the sin of my people, pleading with the LORD my God for Jerusalem, his holy mountain. As I was praying, Gabriel, whom I had seen in the earlier vision, came swiftly to me at the time of the evening sacrifice. He explained to me, "Daniel, I have come here to give you insight and understanding." (Daniel 9:20-22, NLT)

When we pray, we are acknowledging that we are living in or between two worlds. Jesus taught his disciples that when we pray we are seen by our Father in heaven, who sees what is done in secret (Matthew 6:6). To seek after God in prayer, out of sight of the world, is a deliberate act in this visible earthly realm of coming before our unseen heavenly Father and finding great reward in so doing..

Daniel knew what it was to live between these two worlds. He served in the court of the Babylonian king and yet he was both devoted to and deeply aware of the kingdom of heaven. Daniel lived under the scrutiny of those who observed him and his friends for their acts of defiance. Their prayers and worship went against the flow, even against the laws. Yet still Daniel prayed, for he knew he was also under the gaze of the Lord, the Most High.

In these verses, Daniel's prayer is heard and the answer is coming before he has finished praying. The angel Gabriel appears and speaks to encourage and direct this faithful man of prayer. Daniel will receive divine wisdom and insight as a direct consequence of his prayers.

Prayer connected Daniel with God's power and purposes. Prayer releases resources from heaven to sustain, guide and equip God's people. Daniel's experience may seem dramatic, and we might not have stories of angels (some do), but something of the potential of prayer in his life is made plain for us today.

Prayer connects the visible world with the invisible, the kingdom of this world with God's mighty and glorious kingdom. His God is our God, only now we can know him more fully through the Lord Jesus.

Like Daniel, we don't move on from the need for humble confession, the need to seek God's mercy over our sins, as we recognise God's holiness. But like Daniel, our heavenly Father hears and answers, so we might see the kingdom of God come in the midst of the kingdoms of this world.

Praying from the depths

"To the roots of the mountains I sank down; the earth beneath barred me in forever. But you brought my life up from the pit, O LORD my God. When my life was ebbing away, I remembered you, LORD, and my prayer rose to you, to your holy temple." (Jonah 2:6-7)

A friend of mine once said, wisely, 'Don't make any major decisions at 3 a.m.' When our sleep is disrupted and we wake up to find the demands, concerns and plans for the day or the worries of life all clamouring for our less than fully awake attention, that is not the time to resolve them. We need the perspective that comes with the new day, with daylight, with a clearer mind, perhaps after the first tea or coffee too!

Jonah's prayer comes from an extraordinary place. He has run from God, run from God's call and command, and run to the sea. He's gone down to the docks, down into the boat and has continued his descent into the sea and now into the belly of a great fish. Physically, spiritually and emotionally he has gone down to the depths. He can't get lower. He feels like he has been brought to the 'roots of the mountains', to 'the pit'.

His prayer reflects that it is in this dark, deep and despondent place that the rebellious prophet gains a remarkable new perspective. This is his 3 a.m. moment, but in his case it is not time to roll over and try for sleep but to rejoice as true clarity and wisdom break into the gloom.

Jonah is in the fish but his eyes are set elsewhere – on God's holy temple. In his mind, he is there, for he remembered God for who he was – merciful, compassionate, holy, glorious, good – and cried out in prayer. God heard (as he hears our cries) and rescued.

But Jonah is still in the fish. He has not yet been freed from his dark aquatic prison. His circumstances haven't changed, but his heart and hopes have, and he will soon be back on dry land.

As we pray, God can bring fresh perspective, lift our burdens and remind us who he is and of his great promises and presence. The Lord can bring us new wisdom, peace and hope. May we find this in our own experience, and not just at 3 a.m.

Have mercy!

As Jesus went on from there, two blind men followed him, calling out, "Have mercy on us, Son of David!"

When he had gone indoors, the blind men came to him, and he asked them, "Do you believe that I am able to do this?"

"Yes, Lord," they replied.

Then he touched their eyes and said, "According to your faith will it be done to you"; and their sight was restored. (Matthew 9:27-30)

The two men couldn't see Jesus. Perhaps they could hear him speaking. They would almost certainly be aware of the crowd and the talk about this Jesus of Nazareth. Since returning to Capernaum, Jesus had restored a paralysed man and declared his sins forgiven, shared a meal in the company of Matthew and other tax collectors and social outcasts labelled as 'sinners' (like a doctor amongst the sick), spoken of himself as heaven's bridegroom, and then healed both a woman who was ill and a young girl who was dead!

It is inconceivable that the two blind men had not picked up on some of these stories that were surely spreading like wildfire through the community. They longed to see Jesus.

Their prayer reveals that they truly 'see' who Jesus is, the 'Son of David' – a messianic title. They are the first to use this title in Matthew's gospel. Faith sees who Jesus is; true faith perceives who he is as Saviour and Lord, as the Son of God. Such faith begins then to grasp what he is like: the God who saves, full of mercy, compassionate to those in need, the source of all healing, a friend to sinners, God who comes alongside as one with us.

We have no idea how much or how little these two blind men understood but we do have the record of their prayer. It is short, direct and heartfelt. It is directed to Jesus. It seeks God's mercy.

Their faith doesn't end there. The follow Jesus indoors, away from the crowd perhaps. There they receive the reward of their faith from Jesus in person. Sight is restored.

We have the privilege of seeing who Jesus is far more clearly and fully, because we see him revealed in the gospels in his words, his life, his miracles, his sacrificial death, his glorious new life and his ascension to rule from heaven. By faith we will receive that reward of seeing him face to face. We can also be assured that he hears our prayers. It is faith that counts, a faith in Jesus the Son of God.

Grasping the love of Christ

... that Christ may dwell in your hearts through faith. And I pray that you, being rooted and established in love, may have power, together with all the saints, to grasp how wide and long and high and deep is the love of Christ. (Ephesians 3:17-18)

Daytime TV is full of quiz shows. The evening slots have their fair share too. From *Pointless* to *Mastermind*, *University Challenge* to *The Wall*, you could spend a fair amount of any given week learning useful or fairly useless facts, as well as enjoying watching other people try to answer questions.

Growing as a Christian includes growing in knowledge and understanding. It includes a certain amount of facts, or more broadly, truths: truth about God and salvation, about ourselves and human nature, about God's promises and purposes, about his Son! Reading and reflecting on the Bible, hearing and responding to the preaching of God's word, sharing with others in a small group – these can all help with this spiritual formation. It's important and healthy for our spiritual health and encourages us, for what we learn about God is good news!

But knowledge and understanding are not the **ultimate** goal, good as they are. The apostle Paul's prayer in Ephesians 3, is for knowledge of God's love by *experiencing* it. To have Christ 'dwell in our hearts', to 'grasp' the greatness of the love of Christ, is tied to knowledge, it flows from trusting faith, but it is also to *experience* it.

You might receive a postcard from a beach or a mountain top. You 'know' something of what that place is like, but the postcard is not the reality. The experience is far richer. So also, knowing God's love in Christ is something to grow in experience of, to 'taste and see' in our lives. Knowing about it isn't the same thing.

God loves to grow our understanding or knowledge, but even little children – lacking much 'factual knowledge' – can experience deep love. So today and as you continue to follow the Lord, may you be encouraged as your knowledge of God grows, but may you also know in your experience, *really grasp*, something new of the love of God towards you found in Christ Jesus.

11

GOD'S UNLIKELY RECRUITS

We can read the Bible through different 'lenses' or with a variety of points of focus. Look at the character of God and we find that he truly is compassionate and gracious, abounding in love, slow to anger. He is holy and just, awesome in power, full of goodness and mercy. We see this throughout the scriptures. We see him most clearly in the Lord Jesus Christ, God in the flesh.

Another lens might look at the people upon whom God chooses to set his favour, those he calls into his service, those to whom he speaks , saves, empowers or to whom he simply chooses to reveal his great grace and loving kindness. When we pause to look at the cast of such characters, we can't fail to notice how fallible they are. We would say they are so 'human', rather than extraordinary. They are often remarkable for the qualities they lack, rather than their exceptional human greatness. Many are exceptional only for how very unqualified they seem for the roles God asks of them, or to be found amongst God's chosen people.

This is the nature of grace. He chooses because he loves, not because of merit or performance. We are all saved by grace and not by works. We are all unlikely recruits of the living God, surprised by grace as we become children of our heavenly Father, citizens of heaven, friends of the Lord Jesus Christ.

The following twelve reflections offer a snapshot of this great grace, the wide and open reach of God, that calls, reaches, equips and blesses many who might seem so unlikely yet find themselves secure in God's love in Christ.

Genesis 50:19-20   Joseph, on the path of God's purposes

Exodus 4:11-13   Moses, the reluctant leader

Judges 6:12-15   Gideon, least of all

1 Samuel 17:32-50   David, the unlikely giant killer

2 Kings 5:13-15   Naaman: powerful man, powerful cleansing

Esther 8:3-4   Esther, beautiful and brave

Matthew 27:55-28:5   Mary Magdalene

Mark 5:2-20   Living among the dead

Luke 23:42-43   The thief on the cross

John 21:15-17   Simon Peter, the failed friend

Acts 9:11-15   Ananias, fearful yet faithful

1 Corinthians 1:26-27 God's unlikely chosen ones

Joseph, on the path of God's purposes

But Joseph said to them, "Don't be afraid. Am I in the place of God? You intended to harm me, but God intended it for good to accomplish what is now being done, the saving of many lives." (Genesis 50:19-20)

Joseph would become saviour of the nations. Through his high office, second only to Pharaoh in Egypt, he exercised considerable power and great wisdom to provide grain during a widespread famine. Egypt's power and influence were increased; the people were saved from starvation. Joseph's own family were amongst those seeking help. His personal prestige and honour were very great as a result.

A recurring line in the story of Joseph is that the Lord was with him. In highs and lows, the source of wisdom, comfort or resilience in difficult times was derived not merely from Joseph's resourcefulness but from the company, provision and protection of God.

Yet the path to this 'happy ending', with his family reunited, significant personal riches and status, and the thanks of a nation was far from smooth. It was hard and painful for Joseph, including times of being abandoned, alone, enslaved, falsely accused and imprisoned.

We might find ourselves in situations where we wonder if God is still there, why we are experiencing tough times, or 'what on earth is happening?!' Joseph shows us that God can use someone rejected by his family, sold into slavery, his integrity maligned, who endured prison, whose own brothers continued to lie to him, but one whom God took from the lowest place to the highest and saved the nations through him. All of which is a pattern of Jesus.

Wherever we find ourselves, God can use us and work out good purposes even there. Like Joseph, we can know the Lord Almighty with us, and that makes all the difference.

Moses, the reluctant leader

The LORD said to him, "Who gave man his mouth? Who makes him deaf or mute? Who gives him sight or makes him blind? Is it not I, the LORD? Now go; I will help you speak and will teach you what to say." But Moses said, "O Lord, please send someone else to do it."

(Exodus 4:11-13)

Being a leader is not everyone's 'cup of tea' or calling. Not everyone can or should lead. Some leaders are in the wrong role and you wonder how they got there. Others are natural leaders without ever being given a formal title or position; they lead effectively out of their character, gifts, personality, knowledge and charisma. Great leaders serve well, empowering and equipping others with encouragement, direction and support.

Moses was a great leader. He was one of the most significant leaders in all of Israel's history, arguably in all of human history. He is honoured within scripture itself (e.g. Hebrews 3:2-5; 11:24-28; John 1:17) and he appears at the transfiguration of Jesus. He was used by the Lord in the epic salvation events of the judgement on Egypt, the Passover, the mass exodus of the rescued slaves, crossing the Red Sea, receiving God's law on Sinai then leading the rebellious tribes through the wilderness as their teacher, judge and leader.

He faced monumental practical challenges, moments of terrifying peril, constant spiritual waywardness and sin from the people in his care, and regular criticism. How did he sustain his leadership? The friendship of the Lord. He enjoyed a close walk with God; he displayed humble dependence for everything on the true Teacher, Judge and Leader of Israel. God 'had his back'.

However, the conversation in Exodus chapter 4 does not mark him out as a confident leader, far from it. In a to-and-fro question and answer session, Moses offers reasons not to accept the call and queries both the plan and his abilities. "Who am I?" (verse 11) is met with "I will be with you" (verse 12). Still Moses ducks and dives, finally asking directly for a replacement: send anyone but me.

God has experience with those who can only see their weakness, who feel inadequate, who wish to opt out. A healthy measure of weakness is a good thing; obstinate doubting of God's call is not. In your calling, wherever he has placed you, find fresh joy and confidence in knowing that he is with you, that you can lean on him for all that you need, and be open to his leading.

Gideon, least of all

When the angel of the LORD appeared to Gideon, he said, "The LORD is with you, mighty warrior."

"But sir," Gideon replied, "if the LORD is with us, why has all this happened to us? Where are all his wonders that our fathers told us about when they said, 'Did not the LORD bring us up out of Egypt?' But now the LORD has abandoned us and put us into the hand of Midian."

The LORD turned to him and said, "Go in the strength you have and save Israel out of Midian's hand. Am I not sending you?"

"But Lord,'" Gideon asked, "how can I save Israel? My clan is the weakest in Manasseh, and I am the least in my family."

(Judges 6:12-15)

Gideon is not a mighty warrior. But the angel of the Lord says he is. Which is it to be?

The angel speaks of what God will do, of who Gideon will become, that he will have the glory, power and prestige of a mighty warrior. The word of the Lord will not fail. But Gideon had questions.

Gideon was timid rather than bold and brave. Gideon was a young man and not obviously warrior material. His clan was not strong but the weakest, and Gideon himself was the least in the pecking order for a leadership role within his own family. (What was the Lord thinking?!)

Yet God delights to use the weak things, the apparently foolish things and the people who lack earthly honour or prestige. He does this so that it is plainly his glorious power at work and not our great ideas, wits, resources and skills. He also does this so we can serve with great confidence despite our lack of incredible ability or worldly prestige.

He does this because he delights in those like Gideon, who come with humility and don't consider themselves worthy or even ready.

God continues to raise up the humble and do great things, acting in his mighty strength through us, weak though we are.

May you know the joy of service, the honour of being his, the encouragement of his calling, you mighty warrior!

David, the unlikely giant killer

David said to Saul, "Let no one lose heart on account of this Philistine; your servant will go and fight him." Saul replied, "You are not able to go out against this Philistine and fight him; you are only a boy, and he has been a fighting man from his youth."

David said to the Philistine, "You come against me with sword and spear and javelin, but I come against you in the name of the LORD Almighty, the God of the armies of Israel, whom you have defied."

So David triumphed over the Philistine with a sling and a stone; without a sword in his hand he struck down the Philistine and killed him. (1 Samuel 17:32-50 selected verses)

David vs. Goliath. The showdown in the Valley of Elah.

Shepherd vs. Giant. Boy vs. Man.

This is such a familiar story in the outline and the outcome that perhaps we miss how simply amazing and unlikely it is. The one-on-one combat of the two representatives is actually a battle of Israel versus the Philistines, which, in turn, we find is the confrontation between Yahweh, the Almighty and living God, against Dagon, a dumb stone idol. Only David, the shepherd boy, seems to have kept this perspective in plain sight.

The Lord had a whole army gathered – seasoned warriors, wearing armour and carrying swords, axes, javelins, etc. He had a king, Saul, whom the Spirit of the Lord could have employed to deal with Goliath's loud and proud insults. But God chose the shepherd boy.

Here, in the valley, the giant fell and the triumph was for the Lord Almighty, but the fame and honour of the day went to the young lad who had knelt by a stream and picked his smooth stones. The king and his warriors would not win glory that day, and the shepherd would one day become king, the shepherd over God's people.

God does not need to choose those with obvious influence, skill or earthly positions of power to achieve his ends. In fact, he delights to choose the unlikely, those with a heart set on him, with a clear faith, with godly courage, who do not seek glory for themselves but delight to give glory to God.

Where has God placed you that you might serve? How might your actions serve to give honour to the Lord? Where might you need courage? For the Lord delights over those who look to him.

Naaman: powerful man, powerful cleansing

"'Wash and be cleansed'!" So he went down and dipped himself in the Jordan seven times, as the man of God had told him, and his flesh was restored and became clean like that of a young boy.

Then Naaman and all his attendants went back to the man of God . He stood before him and said, "Now I know that there is no God in all the world except in Israel. Please accept now a gift from your servant."

(2 Kings 5:13-15)

Naaman was the commander of the army of the king of Aram, a proven warrior and successful leader, with status, power and wealth. 'He was a valiant soldier, but he had leprosy.' (v. 1) This was not just a serious skin disease, but also a social barrier in many cultures.

Help comes from several unexpected quarters in this story: his young Israelite slave girl speaks to his wife to suggest that her master see the prophet in Samaria and be cured.

The king of Aram supports the plan and sends Naaman to the king of Israel with a vastly expensive set of gifts. Israel's king is outraged, thinking this is a ruse to restart a military offensive, but the prophet Elisha hears of the request and issues instructions for Naaman to go to the river, dip himself in the water and be clean: be healed. Elisha doesn't go in person, he sends a messenger. Still, Naaman the great warrior has not met the prophet, the man of God.

Wash seven times in the river Jordan? Naaman finds this preposterous, beneath him, and goes off in a rage. However, he is then convinced from another unlikely source: his servants. So he goes to wash, seven times, and is miraculously completely healed.

This man of such status and influence, a proud and capable warrior, receives the powerful healing and restoration of the Lord. But only via the working of God's mercy through a young slave girl, his wife, his king, a messenger, his servants, a river, and obedience. Naaman was right, Elisha possibly could have just waved his hand and called on the Lord (v. 11), but that's not how God chooses to work.

No matter how powerful we are, how high our status, we need the Lord's cleansing too. We need the forgiveness and healing of our sins. Our method of cleansing will seem preposterous to some – a crucified man – but here is full salvation.

No matter how lowly we are in the eyes of the world or how far we seem from influence or power, like the various servants in this story, God can and does use us in his purposes.

Esther, beautiful and brave

Esther again pleaded with the king, falling at his feet and weeping. She begged him to put an end to the evil plan of Haman the Agagite, which he had devised against the Jews. Then the king extended the gold scepter to Esther and she arose and stood before him. (Esther 8:3-4)

Some people rise high in their career by their training and technical skills (e.g. surgeons, pilots, engineers), others by their entrepreneurial abilities (many self-employed people and business owners), others by knowledge (scientists, educators) and others by physical abilities (athletes, those in elite sport, dancers). There are many routes to the 'top' and many rise up in their career through a mix of these factors and experience, training, grit and opportunity.

As Christians, we also recognise that God plays his role in this. Providence, his direction, his provision, words of scripture, the timing of conversations or prompting are all means by which he can direct our paths.

Esther rose stratospherically high in some ways: from a sex slave to a queen. Not a path she chose, one where a king with absolute power dictated her place and elevated her to his court, his side and her title. A young Jewish girl of great beauty became the favoured partner of the ruler of the kingdom. She achieved this through her beauty, something she had no control over, a circumstance of genetics and a gift from God yet used by him in his purposes.

Esther the beautiful queen was called to display great bravery. Would she stand up for her people? Would she speak up for the Jews, at great risk of her own life? If not her, who? (Esther 4:14)

Esther proved her courage, standing in the place of immense peril and uncertainty, against dark forces and the potential death of her and her family, as she spoke up for the Jews. God honoured her, saving her and his people.

She wholly depended on an earthly king, received his royal favour, was honoured in his presence, and stood – saved – before him. God can and will use his people to bring about salvation for others. We carry a gospel of saving power.

We, too, depend wholly on a king, our King Jesus. We have also received royal favour and we are crowned with honour as those sealed as his own by the Spirit in us and saved by God. So we can stand confident before him and the world, wherever he sends us.

Mary Magdalene

Many women were there, watching [the crucifixion of Jesus] from a distance. They had followed Jesus from Galilee to care for his needs. Among them were Mary Magdalene, Mary the mother of James and Joses, and the mother of Zebedee's sons.

Mary Magdalene and the other Mary were sitting there opposite the tomb. ... After the Sabbath, at dawn on the first day of the week, Mary Magdalene and the other Mary went to look at the tomb.

So the women hurried away from the tomb, afraid yet filled with joy, and ran to tell his disciples. (Matthew 27:55-28:5 selected verses)

If you could witness any moment or event in history, what would it be? A sporting occasion – Wembley 1966, or one of Federer's many triumphs? A political event – a famous speech by Churchill, JFK, MLK or Mandela? Or just the fascination of meeting Julius Caesar, Joan of Arc, Henry VIII, Shakespeare, Jane Austen or Einstein?

As a Christian, it would be incredible to witness at first hand some of the life of Jesus, humbling and distressing to witness his death, amazing to be at the garden tomb on Easter morning.

The four gospel accounts record one group who are consistently with Jesus throughout his ministry and most notably as witnesses to the crucifixion, his burial and the empty tomb on the third day: 'the women.' An often unnamed group, but some names occur in various texts and one name stands out: Mary Magdalene.

In a society where women were overlooked, not empowered or honoured, barely given dignity, the company of Jesus and notably those who are listed as the key witnesses, makes for a stunning contrast. And Mary Magdalene is prominent.

Luke tells us that she had personally experienced the grace and power of Jesus. Her life had been delivered from the grip of seven demons (Luke 8:2). How would this reputation and former life trail behind her in the eyes of the world? We don't know, and it pales into insignificance beside her incredible devotion to Jesus in his life and death, and her incomparable place amongst the first witnesses to history's greatest turning point: the resurrection of Jesus Christ.

After Mary meets the risen Christ, (John 20:10-18), she rejoices that she has "seen the Lord!" Those who have received God's salvation, whose lives have been transformed, share her joy. We have 'seen the Lord'; by faith we know him. All history honours this Mary and the other women for their witness, entrusted as God's story-bearers.

Living among the dead

When Jesus got out of the boat, a man with an evil spirit came from the tombs to meet him. This man lived in the tombs, and no one could bind him any more, not even with a chain. ... Night and day among the tombs and in the hills he would cry out and cut himself with stones.

"Go home to your family and tell them how much the Lord has done for you, and how he has had mercy on you." So the man went away and began to tell in the Decapolis how much Jesus had done for him. And all the people were amazed. (Mark 5:2-20 selected verses)

If there were a census or report card on the impact of Jesus visiting particular towns or cities, detailing the number of lives changed, this one would raise some eyebrows: only one man received the ministry of Jesus and 2000 pigs died.

Was it the most 'efficient' use of Jesus' time? No, not if we measure that day by modern economic thinking, but that's not the right measure. Jesus considered it worthwhile to cross the lake, visit a graveyard, rescue one man, even for the sake of the local pig economy taking a major downward turn (literally). Then he returned across the lake.

Jesus would do all this for just one man.

And what was this man like? He lived amongst the dead, a ritually unclean and socially excluded way of life. He was demon-possessed, of scary strength, deeply disturbed and self-destructive. An incredibly sad existence. Yet Jesus went there, knowingly into this unwelcoming place of stigma, even into discomfort and danger, and brought life-transforming healing through the compassion and salvation of God.

The transformation of the man sparks fear in the onlookers (who *is* this Jesus?) For this most unlikely recipient of a very focused visit by Jesus, it brings deep peace, new life and evangelistic zeal to tell of what Jesus has done.

No one is out of bounds for Jesus, no matter how tough, painful or dark their circumstances, nor how socially excluded they seem or feel. The power and mercy of Jesus are not bound by our limits or understanding. Often his glory is shown more brightly in those who know how great, how wonderful, their salvation story has already been.

What might this man's experience have to say to you?

The thief on the cross

Then he said, "Jesus, remember me when you come into your kingdom."'

Jesus answered him, "I tell you the truth, today you will be with me in paradise." (Luke 23:42-43)

Some of those who become followers of Jesus, or worshippers of the living God before the time of Christ, are 'unlikely' disciples in terms of their past. Others might be surprising 'recruits' in terms of their position in society. For yet others, it is their present circumstances that seem so unpromising. The thief on the cross is a clear example to us of all of the above.

His past life has led him, whether justly or unjustly, to being condemned to capital punishment. We are told he was a 'criminal'. Other versions refer to a thief or a robber. He may well have been guilty of violent crime. The cross was both a punishment and a means of deterrent, displaying the power and harsh justice of the state against their enemies.

His position in society was now that of one being despised, an outcast, guilty in the eyes of the authorities and humiliated in the eyes of the public.

His circumstances are dire: he is nailed to a cross. He is dying, an excruciating death too. He is in no place to offer any religious ritual, to do any good works for society, to attend a discipleship course or to try to improve his life. His life is virtually over.

In all these unpromising ways, he is in plain sight before the Lord Jesus, and in response to a simple request for some measure of mercy, he receives a staggering, cast-iron promise of great honour and wonder: Jesus will welcome him into the kingdom, today.

Nothing in our past or present is great enough to bar us from God's welcome, if we come to Jesus in humble repentance and turn to him for mercy. No one is completely beyond his reach or rescue. No situation can fully obscure God's grace if we turn to ask. We need only truly recognise our great need and this great Saviour. He would welcome us too.

Simon Peter, the failed friend

When they had finished eating, Jesus said to Simon Peter, "Simon son of John, do you truly love me more than these?"

"Yes, Lord," he said, "you know that I love you."

Jesus said, "Feed my lambs."

Again Jesus said, "Simon son of John, do you truly love me?"

He answered, "Yes, Lord, you know that I love you."

Jesus said, "Take care of my sheep."

The third time he said to him, "Simon son of John, do you love me?"

Peter was hurt because Jesus asked him the third time, "Do you love me?" He said, "Lord, you know all things; you know that I love you."

Jesus said, "Feed my sheep." (John 21:15-17)

Have you ever played Top Trumps? It's a card game where each card rates the object in various categories and you see whether your card 'trumps' the scores of your opponents. It could be a set of cards based on Disney characters, superheroes, WW2 tanks, Premiership footballers, or just about anything.

I've not come across this game for the twelve apostles. If we were to rate them for patience, loyalty, honesty, team spirit, etc. then it takes little imagination to put Judas Iscariot at the bottom of the score chart, the worst card of the pack. He is rightly remembered for an act of betrayal, of singular wickedness and unthinkable magnitude.

However, perhaps we forget the other eleven in that time where Jesus needed support. We are told that they all ran away as Jesus was seized (e.g. Matthew 26:56). None of them stood with Jesus or for Jesus in his hour of greatest need. They couldn't even stay awake while he prayed.

Simon Peter emerged as the leader of the apostles during Jesus' ministry, but having fallen asleep in Gethsemane he is also remembered for his own act of betrayal after Jesus' arrest. He denied even knowing Jesus, disowning his Lord with oaths and curses.

So the breakfast scene on the beach from John chapter 21 is all the more remarkable. Jesus does not merely forgive his friend or forgive the offences; he reinstates and recommissions Peter to the role to which all pastors are now called. The feeding, leading and care of the sheep was given to this headstrong man who had slept through his watch duty, run away from trouble and from Jesus, and then repeatedly lied to protect himself and distance himself from the Lord.

Jesus only had fallen, imperfect and occasionally really unfaithful disciples from which to choose. And the wonder is that he still does choose imperfect people, who he calls and forgives and then empowers. To be of service, all that matters is that we truly love him, that we put that love for him at the centre of following him. Then we find that, like Peter, we are secure in his love.

Ananias, fearful yet faithful

The Lord told him, "Go to the house of Judas on Straight Street and ask for a man from Tarsus named Saul, for he is praying. In a vision he has seen a man named Ananias come and place his hands on him to restore his sight."

"Lord," Ananias answered, "I have heard many reports about this man and all the harm he has done to your saints in Jerusalem. And he has come here with authority from the chief priests to arrest all who call on your name."

But the Lord said to Ananias, "Go!" (Acts 9:11-15)

God does not need us. He does not need any disciples, believers, followers or servants. He is entirely capable of achieving his purposes with a word. Yet he chooses to involve us. We are intrinsic to his plans and kingdom purposes.

The apostle Paul would prove to be the greatest pastor, church-planter, theologian and missionary of the new Jesus movement. A man of rare abilities and a true intellectual heavyweight, morally and culturally steeped in the scriptures of Israel as a 'Hebrew of Hebrews' (Philippians 3:5). From his hand, head and heart come much of our New Testament. God surely chose him well. And he had an unlikely background, from hunting down the Christians to preaching Christ crucified.

Yet God did not simply appoint and then send the great apostle. Instead God chose to involve Ananias. He did not need to, but consider the impact on Ananias.

He is summoned to go and find Saul, persecutor of Christians, to lay his hands on Saul and restore his sight. Ananias wants none of it. Saul was a dangerous man and had caused great harm to the Lord's people. It was a terrifying prospect and sounded absurd.

At this point, Ananias stands in a long and familiar line of God's servants (Abraham, Moses, Gideon, Jonah, Peter, etc.) who question God's ideas or commands. But God has been here before too. He can speak into fearful hearts, summoning the unsteady and uncertain servant into action. Ananias is told to 'go', and he goes.

Saul gets his sight restored and will indeed be God's great instrument for the gospel. Ananias recognises in him, a brother in Christ. But Ananias has also had the joy and faith-building experience of stepping forward in obedience, despite the questions and the risks, and being part of God's great purposes.

God didn't have to, but he chose Ananias. He could have found another way. May we choose faith over fear, obedience over convenience, service over spectating, and enjoy the blessings and encouragement that follow.

God's unlikely chosen ones

Remember, dear brothers and sisters, that few of you were wise in the world's eyes or powerful or wealthy when God called you. Instead, God chose things the world considers foolish in order to shame those who think they are wise. And he chose things that are powerless to shame those who are powerful. (1 Corinthians 1:26-27 NLT)

The Christians of the church of Corinth were so shaped by the values of their world, they were sucked into the pointless comparison game of status-seeking. In the Roman Empire, honour was everything. This was measured by one's family connections ('noble birth'), by a reputation of intellectual prestige (being 'wise') or by the fleeting appearance of physical beauty or strength.

Paul revels in demolishing these notions and insisting on brand new foundations for God's people, values that seem utterly foolish, absurd or blasphemous. To the wider society of Jews, Greeks or Romans, the cross provokes all these reactions, yet Paul claims it as the centre of his confidence and message. From this scandalous, foolish display of God's power in weakness, greatness in humility, victory in defeat, he turns his attention to us: the disciples.

God chose us. He chose the foolish, the weak. He knows that is what we seem to be, and chose us anyway. He does not measure his people by the value system of our social status, our background, our educational achievement, our wealth, our health or strength. He chooses us in Christ, from across every possible strata of society and starting point, and delights to have us in his service and in his family.

God chose us, unlikely as we might feel, yet exactly with his purposes in mind and for our greatest joy of belonging to him. We are all 'unlikely recruits', sinners saved by grace, called and created in Christ for the good works God has prepared for us (Ephesians 2:9-10).

What greater honour can there be than to know that through Christ, God chose you? There is our significance, security and joy, however we might seem in the world's eyes or however unlikely we consider our place amongst God's people.

12

GOD'S LIFE IN US: THE FRUIT OF THE SPIRIT

To become a Christian is to receive new life from God, eternal life as a gift. This life is of a wholly new quality not simply quantity, it is as Jesus said to be 'born again', born of the Spirit.

The remarkable life of the Spirit is seen in a chosen few of God's people in the Old Testament given divine power to lead or rescue, in miraculous strength or new-found courage, in great wisdom or artistic ability. God can and does still give many remarkable gifts, now with a greater abundance. He also promises to do the work of new creation in every believer.

Every Christian receives not simply a new life but specifically the life of God, the Spirit uniting us to the Son of God and his life now found in us. His character is therefore being formed in us. We are becoming the people of God, changed on the inside and being transforming in how we live.

The following nine reflections take the fruit of the Spirit as the starting point. The first three touch on our relationship to God (love, joy, peace), the next three are in relation to our life with others (patience, kindness, goodness) and the final three speak to who we are in ourselves (faithfulness, gentleness and self-control). Each reflection focuses on the character of God, to help us to dwell on who he is shaping us to become and the good work he seeks to do in and through us.

Galatians 5:22-23	The fruit of the Spirit is love ...
Nehemiah 8:10	Sustaining joy
Proverbs 14:30	A heart at peace
2 Peter 3:9	The patience of God
Titus 3:4-5	God's merciful kindness
Psalm 27:13	Noticing the good news
2 Corinthians 1:20	Promise-keeping faithfulness
Matthew 11:28-30	Our gentle Saviour
Romans 12:19	Self-control

The fruit of the Spirit is love ...

But the fruit of the Spirit is love, joy, peace, patience, kindness, goodness, faithfulness, gentleness and self-control. Against such things there is no law. (Galatians 5:22-23)

Some of the most familiar words of the apostle Paul. Famous words even. The 'fruit of the Spirit'. Do you know them? Could you recite them, all nine, in order? This is not a test; there is no prize!

These words are so engaging because they describe something utterly wonderful, deeply attractive, eternally relevant, and quite lovely. We LOVE to encounter these qualities in other people. Life is happier, more contented and fruitful when we see them growing in our own character too. These fruit bear further good fruit.

We might well notice them by their absence: a mind without peace is anxious and troubled; a workplace without kindness is tough and demoralizing; a friend without gentleness can be taxing or create distance between you.

Much as we can pray for God to grow these in us (our Father in heaven is the expert Gardener, after all), today can I encourage you to recognise how these all reflect the person of the Lord Jesus Christ. He is full of each of these to the limit and beyond. God is love and in Jesus we see that love for God, for his word and for those he encounters to the full.

You will never meet anyone like Jesus whose love is so wholly joyful, peaceful, patient, kind, good, faithful, gentle and self-controlled. As the 'fruit' belong together, so his love is all these – utterly good, Godly, always for our good, gentle yet unbreakably strong, kind yet never yielding to sin or temptation.

Today, appreciate God's good work to grow you to be more like Jesus, but also marvel at his amazing love towards you.

Sustaining joy

Nehemiah said, "Go and enjoy choice food and sweet drinks, and send some to those who have nothing prepared. This day is sacred to our Lord. Do not grieve, for the joy of the LORD is your strength."

(Nehemiah 8:10)

The first three fruits of the Spirit from Galatians 5:22 are love, joy and peace. God wants to grow these in our hearts, in our innermost being. They each relate to our relationship with him – **love** for God, **joy** in knowing him and his presence, **peace** with him, peace as we receive his forgiveness, peace as a gift from him. These are the work or fruit of the Holy Spirit. He will do this good work, as we grow in our life with Christ.

Today's verse speaks of 'the joy of the LORD', a joy that comes from him as a gift to his people, a deep experience in that moment but also a lasting blessing.

Nehemiah had witnessed the rebuilding of the walls of the city and was now rebuilding a community of faith. They had rediscovered the Scriptures having previously ignored them and left them at the margins of their life for generations. On this day, they rediscovered them and heard them read and taught; it moved them deeply. They grieved for the days lost and blessings missed, for having wandered from the good paths, but Nehemiah tells them to celebrate for now they have God's word in their life again. And the result: joy!

God's joy sustains us. It can carry us through our challenges, sorrows and failings. It is fuel for the journey of faith. 'The joy of the LORD is your strength.' Joy comes from knowing him, finding him afresh in the midst of any trial.

Like coming to a deep well that never runs dry, take time to bring yourself before the Lord today and be refreshed. Pause and pray. Know that he loves you and wants to guide you, and may you know his joy as you do so, which will strengthen you.

A heart at peace

A heart at peace gives life to the body, but envy rots the bones.
(Proverbs 14:30)

We are made as whole people. We don't 'have' a body, a mind and a spirit as separate parts, like components of a car. We are embodied beings with a soul and a mind, all deeply interconnected. This is how God has made us, 'fearfully and wonderfully made' (Psalm 139:14).

So it should not surprise us that when our mind is anxious, our digestion may be disrupted. When our inner thoughts are dwelling on anger, sadness or how we have been annoyed, our sleep will suffer. 'Envy rots the bones' – indeed!

If we are laid low with physical illness, we can find our mental and spiritual well-being suffer too. Not always, but sometimes. Pain can also draw us to seek God more urgently.

Today's verse is a great encouragement that God can give us 'a heart at peace'. He cares for us; he is able to carry our burdens for us or with us. In the midst of storms, he can bring stillness. He has the power to heal, to restore, to forgive, and to help us see ourselves or others with more compassion and kindness. This and more come when we find rest in God and a heart at peace. And this can give 'life to the body' – renew our smile, rest our minds, lift our energy levels.

May you know the gift of God's Holy Spirit working in you and your circumstances today – a heart at peace – and your mind and body blessed along with this.

The patience of God

The Lord is not slow in keeping his promise, as some understand slowness. He is patient with you, not wanting anyone to perish, but everyone to come to repentance. (2 Peter 3:9)

One aspect of the fruit of the Spirit that God wants to grow in us is **patience**. Within that list of beautiful and desirable character traits in Galatians chapter 5, patience is one that we see in action towards other people. It is very easy to be patient when you don't have to wait for anything or on anyone to respond! Try it – you can become an elite level patience-displayer very easily, until something or someone tests your patience!

Patience enables us to show grace to one another, to extend kindness to others rather than a sharp word, quick criticism, thinking ill of them or rapidly withdrawing to a safer emotional distance. As God grows our patience towards our family and friends, towards colleagues or our boss, to customers or pupils, to the terrible driver or the person endlessly holding up the queue ahead of us, we find he also grows our resources of kindness. We become more like Jesus! (We might also find that, with such patience, life becomes less stressful and more enjoyable.)

Today's verse reminds us not of **our** patience (or need of it) but remarkably of the patience of **God**. He can appear slow to act, but that is because he is patient. He is patient with us, allowing room and time for repentance. Allowing scope and space for our genuine sorrow over sin and turning back to him, for our recognition that we need God's grace and to return to our Father, God is patient. He is ready for all who come in repentance, who truly seek him. So, patiently, he waits, and calls all to repent.

He is still patient, wonderfully so. His plans and promises will all be fulfilled. We can trust him with the troubles of today and find he is always ready through Jesus to give us grace and mercy again.

God's merciful kindness

But when the kindness and love of God our Saviour appeared, he saved us, not because of righteous things we had done, but because of his mercy. (Titus 3:4-5)

The Bible tells us to bear with one another, forgive one another, encourage one another, carry one another's burdens. There are apparently no less than 59 separate commands in the New Testament for how we are to relate to "one another". The Bible is not simply for me, or for you, but for us, for life with God and from God with one another and in God's world.

Many of these actions for the sake of one another might be labelled as acts of **kindness**. To 'do good' towards others, especially believers, and not to give up (Galatians 6:9-10) is to act with kindness.

God grows kindness as a fruit of the Spirit as we let him shape us, as we allow him to soften our hearts with his compassion and equip us to serve others. Kindness may be a 'soft' quality in some ways – it should also be gentle – but is also tough in others. Kindness to others requires setting aside some of our own needs or wants at times, a tough persistence. Kindness to friends and children also involves telling them what is true and good, stopping them doing what will harm them, even if they don't like it! Kindness may look like tough love. Kindness is not a pushover. It is love in action, for the sake of others. Such kindness honours God.

Today's verse from Titus points us to Kindness in person – Jesus appearing on earth was God the Son who displays all the 'kindness and love of God'. He unfailingly served others at such great cost. He unfailingly spoke the truth, even when people didn't want to hear it, even as they despised and rejected him. He was kind to all without fault, tender and tough, strong yet gentle.

May God give us opportunity to show kindness to others today.

Noticing the good news

I am still confident of this: I will see the goodness of the LORD in the land of the living. (Psalm 27:13)

As you switch on the news on the TV or radio, or swipe for the news on your phone, you are presented with the headlines. Stories of war and disaster sit alongside sporting triumph, weather news, bizarre celebrity antics, cute animal videos and serious political announcements. It can all be a bit disorientating. And the news cycle is such that major events far away (e.g. a famine in East Africa affecting 300+ million people) disappear quickly from our view.

Today's verse reminds us that there is something to be seen in each day which may not grab the headlines, which we might miss ourselves, but is well worth giving attention to: the goodness of the Lord.

God is always at work, his kingdom is growing, but like a well seeded and watered field this growth might not always be spectacular or visible even. But it's happening. His Spirit is always active, sustaining and blessing God's people, growing faith, prompting kindness, bringing peace and comfort, granting courage and wisdom, guiding the church, revealing Jesus. This is the good work of God, in small and large ways.

When we see the goodness of the Lord, our hearts are more glad, our worries diminished, our resolve stronger, our hope more confident.

God is good, all the time. May we lean on him and pray for those news stories where suffering, evil and sorrow are obvious. Let us pray for mercy and justice.

May we also notice something of the good news of God in our own stories, recall his goodness to us, notice what is good in our world today, and may it give us fresh confidence in him.

Promise-keeping faithfulness

For no matter how many promises God has made, they are "Yes" in Christ. And so through him the "Amen" is spoken by us to the glory of God. (2 Corinthians 1:20)

One of the songs we sing often at church is called 'Yes and Amen'. The chorus line goes, 'All your promises are Yes and Amen.' It draws from this verse, from 2 Corinthians. The apostle Paul reminds them and us that all God's promises find their fulfilment, their answer, in Christ Jesus. All of them. God is **faithful**.

What does that mean about **Jesus**? It puts him at the centre of all God's plans, all his great and good purposes. At the centre of God's plans for humanity, for the cosmos, for the renewal of creation, for salvation from sin, for judgement, for now and forever. Jesus is the 'Executor' of God's full and final will and testament, the one who opens the scrolls in the Book of Revelation so the plans are fulfilled. You won't see or experience any good thing from God without going through Jesus Christ.

What does this mean for **us**? It calls us to bring our lives and unite them to Jesus by faith. When we do, we have the joy of being recipients of his good promises: the promises of new life, of lasting joy, of forgiveness and hope, of God's strength and peace for us and with us, of his eternal friendship. All this, through Jesus, where God says "Yes and Amen" to his own promises, fulfilled by God the Son.

And as we live for Jesus in this world, we faithfully witness to him in our words, deeds, character and priorities: *And so through him the "Amen" is spoken **by us** to the glory of God.*

Men, women and children who show that they love and trust Jesus are saying "Amen" back to God, to bring glory to God.

May we trust God's faithfulness today. He keeps his promises. He is faithful to us and for our sake. May we be those in whom such faith is clear and real, as the Spirit deepens our life in Christ. Yes and Amen.

Our gentle Saviour

"Come to me, all you who are weary and burdened, and I will give you rest. Take my yoke upon you and learn from me, for I am gentle and humble in heart, and you will find rest for your souls. For my yoke is easy and my burden is light." (Matthew 11:28-30)

The God who created all things and rules over the cosmos is immeasurably powerful; nothing and no one can rival him or resist his good purposes. Yet he has revealed himself to us in person, in the form of God the Son, who shows us God's heart, his character.

Jesus is our gentle and humble Saviour and Lord. He is no less powerful for being gentle, no less awesome for being humble. He is no pushover for those who are proud or certain of their self-righteousness, those who bat away all criticism of themselves and are quick to point the finger at others. Such people will find Jesus to be a stern, implacable and just judge, who longs for his followers especially, to be gracious, loving, kind and tender towards others.

But to those who come feeling 'weary and burdened' – by life, by sin, by fears or questions, by shame, by the unjust words or unkindness of others – we find that Jesus longs to give these people his rest. Real and deep refreshment, the safety and peace of his welcome. The rest of knowing a great freedom by being led by him and not bearing the burden of leading ourselves. He does so as the gentle king.

As we look to see the fruit of the Holy Spirit grow in our lives, let us seek after gentleness, and see that Jesus himself is the gentle Lord we need to restore us and to lead us. He calls us to come to him.

Self-control

Do not take revenge, my friends, but leave room for God's wrath, for it is written: "It is mine to avenge; I will repay," says the Lord.
(Romans 12:19)

There are days when things happen to us or to people we care for that are caused by thoughtless or destructive behaviour, by deliberate unkindness or selfishness, even by violence. Sin has many forms. There are other times when we look on events in the world and we can discern evil – the massacre of innocents, cruelty on a large scale, the impact of corruption, systematic abuse or state violence.

Whether close to home or far away, we see that we live in a world still stained by corruption, by rejection of God's ways and his authority. Original sin is real, but sin is rarely that original, sadly.

I wonder what the apostle Paul had in mind as he wrote today's verse: 'leave room for God's wrath.' He had surely endured so much personal suffering at the hands of wicked and violent people. He had also previously dished out the violence himself.

His words are a comfort and encouragement to us that God sees and is a just Judge. His wrath – his personal, just, holy and pure judgement – is ready to respond. His 'self-control' is perfect. He never lashes out, whereas our lack of self-control can swiftly seek revenge or trigger a reaction that only adds to the problem.

There will be a day when this Godly wrath and justice are seen and done, perfectly (Rev. 6:16-17). So amidst our hurts and tears, our righteous anger or sense of injustice, we need not lash out. Instead, we can leave it with our Father God, the Lord Almighty. We can learn new trust and patience.

His wrath will deal with all wrongdoing. His grace, mercy and comfort are always there for those who look to him and cry out for relief. Let's pray on – 'may Your kingdom come.'

13

SHINE LIKE STARS:
THE WITNESS OF GOD'S PEOPLE

To become a Christian in the first two centuries after Christ was to choose to go against the flow. This is still the case around the world today, dangerously so in countries dominated by other religious worldviews, but it was a decision with stark consequences in the early church. It frequently led to being socially rejected and considered strange, suspect or even a threat to the order of society. It was not unusual to suffer economically or physically. You could be made jobless, arrested, sent to the mines or even killed for declaring allegiance to Christ as Lord.

So, why would people become Christians?

Part of the answer is the work of God, the activity of the Holy Spirit in changing hearts and minds. Another answer is the 'pull' factor of the sheer wonder of the gospel and the wonderful promises of grace – of forgiveness, of hope, of God's welcome and adoption, and of a new identity in Christ.

A key reason that the Bible offers for people choosing an often hard, narrow, unpopular path of declaring faith in God is the compelling, attractive witness of God's people. Disciples make disciples.

People are drawn to faith in Christ in part by those who already live out that faith, whose lives have been shaped by God, whose new priorities, character and faith shine out in some way.

In God's plan of salvation, he chose to use us to display the kindness and love of God and to declare the good news. The following 14 reflections explore this theme. May these equip and encourage us to witness faithfully, clearly and confidently to a needy and often dark world.

Exodus 20:1-3	No other gods
Joshua 24:15	Choose for yourselves
1 Kings 19:13-15,18	Not alone
Daniel 3:16-18	Courage to stand
Matthew 5:13-16	Salt and light
Matthew 28:19-20	The Great Commission
John 15:15-16	Fruitful disciples
John 17:14-18	Sent into the world
Acts 1:8	Power to witness
Romans 10:14-15	How can they hear?
2 Corinthians 8:7	A new generosity
Philippians 2:15	Shine like stars
1 Peter 2:12	Attractive witness
1 Peter 3:15-16	Questions and answers

No other gods

*And God spoke all these words: "I am the L*ORD *your God, who brought you out of Egypt, out of the land of slavery. You shall have no other gods before me." (Exodus 2:1-3)*

To become a Christian is to adopt a brand new loyalty: a singular devotion such that God alone is at the centre; only he is God over our life. We can all be drawn to make other things our god, the focus of our true security, the source of our peace, and the thing to which we give time, attention and loyalty – in other words, what we love.

God spoke to Israel and reminded them who he was, not just the LORD but *their* LORD, *their* God. He also reminded them what he had done for them: rescued them from Egypt, from an existence of fear, oppression, hopelessness and death. 'Out of the land of slavery.' He is the one true God; he calls people into a relationship with him. He does so still, by rescuing them from sin and death and into new life, and he does all this through Jesus.

To give God his rightful, central place in our life doesn't mean that nothing else is important in life, only that nothing else is ultimate. We should rightly recognise lots of other good things that we are given to enjoy, protect, develop or serve, such as a marriage or family, children, a job or vocation, friendship, health, possessions, skills and interests. These can be truly good, genuinely appreciated as gifts from God, but they are not gods. They can't ultimately save us or make us whole. They can't carry that weight. It isn't fair on people to have that expectation to deliver all that we need. It isn't reasonable, loving or God-honouring to live like that either.

The great prayer of Israel as they began life as a nation was to their one God: *Hear, O Israel: The L*ORD *our God, the L*ORD *is one. Love the L*ORD *your God with all your heart and with all your soul and with all your strength.* (Deuteronomy 6:4-5)

To be a witness to the living God, our heavenly Father, and to his Son the Lord Jesus Christ, is principally an act of love. We love God and love no other like him, meaning only in him is our whole being, our past, our present and our future resting. Only he has the right to lead our life, for he loves and rescued us.

When we choose this central love we also find, in God's goodness, that our love for all the other good things in life becomes richer, more selfless, rooted in the fact that we are truly loved and secure in God already. May he shape and lead us. May our love for him grow.

Choose for yourselves

"But if serving the LORD seems undesirable to you, then choose for yourselves this day whom you will serve, whether the gods your forefathers served beyond the River, or the gods of the Amorites, in whose land you are living. But as for me and my household, we will serve the LORD." (Joshua 24:15)

To stand for God in the midst of the world is to choose to live by faith not by sight, when our mind and eyes might tell us that living for ourselves is a lot simpler or more comfortable. To stand for God will inevitably bring us against the flow of the world's values, against the opinions of some family and friends, into conflict with what the media or culture wants to celebrate or promote. Is it worth it? Does it seem 'undesirable'?

Jesus said we would be persecuted, insulted and rejected on account of him, if we follow his name. The apostles were physically persecuted; some were killed, yet they died honouring the name of Jesus. Across the world today, millions of Christians make everyday choices to stand with Jesus despite the cost – loss of job, friends, family ties or social status, perhaps even losing their life. It's humbling. Joshua's situation was not new and speaks to today's world.

Wherever we live, there will be points at which we need to reaffirm again whom we will choose: will we choose to serve God – to honour him in our lives, to reflect his love and leading in our actions and priorities, in our connection to his church (his people), in our giving and spending? Or will we choose other gods, to take our lead in life from ourselves or the world?

Joshua spoke to Israel and laid these two choices before them: the LORD, the one true God, or the gods of the Amorites. One had saved them, led and fed them, taught and blessed them. The others had done none of these and brought death. It seemed a plain and simple decision, yet they – and we – need to make the active choice, to follow the Lord and serve him.

When we do, we find renewed joy from God! We can find gladness of heart, the security of the soul, hope now and beyond death, the friendship of the Lord as he walks with us, giving us wisdom in our ways and strength for each day. The choosing doesn't create these, it reminds us who he is and who is with us.

So choose well and find that in serving him there is great joy!

Not alone

Then a voice said to him, "What are you doing here, Elijah?"

He replied, "I have been very zealous for the LORD God Almighty. The Israelites have rejected your covenant, broken down your altars, and put your prophets to death with the sword. I am the only one left, and now they are trying to kill me too."

The LORD said to him, "Go back the way you came ... I reserve seven thousand in Israel—all whose knees have not bowed down to Baal and all whose mouths have not kissed him." (1 Kings 19:13-15,18)

The story of Elijah is a stirring tale of great courage and faith, of miracles and God's provision. When hungry, he was fed both by ravens and from a miraculously never-empty kitchen of the widow of Zarephath. He prays and it doesn't rain, he prays and it does rain: God's power was evidently with Elijah. He challenged the authority of a cruel and powerful king, Ahab, and his angry and vicious wife, Jezebel. He stood in God's strength and witnessed an overwhelming victory over the false prophets and their idol, Baal.

We might expect Elijah to have been brimming with godly confidence, or at least have a steady sense of well-being. Not so. Immediately after the mountain-top showdown with Baal and his 400 followers where the outright supremacy of God and his prophet were affirmed, Elijah ran for his life, afraid and ready to end it all.

The Lord God came alongside him with tender and practical care of hot food, water, sleep and reassurance. What a lovely picture that is of God and also of what we need at times. But still Elijah shared his dark thoughts and a deep sense of loneliness: "I am the only one left."

My guess is that none of us have experienced a fraction of Elijah's more exhilarating, scary or spiritually miraculous moments. But many of us might have had this sense, of spiritual isolation or loneliness. We might be very aware of being the only Christian in our office, our team, our department, our school, our friendship group or our family. We might feel alone.

So may these words be our comfort. God is always with us, the greatest reassurance possible. But, as Elijah needed to hear, God has many who know and follow him. 'Elijah, meet your 7000 friends.'

We are surrounded by a great cloud of witnesses to cheer us on and encourage us (Hebrews 12:1). We are numbered amongst the people of God yet known by name. God is with us. We are never, ever alone.

Courage to stand

Shadrach, Meshach and Abednego replied to the king, "O Nebuchadnezzar, we do not need to defend ourselves before you in this matter. If we are thrown into the blazing furnace, the God we serve is able to save us from it, and he will rescue us from your hand, O king. But even if he does not, we want you to know, O king, that we will not serve your gods or worship the image of gold you have set up." (Daniel 3:16-18)

To be a disciple of Jesus is to become a changed person. He *accepts* anyone as they are when they come to him in humble repentance and faith, but he *leaves* no one as they are. They – we – all need change, transformation. God is forming us to be more like Christ.

He changes us in our innermost being, in our character, and this will be noticed by family, friends, work colleagues and fellow Christians. Some changes happen rapidly, even immediately, sometimes miraculously. Others often take longer: the gradual softening of rough edges, the deeper work of becoming more gracious, kind or patient, with his power transforming our attitudes, habits or values.

Some changes are only revealed under great pressure. Today's verses are certainly from a highly pressurised situation. Daniel's friends have refused a royal decree to bow before a large golden statue. For this crime they face the death penalty. They knew this potential outcome so it was a clear and deliberate choice on their part, as their response reveals. To bow would be to dishonour the one true God, to break the first two of the Ten Commandments. They serve him; they will serve no other god.

Their plea before the king is clear, logical, respectful and unmoving. Even facing the prospect of being thrown into a fiery furnace, still they will not change their stance. They might die, God surely could save them, but even if he does not they stand by their actions.

What has God done in them? He has given them courage. This is an incredibly brave response. Facing almost certain death and a painful one at that, they stand loyal to God. Some things are more precious than life, some things are worse than death.

Many Christians around the world today face the prospect of violence, exclusion, punishment or death for professing faith in Jesus Christ. May we pray for their courage. For those of us spared physical persecution, may we find courage from God to stand clearly for him, whatever the cost.

Salt and light

"You are the salt of the earth. But if the salt loses its saltiness, how can it be made salty again? It is no longer good for anything, except to be thrown out and trampled by men.

You are the light of the world. A city on a hill cannot be hidden. Neither do people light a lamp and put it under a bowl. Instead they put it on its stand, and it gives light to everyone in the house. In the same way, let your light shine before men, that they may see your good deeds and praise your Father in heaven." (Matthew 5:13-16)

Have you ever mistaken salt for sugar? A salty cake or coffee is not a happy experience! Sugar on chips is not something I've tried and sounds better than salty cake, but is not ideal!

Salt was considered as a valuable commodity in many parts of the ancient world, precious even. Packing the meat with salt could preserve it from decay. It could add or bring out the good flavours of other ingredients in a meal. Other forms of salt were used as fertilizer, spread on the ground to promote growth. The success of this relied on the salt being ... salt! Salty salt, salt that has not lost its saltiness, could hinder decay, add distinctive flavours or promote growth.

Jesus says to his disciples: you ARE the salt of the earth. Not that we could be, or under certain conditions we might be. We are. As we reflect the kingdom of God in our lives, so we act within God's world as the salt of the earth, to restrain evil and spiritual decay, to bring out what is good in the world around us and to promote God's good work of the kingdom and its growth. If our lives are not shaped by the kingdom, we are unable to be this salt.

The Lord Jesus says we are not just distinctive as salt but also as bright lights. He is the great light, the light of the world (John 1:7; 8:12). We are now his light, reflecting or carrying his light (Ephesians 5:8-9). This light is to be lifted up high, not hidden. What use is a light under a bowl? It would snuff out!

To be a light is an image of purity and goodness, of knowledge of God rather than ignorance, and of revelation by shining into the dark. God has made us to be lights in his world.

Salt and light. Both stand out, both are distinctive. This is our calling. As we grow more like Christ, may our salty and bright lives bring him glory.

The Great Commission

"Go and make disciples of all nations, baptising them in the name of the Father and of the Son and of the Holy Spirit, and teaching them to obey everything I have commanded you. And surely I am with you always, to the very end of the age." (Matthew 28:19-20)

What is the church for? Many a denomination or church will have its own strapline, mission statement or a way of expressing its vision: what is its purpose, what are the central aims? For the church I serve with it is: 'Helping people meet Jesus Christ and become his fully devoted followers.' This is what we are there for, what shapes and drives our church life. We can then ask: how can we do this more effectively, creatively, boldly or clearly? If one of our activities isn't really seeking that goal, why are we doing it?

Regardless of a church's vision statement, we already have our very clear marching orders from our Commander-in-Chief. Every disciple is a follower and Jesus has already marked out the direction of his leadership. His final words in Matthew's Gospel (and final words are always worth noting) are these: 'Go and make disciples.' The central purpose of the church is to bring people into a relationship with Father, Son and Holy Spirit – our new life with God.

Who are the beneficiaries? 'All nations', everyone everywhere. It's good news to all people, to be shared widely. We 'go' into our world, into offices, schools, wards, homes, conversations and vocations, to be his disciples. Representing Jesus, we also make disciples.

What is the strategy? 'Baptising them... and teaching them to obey everything I have commanded you.' It's not complicated. Bring people to a point of personal repentance and faith, the Christian faith in the Triune God of Father, Son and Holy Spirit, and to baptism as the sign of that faith. Grow those disciples through teaching: grow them in faith and knowledge, in confident joy and in God's commands, through teaching, preaching and exploring God's word together. It's not novel; constant innovation is unnecessary or distracting. It is life-transforming. It is a command with the authority of Jesus. And it is not simply reliant on us. The command comes with one of the greatest of promises. He is with us, for us, always.

This is the mission, our joyful and clear commission from the Lord of the church. May we find great confidence as we seek to serve him, keep our focus, relying on his presence and power as we go and make disciples.

Fruitful disciples

"I no longer call you servants, because a servant does not know his master's business. Instead, I have called you friends, for everything that I learned from my Father I have made known to you. You did not choose me, but I chose you and appointed you to go and bear fruit— fruit that will last. Then the Father will give you whatever you ask in my name." (John 15:15-16)

There is a principle that is basic to forensic science and the study of crime scenes called Locard's principle. It states that when two objects come into contact with each other something is exchanged and taken away by both objects. This is the basis of the transfer and recovery of all scientific physical evidence. If you like crime dramas, this is what is going on with finding the footprint in the garden, the fingerprint on the handle, the DNA from the glass. Every contact leaves a trace.

The same is true, only far more wonderfully and positively, with our life in Christ. Our contact with him leaves not just a trace but also a deep and lasting impact, ongoing change, and one that affects the world around us. Our lives as God's people have many contacts with the world and never leave it unchanged.

Jesus chose an agricultural metaphor for this, or rather a viticultural one. He is the true vine, we are the branches (John 15:5), so the impact of the vine is seen in our lives in fruitful growth. He has chosen us and appointed us 'to go and bear fruit – fruit that will last.'

When we remain with our lives rooted in Jesus, obedient to his word and commands, we will have his life sustaining us. We will remain in his love. And we will bear fruit. We will be changed, we will grow and be transformed, but we will also have a lasting impact for the kingdom. We will not see all this impact, we may not hear of how God used us, but Jesus chose us for this and his words do not fail.

So, friends of Jesus, where are you having contact, leaving traces of the kingdom of God? For there too, he will make you fruitful.

Sent into the world

"I have given them your word. And the world hates them because they do not belong to the world, just as I do not belong to the world. I'm not asking you to take them out of the world, but to keep them safe from the evil one. They do not belong to this world any more than I do. Make them holy by our truth; teach them your word, which is truth. Just as you sent me into the world, I am sending them into the world."
(John 17:14-18, NLT)

As Christians we are in the world but not of the world.

We are unquestionably in the world. We inhabit time and space, the same physical reality as everyone else we meet or live amongst. We are in the world that God made, a beautiful and fascinating creation even though it is marred and broken in part, not least by our impact. This is the world in which we are called to live for God, as servants of Christ. The world is also the people, loved by God even as a rebellious world in need of saving (John 3:16).

We are in this world to seek the flourishing of God's kingdom and of community, to pray and work for the blessings of God in the home, in our families, with friends and work colleagues, alongside our neighbours or towards strangers. A place to express God-given creativity and skills, to bring beauty and justice. This is the world God has put us in, a world known and loved by him, where our days are in his hands and our work really matters.

This world is also a spiritual battleground. The land itself is not the target of enemy action; the devil is not seeking to conquer countries. The focus of his evil assaults is God's people. Because we are definitely *in* this world but we are without doubt not *of* this world: we have another allegiance, a new identity. We belong to Jesus.

So Jesus himself prayed for all those who follow him, who believe in his name, who have become children of his heavenly Father. He prayed for our protection from the evil one, and his prayer is powerful and effective. We can be impacted by discouragement, doubt, lies or dark thoughts, but they will not have ultimate power over us – we remain securely in the care of God, held in his hand.

Jesus prays for us as his own; for our protection. He prays for us as we go out in his name. He was sent by the Father, so he also sends us. May you know the assurance of his power, presence, favour and prayers with you and for you in this world.

Power to witness

"But you will receive power when the Holy Spirit comes on you; and you will be my witnesses in Jerusalem, and in all Judea and Samaria, and to the ends of the earth." (Acts 1:8)

Once or twice I have found myself perilously close to the car running out of petrol, with the dial right at the bottom or showing 'miles left' as just 2 or 3. It's very unnerving.

Many times my phone or laptop have run out of battery power just when I needed to send a message, find somewhere on a map or complete a task. Quite frustrating.

On a few occasions in my life I have felt completely physically exhausted, to the point of near collapse: after a day walking many mountainous miles in the Yorkshire peaks in blizzard conditions; after helping friends move house and spending the day lifting heavy objects (which felt like an 8-hour gym session); and after making the 'epic' journey on crutches from a car into my home and then upstairs after major surgery – feeling just like someone had taken my batteries out!

When you don't have the power, you can simply grind to a halt.

As God's people, we have access to power beyond ourselves: the Holy Spirit. He is the power and presence of the living God, alongside and within the body of Christ to enable us to fulfil all of God's purposes through us. He brings power to change hearts and minds, to open the eyes of the spiritually blind, to set the prisoners of sin free from guilt, addiction, dead-end thinking, destructive habits and shame. He has power to sustain the church, so that the gates of hell will not prevail against it. He has power to enable each Christian to keep on walking with Christ, not in their own strength but in his.

He is also the power behind our witness. He enables our words and actions to point to the Lord Jesus, to the gospel itself, which is the power of God for the salvation of everyone who believes (Romans 1:16). He is the power to take mere words and enable spiritual transformation as they are heard and believed. It is his power that sustains the church in the face of persecution, ridicule or the indifference and intolerance of the world.

This power, this Holy Spirit, is for us today. Like those first disciples, we should watch, wait, receive and then witness. He is with us.

How can they hear?

How, then, can they call on the one they have not believed in? And how can they believe in the one of whom they have not heard? And how can they hear without someone preaching to them? And how can they preach unless they are sent? As it is written, "How beautiful are the feet of those who bring good news!" (Romans 10:14-15)

When surveys are compiled of people's greatest fears, the top answers are often social fears, e.g. fear of change (except from vending machines!), of rejection, of loneliness. Close behind these are physical fears, e.g. fear of the dark, of heights, of confined spaces, of snakes or spiders, of dogs or needles. Amongst the lists of such things is another common answer: public speaking. The most chatty and confident person can go pale and silent at the thought of standing on a stage behind a microphone.

These verses from the apostle Paul to the Christians in Rome can often be misunderstood to refer only to public speaking. As if Paul means, 'How can people believe? Only with someone preaching to them' However, he means someone declaring or sharing the good news, with or without a stage, a microphone or a job title.

Faith comes by hearing the message of Christ (Romans 10:17), and preaching is a God-given means, commanded and commended to the church to build faith. Preaching is found throughout the Bible, unleashing God's power to change hearts and leading to new life. Faithful preaching is part of the life of any healthy church. But it is not the only way to get a message heard. Paul has in mind that the good news be shared widely, everywhere, with everyone.

How will people believe? By hearing the gospel, the good news of what God has done through Jesus Christ, of the kingdom of God's Son, of forgiveness of sins, God's friendship and eternal life. How will they hear? Simply by someone telling them. With words.

To be a witness is to tell others about God, to testify to this good news. We don't need all the words, we don't need long words, we won't be able to tell the whole story in one go. But as we tell the story, perhaps our own story of how we have met Jesus and now know the difference he has made, our words will be used by God.

So do not fear and let God give you words, opportunities and confidence.

A new generosity

But just as you excel in everything—in faith, in speech, in knowledge, in complete earnestness and in your love for us—see that you also excel in this grace of giving. (2 Corinthians 8:7)

One of the most remarkable and perhaps tangible changes that God works in his disciples, especially in the rich nations of the West, is our attitude to money and wealth. He sets us free.

Many a society seems completely given over to the pursuit of stuff, to the accumulation of wealth and material resources, where more people worship in shopping malls than in cathedrals and success is measured in the number of cars you own, the size of property or the extravagance of holidays. The economics of God are so different as to seem bizarre. And all this in a world where billions lack clean water or live with food insecurity.

Jesus warns us not to worry about wealth (or clothes, food, or indeed anything else). He knows we do worry and will worry, yet he loves us too much not to warn us how material things could be a source of anxiety and how the 'deceitfulness of wealth' will stunt or kill our spiritual growth (Matthew 6:25-34; Mark 4:19). He tells us that we cannot serve God and money, and obviously only one of these makes a good master; only one of these will love us.

The apostle Paul describes the love of money as the root of all kinds of evil. It leads many away from faith and into all kinds of grief (1 Timothy 6:10). Wealth is a gift from God, a tool for immense blessing and with great potential in the kingdom of God, but to be used and stewarded, not revered and hoarded. To give is also to be blessed.

God changes our hearts and one of the new Christ-like traits is this: to excel in the grace of giving. To have a freedom, a joy, a spirit concerned for God's people and kingdom that is seen in financial generosity. And to recognise that it all comes from him and is all for him, whether we keep it or give it away.

Jesus owned next to nothing but was immeasurably rich in spiritual terms. He gave it all away that we in our poverty might become rich. He didn't grasp after wealth. He would not have us gripped by a love of it either, but rather know the joy and grace of God in us as we give generously.

Shine like stars

Do everything without complaining or arguing, so that you may become blameless and pure, children of God without fault in a crooked and depraved generation, in which you shine like stars in the universe as you hold out the word of life—in order that I may boast on the day of Christ that I did not run or labour for nothing. (Philippians 2:14-15)

Christians belong to Jesus, the light of the world, and as such we are carriers or bringers of his light (Matthew 5:14). And so we will shine, shine like stars.

As you look upwards on a clear and cloudless night, if you are far enough away from streetlights, you will glimpse the stars. If you are somewhere with a truly dark sky, somewhere remote or at high altitude, the starry sky can be breathtaking. The pinpoints against the vast inky backdrop stand out sharply, each a distinct source of light reaching us from unimaginable distances. The light of stars, the cosmic furnaces like our own sun, or the reflected light from planets within our solar system, shine distinctly.

Have you ever stopped to think that Moses, Daniel, David, Jesus and Paul will all have seen these same stars, witnessed the beauty and vastness of the heavenly lights?

In God's eyes, we are his distinct lights, scattered in a dark world, a morally dark place or a 'crooked and depraved generation' (Deuteronomy 32:5) that has lost its way, rebelled against God, and turned to destructive, foolish and even evil ways at times. In this darkness, Christians shine with the light of their new lives.

We can shine as God's people where we stand out against a morally confused and corrupted world, as people who are 'blameless and pure'. Not that we are sinless or without fault, but with lives marked by godliness, integrity, purity, truth, wisdom and the fruit of the Spirit we reflect God's light. We don't have to make these characteristics shine, they just will. Paul says 'you shine' already.

We also offer the light of the gospel. As we 'hold out the word of life', we are letting the light of Christ shine. We are lifting Jesus up, the blazing light of the world, the light of life himself. As we do that, we shine, and people will be drawn out of the dark and into the great light. Not ours, but his.

Shine, Jesus, shine, and may you shine both in our lives and your world more and more.

Attractive witness

Live such good lives among the pagans that, though they accuse you of doing wrong, they may see your good deeds and glorify God on the day he visits us. (1 Peter 2:12)

The first adverts to appear on radio, billboards and screens tended to focus on what a particular product was and how well it worked – even whiter clothes/teeth, a faster car, a smoother taste. Over time this changed from a focus on *performance* to the *experience* or even lifestyle that the product would give you: a happy meal, 'the best a man can get', 'because you're worth it'. How does this product make you *feel*?

Some adverts nowadays are so abstract, initially so far removed from the product, that you can watch the first 20 seconds of a 30 second advert and be none the wiser whether it is for shampoo, a car, beach holidays, a cruise, toothpaste or central heating.

But a good advert makes you want to experience it, to buy it, to enjoy it.

1 Peter 2:12 reminds us of the attractive power of a life shaped by God, the effective witness or 'living advertisement' for the gospel. As we go about our lives, our everyday and not particularly dramatic Christian lives, by the Holy Spirit the goodness of God is able to shine in us and through us into the world. People notice. And they are attracted, not to our lives alone but by God in us.

The apostle Peter's audience were 'strangers in the world' (1 Peter 1:2) but chosen by the Father, being sanctified by the Spirit, and obedient to and marked out by Christ and his blood (his saving death). They were a distinct people. Under persecution, facing ridicule and social stigma, possibly violence, they continued to live godly lives. Their good deeds shone brightly for Christ.

In every age and society, this has been part of God's good plan through his people: the attractive power of the gospel as it shapes lives and draws others to Jesus. Take heart: your everyday faithfulness, kindness, patience, compassion, love for others, grace under fire, generosity to those in need and integrity at work – God can use these for his glory.

Questions and answers

But in your hearts set apart Christ as Lord. Always be prepared to give an answer to everyone who asks you to give the reason for the hope that you have. But do this with gentleness and respect, keeping a clear conscience, so that those who speak maliciously against your good behaviour in Christ may be ashamed of their slander. (1 Peter 3:15-16)

Sooner or later every Christian will be asked a question about faith. It might be from a child at school ('How big is God?' 'Where does God live?') or an adult at work ('Why are you a Christian?', 'Do you think God hears my prayers?'). These are questions I've been asked and attempted to answer, but usually I think of an even better response much later! Isn't that just the way of it though, that with a bit of time and thought, we can come up with fuller, clearer answers to other people's questions?

Notice that when the apostle Peter wrote to Christians scattered across the Roman empire, under growing persecution for their faith, he didn't require them to give the fullest possible answer, or even the most thought-through and brilliant answer. He encouraged them to give 'the reason for the hope' that they had, and answer with gentleness and respect. A simple answer, given in a godly manner, has great value. At times, less may be more.

What is the reason for the hope we have? The Lord Jesus Christ, and all that God did and promised through him. He is the reason for our hope. All our answers, eventually, connect to Jesus. That doesn't mean he is the answer to every single question, but behind every good question about faith, God, life, Christianity, the Bible, prayer, death, hope and more stands the person of Jesus. The cornerstone of faith, the author of life, the anchor for our soul.

Questions can come from many places: from grief and sorrow, from past hurt or failure, from confusion with faith and genuine searching, from mocking distrust and intellectual pride, or from a humble, open attitude of spiritual hunger and thirst for life and purpose. The shape of our answers might vary, but Peter's words remind us that our witness will shine brightly, not so much from clever or even sensible answers (we might not know, and that's ok), but from how we speak.

An answer given with love, humility, patience, kindness, gentleness and respect will often have a great impact in a world starved of grace and filled with need. May we welcome questions, in the confidence that it does not all rest on us to give the answers, for Christ is Lord.

14

TRANSFORMED:
OUR NEW LIFE IN CHRIST

Therefore, if anyone is in Christ, he is a new creation;
the old has gone, the new has come!

(2 Corinthians 5:17)

To become a Christian, or as the apostle Paul often puts it, to be 'in Christ', is to receive a radically new identity, to live under brand new ownership and to be subject to a completely different relationship to our Creator and Redeemer. The New Testament speaks of this new reality with a wealth of wonderful insights.

In the following 25 reflections, the focus here is on how we are being and becoming the people of God in Christ. We explore some of the many beautiful and practical facets of God's good work in us. We will hear some of the promises of God that speak of our new-found confidence and joy, of God's presence and equipping, and of his leadership and comfort.

Each of us is a precious new creation, born again of the Spirit, being renewed and transformed in Christ amongst his body, the church.

May we take time to let his words take root and trust that the good work he has begun will not fail but continue, despite doubts or hardships, for God is faithful.

Genesis 28:15	I am with you
Matthew 5:9	Peacemakers
Luke 21:33	Jesus' enduring words
John 10:28	Safe and secure
John 14:16-17	The Father will send the Spirit
Acts 7:37-38	God's living words
Romans 8:19	Creation is longing
Romans 12:1-2	Renewing your mind
Romans 15:4	The past is our teacher
1 Corinthians 1:9	God is faithful
1 Corinthians 10:13	Resisting temptation
1 Corinthians 12:4-6	Generous diversity
1 Corinthians 15:58	Working for the Lord
Galatians 4:6	"*Abba*, Father"
Ephesians 5:18	God's abundance
Ephesians 6:10-11	Stand strong
Philippians 2:12-13	God at work in you
Philippians 3:20	Citizens of heaven
Colossians 1:29	God's rule, our responsibility
Colossians 3:12-14	Wardrobe change
1 Thessalonians 4:11-12	Godly ambition
1 Thessalonians 5:16	Always joyful
2 Peter 1:19	The morning star
Revelation 3:11	I am coming soon
Revelation 3:20	I stand at the door and knock

I am with you

"I am with you and will watch over you wherever you go, and I will bring you back to this land. I will not leave you until I have done what I have promised you." (Genesis 28:15)

There are some very unlikely candidates for receiving God's promises in the Bible. You might think our wise God would find some reliable, honest, decent and courageous people. Faithful ones, even! But time and again we find that the people receiving these stunning promises are not like this, sometimes far from it. After all, God only has fallen people to use (with one exception – Jesus).

Jacob was a deceiver. He had cheated and manipulated his family; he had taken God's rule as something he could ignore. God breaks into his life here and calls Jacob afresh to obedience and blessing.

"I am with you and will watch over you wherever you go, and I will bring you back to this land. I will not leave you until I have done what I have promised you."

Do these words sound familiar? Recall the final words of the Lord Jesus in Matthew's Gospel: "Surely I am with you always."

God's promise to Jacob was to a most unlikely follower. Jesus' promise to his disciples as he left them was very similar, but they had proved an 'unlikely' bunch too. Yet God's promises are the same, then and now: "I will be with you always. Wherever you go."

The promise to Jacob continues further to his people. The Lord has great purposes in mind, not just to be with us but also to work in and through us. Jacob would see and experience God's power, loving kindness, provision and forgiveness. He would see the Lord's ability to rescue from seemingly hopeless situations, even to reconcile him to his brother.

He is the same God today; he is with us, and still working out his purposes. May we look to him, listen to his word and lean on him, putting the past behind us and walking in faithful trust. He is with us.

Peacemakers

"Blessed are the peacemakers, for they will be called sons of God."
(Matthew 5:9)

Some friends of mine live and work in South Sudan. It is currently the second-poorest country in the world as measured by GDP per capita; only Somalia has a lower value. It is a fragile country, wracked by the impact of civil war, ethnic violence, famine, flooding, corruption and the poverty that often comes with these. It is also a country of outstanding natural beauty, with great potential, and loved by God. He is also at work in the peace-making and peace-keeping, including that work done through many NGOs, the church, the government, the UN, people of goodwill, and through prayer.

One such avenue of bringing new peace is through peace and reconciliation workshops as part of an initiative called 'Healing Hearts, Transforming Nations'. Community leaders are brought together, often from previously opposing or literally warring factions and groups. They are then enabled by trained facilitators coming alongside them, to hear and explore the gospel message: how the cross is where God bears our sins and those sins committed against us, how he knows our hurts and fears, how forgiveness from God flows from the cross, and how we can receive that forgiveness and be empowered to forgive others. It is possible to break the cycle of revenge killing, of blood feuds, of habitual violence and generational hatred seen in some of these places. (See hhtnglobal.org)

Peacemaking can stop the killing, but also enable living. It leads, through peace and reconciliation, to new hope, to the joy of being released from fear and bitterness, to the ability to plant crops and grow families, to build communities and make good plans. The change in hearts and plans is a reflection of the power of the gospel.

Jesus' words to us are from the ultimate peacemaker who made peace between us and God (Ephesians 2:15-17). Wherever we work for peace, for the restoration of good relationships and justice, whether between friends or strangers, locally or between nations, we are modelling our Saviour. There is God's blessing, God's favour, on us too.

Jesus' enduring words

"Heaven and earth will pass away, but my words will never pass away."
(Luke 21:33)

Everyday items have a habit of running out or wearing out. The item in your fridge yesterday has mysteriously disappeared. The spare tin or packet in the cupboard you went to reach for ... oh, must have used it. The favourite T-shirt, top or dress ... has a hole in it! The car needs petrol or new tyres.

We live with this as part of everyday life, the routine 'wear and tear'. We also notice the changes in things we were familiar with in our local community or in the world at large. Some of this can be unsettling: a tradition seems to fade away, small habits of politeness become rarer, a trusted institution or person lets us down or is hit by scandal, or society simply becomes noisier, more chaotic, more divided, perhaps ruder or less kind.

Jesus spoke to his disciples on this occasion to warn them to be ready for the end of all things, of all history – the ultimate in 'running out or wearing out'! He said the world would always have signs of sin, of disorder, of wars and corruption. But he also pointed them clearly to that which endures – his words, the very words of God.

God's word still endures; we have the Bible, the teaching, example and encouragement of God through prophets and apostles and supremely from the chief Teacher, Example and Encourager – our Lord Jesus Christ.

Whatever change you see or with which perhaps you struggle, those you navigate at home or work, in health or relationships, know that the Lord Jesus lives forever and he and his word are our unchanging comfort and guide.

Safe and secure

"I give them eternal life, and they shall never perish; no one can snatch them out of my hand." (John 10:28)

I do enjoy heist films, like *Inside Man* or *Ocean's 11.* They usually involve a group of people who conspire to rob a bank, a casino, an art gallery or a billionaire's collection of something absurdly valuable kept in their über-secure fortress, mansion or space station. As the viewer, you get to see both sides. The jeopardy builds as the layers of security are outwitted and as weaknesses in the mad plans are revealed. Invariably the robbers succeed, if Hollywood has its way, although the outcome of *The Italian Job* clearly hangs in the balance!

Earthly security is something we expect for our financial resources, even if we don't own gold bars or Fabergé eggs. We even say that we 'bank' on our money, pension or assets being safe; the very wording refers to the security we expect.

Jesus spoke of himself as the Good Shepherd, the one who keeps us, cares for us, leads us and protects us. He offers us the security of God over that which is far more precious than anything in any bank account: our soul.

He is the source of life for our soul, even eternal life. Without him, we are dead in our sins, enemies of God, objects of wrath, lost – a terrible and fearful predicament. But when we come to the Shepherd over our souls, to the Saviour, he gives us eternal life. We are no longer dead to God but alive, we are no longer enemies but adopted as children, no longer facing wrath but spared and under his blessing, no longer lost but found and brought home.

In Christ, we are now completely secure. No one can snatch us out of God's hand. The Father gives the sheep to the Son, they know and obey him, and we are held by God in eternal life, protected and secure.

Jesus is our Good Shepherd. Our destiny need not hang in the balance. Our soul can be truly secure.

The Father will send the Spirit

"And I will ask the Father, and he will give you another Counsellor to be with you forever—the Spirit of truth." (John 14:16-17)

The Son of God, our risen and exalted king – Jesus the Christ – has not forgotten us. He had us in mind when he went to the cross. The 'joy set before him' was the joy of the victory he would win and the joy of our salvation, our home-coming as God's once-lost children (Hebrews 12:2).

But he wasn't finished there. Having won the battle on the cross and raised to new life from the grave, he asked the Father – our heavenly Father – to send to every Christian an incredible gift: the Holy Spirit. The Trinity, our Triune God, are generous indeed!

So today, every Christian has the Holy Spirit in them and with them. He brings us life from God the Father and God the Son, won for us by Jesus, promised to us by Jesus, and received through the Spirit.

And Jesus calls him 'the Spirit of truth' – the Holy Spirit will lead us into the truth about God, about ourselves, about the world. He does this supremely through God's word, the Bible. So let's go to the word for ourselves often and thank God for his many gifts, but know that the Spirit will speak and lead as we ask him.

God's living words

"This is that Moses who told the Israelites, 'God will send you a prophet like me from your own people.' He was in the assembly in the desert, with the angel who spoke to him on Mount Sinai, and with our fathers; and he received living words to pass on to us." (Acts 7:37-38)

These words come from Stephen's speech after his arrest. He is defending the teaching and actions of this new religious group, followers of Christ, the people of 'The Way', before the Jewish religious leaders. His speech is a rich retelling of the Old Testament storyline. He reminds them of the great prophet, teacher and leader – Moses – and how God spoke through him that there would be another prophet like him. They revered Moses and the Law of God, so Stephen and the Christians with him were clearly saying that they weren't dismissing Moses, the Old Testament law or the traditions of the Jews, but they had something new and better!

Jesus is the fulfilment of the Old Testament. He is the one to whom Moses and the Law point, the greatest of prophets in terms of revealing God, and by his resurrection he has been shown to be the Son of God. He fulfils the Law and the Prophets – all God's promises.

Notice, though, how Stephen describes God's word to Moses and the people of Israel: they 'received living words' to pass on. God's word is alive and life-giving.

To Israel in the wilderness, God's words brought hope, assurance, direction, instructions for their safety, flourishing, spiritual life and physical life. They were words of life in every sense.

God's words for us – from the Old and the New Testament, from prophets and apostles, with Christ at the centre – are for our very life. They speak into every corner of life: work, rest, family, integrity, plans, our speech and spending, our bodies and our hobbies, and our walk with God and our walk with friends. Living words for all of life.

God's words are living words in that they lead us to Jesus, to eternal life from him and with him (John 6:68). As we let the words speak regularly, as we read and reflect and pray into them, we find the living Word shapes our lives through his living words (2 Timothy 3:16-17). His words equip us for the life to which he calls us and speak into our hearts and minds. They address our desires and worries, challenging and changing us.

May we find the word alive to us today. May it deepen, strengthen and enrich our life in Christ.

Creation is longing

For all creation is waiting eagerly for that future day when God will reveal who his children really are. (Romans 8:19)

Have you ever watched something that had you literally on the edge of your seat? A sporting drama perhaps – England's cricket team trying to find those final runs in the last over (thank you, Ben Stokes), or a penalty shootout (both horrible and engrossing to watch), or a rugby team within reach of the line and unable to break through, or the tightly fought final set of Wimbledon. Maybe it's watching a child in a school performance, or a friend's baptism, or the cliffhanger ending of a film.

The tension can leave us a nervous wreck or having to look away!

This verse in Romans pictures *all creation* on the edge of its seat: the 'eager expectation' of all created things, as if the physical world is waiting and straining towards a moment in time and a revelation. It longs, in its own way, for 'that future day', a final moment, when all will be revealed.

And what is the revelation, what's the focus here? It is not a trophy, a match-winning moment, or simply a punchline to a performance. Rather it is when God brings his children to glory, the long-awaited renewal of all things, and the salvation promised for all who believe will finally be fulfilled.

Today, we are one day nearer the hope we have in Christ, the sweetest of victory celebrations to enjoy. One without any sorrow; the ultimate finale with the greatest of endings, and a party like no other. All creation longs for this, and by faith we will be there too.

Renewing your mind

Therefore, I urge you, brothers, in view of God's mercy, to offer your bodies as living sacrifices, holy and pleasing to God—this is your spiritual act of worship. Do not conform any longer to the pattern of this world, but be transformed by the renewing of your mind. Then you will be able to test and approve what God's will is—his good, pleasing and perfect will. (Romans 12:1-2)

If anyone could tell a few stories of how their mind had been changed, it was the apostle Paul. His encounter with the risen Lord Jesus - a blinding light and a voice from heaven - had stopped him in his tracks. His immediate journey plans changed but so did his whole life's direction. God transformed Paul's mind: his viewpoint on Christ and who he is, his priorities, his understanding of God's saving plan for the world and for his place as an apostle in that, his assessment of what really matters in life, and so much more.

These words from Romans are not referring to simply *changing* our mind – an act of intellectual reasoning or a new decision. We can change our mind on many mundane matters (what breakfast cereal we prefer) or with significant life decisions (where to live, a new career direction). When we come to Christ and receive his Spirit, God begins the *renewing* of our mind.

As Paul experienced, God begins the good work of reordering our whole inner being: our values are reconfigured; our motives are reshaped; our desires, hopes and fears are recalibrated, all under the new Lordship of Christ and the direction of the Spirit. In short, our minds are being renewed.

The J. B. Phillips version famously puts the calling to a new way of life of verse 2 like this: *Don't let the world around you squeeze you into its own mould, but let God re-mould your minds from within.*

We face pressure on every side to go with the flow – to act, speak and choose as the world would. We face the temptation to set ourselves back on the throne, in the driving seat, and to set aside anything of God's will that is inconvenient, never mind costly. But Christ has died for us. He has sacrificed his life for us. He has shown us mercy and opened the way to new life; a beautiful and good life in his eyes, and renewing our mind from within is key to that.

Where are you being squeezed into the wrong shape by the world, by others, by your past? Ask God to remake and renew you, to lead you into his freedom and the joy of a life shaped by him.

The past is our teacher

For everything that was written in the past was written to teach us, so that through endurance and the encouragement of the Scriptures we might have hope. (Romans 15:4)

History is our teacher, whether it is our personal history or global history. Difficult experiences we have been through or good things we have achieved can teach us, reveal our strengths and weaknesses, and remind us of God's care and faithfulness. They also deepen our resources.

Past experience can also simply show us what we enjoy or enable our flourishing, where we need to change, or give us ideas for the future. These lessons can be true of individuals, some for entire nations. Humility says we can learn from the past, especially from our mistakes.

It is no surprise that God has many reasons for giving us the Bible, but one of them is simply this: the lessons of the past give us courage and comfort for the present and hope for the future. The past is our teacher.

The apostle Paul wrote to the church in Rome and encouraged them to treasure their scriptures (which for them was what we call the Old Testament). It was 'written to teach.' We now have the fuller, clearer, more stunning story of both Old and New Testament. This is the full account of God's dealing with people, climaxing in God in person, Christ Jesus. In him, God became one like us, to live with us, to die for us, and rose again to bring new life for us.

As we reflect on God's dealings with Abraham, Isaac, Jacob, Joseph, Moses, Rahab, Samson, Ruth, Hannah, David, Daniel, Jeremiah, Peter, Thomas, the woman at the well, Zacchaeus, Paul and countless others ... we see his character towards his people. We see his kindness and power, his plan to save, his ability to restore and his grace freely offered. We hear his invitation and see his kingdom's growth through the gospel.

May God continue to teach us, and so help us endure and flourish. May he encourage us and fill us with hope – for this life and the next.

God is faithful

God, who has called you into fellowship with his Son Jesus Christ our Lord, is faithful. (1 Corinthians 1:9)

To become a Christian is to find your life on completely solid ground. This new ground is the Rock himself, the Lord Jesus, who calls us to build our lives in trust and obedience to his words.

Any building is shaped by the foundations; it takes its lines and angles from the lie of the bricks, concrete or cornerstone on which it is laid. As a Christian, our grounding on God shapes our lives, not least giving us a solid hope through God's promises in this life and for the next. Promises to rely on of his lasting presence, unimaginable power, unchanging goodness, tender mercy, unconditional love and more.

Why is this? Why can we rely on these? Because God is faithful.

The faithfulness of God means this: He is true to his word, all the time, and true to himself, all the time. God is good, all the time. He is kind, every day, in every circumstance. He will only give us that which is for our good and which will enable us to grow in faith, hope and love. He is faithful in the fight as we seek to live his way. He will faithfully, reliably grow our character to be like Christ as we continue to live and rely on him.

God's faithfulness holds the cosmos together, keeps the countless stars in the sky and sustains his people. His faithfulness delivers the promises of the Bible, for history and for us.

Whatever today brings, may we give thanks that the One who made us has called us into the family of God to have fellowship with Jesus Christ. And may our peace and confidence grow, knowing that he is completely faithful. How good he is!

Resisting temptation

No temptation has seized you except what is common to man. And God is faithful; he will not let you be tempted beyond what you can bear. But when you are tempted, he will also provide a way out so that you can stand up under it. (1 Corinthians 10:13)

I wonder how strong you are feeling today. Done your keep-fit routine? Had a good night's sleep? Eaten your porridge, three Shredded Wheat, that first cup of tea or coffee with its magic powers?

God never tells us to "Pull yourself together" if we are not feeling strong, sorted, happy or well. He never tells us that "This is on you", as if we need to simply try harder. He knows that at times we can feel fragile, weak, unwell, lacking in confidence, clueless or overwhelmed.

This is also the case in spiritual matters. We all face temptation to speak, act or respond in ways that are not honouring to God. The temptation is real; the temptation to do what pleases us, to fit in with the world, to make ourselves look better or to get our own way. As for our mistakes, we can be tempted to hide them, deny them or subtly gloss over who was responsible.

In countless small ways and in some large ways, temptation is a life-long challenge. It is of such relevance that we find it included in the Lord's Prayer: "Lead us not into temptation."

Today's verse offers clear encouragement. God doesn't say, "Try harder", he says, "I am faithful."

He always allows us scope for a good, helpful, true and godly response. He can enable us to speak, act or respond in any situation in ways that reflect his character, his kingdom. We don't have to fail, and this is not by being stronger in ourselves, but rather by leaning on our strong God. He is strong, so when he says, "Be strong" it is in HIS strength.

So whatever you had for breakfast, may you know his faithful presence, his enabling, his wisdom and strength today, to keep you from falling.

Generous diversity

There are different kinds of spiritual gifts, but the same Spirit is the source of them all. There are different kinds of service, but we serve the same Lord. God works in different ways, but it is the same God who does the work in all of us. (1 Corinthians 12:4-6)

On my desk at church is a list of 30-40 fellow church leaders, pastors, friends and colleagues who lead churches or Christian mission agencies. Most of them are serving in places across the UK. I am thankful for each of them – grateful to God for the sheer variety of gifts and strengths, for their godly character, for their ideas, stories and encouragement. They also reach and serve where I cannot. I enjoy keeping in touch, sharing ideas and encouragement, praying and planning with them, and keeping one another faithful and 'stirred up' for the kingdom.

The variety I see in this group is also seen in my local church – a great breadth of spiritual gifts, areas of ministry, of godly character, of desire and prayerfulness. I give thanks for a family of faith, for these servant-hearted people, for their generosity and love, as we seek to serve God's kingdom and make Christ known together.

This is seen in what we do together, our mission and service, but also in the way God is shaping people – the everyday acts of kindness, care, listening, encouragement in the gospel, support for one another and the sharing of both joys and sorrows. The Lord Jesus is making disciples through his disciples.

All of this, both here or elsewhere, is the work of God's Holy Spirit. These are signs of the fruit of the Spirit.

Let us give thanks today for the life of the Spirit amongst us: one Spirit, many gifts, varied work.

Who might you be able to pray for or encourage today?

Working for the Lord

So, my dear brothers and sisters, be strong and immovable. Always work enthusiastically for the Lord, for you know that nothing you do for the Lord is ever useless. (1 Corinthians 15:58 NLT)

Nothing we do for the Lord, nothing that we seek to do well -relying on him -is ever useless. 'We do not labour in vain', as another version puts it.

No experience is ever wasted in God's economy. He can, and will, use everything that we do or experience. Negatively, that means even our mistakes or worst choices can be opportunities to really grasp something new of his grace, his forgiveness or his power to restore. Those who are more aware of how unworthy of grace they are, are often more full of joyful gratitude, inspiring joy and faith in others. The apostle Paul is a fine example of this.

Positively, this means we can offer God what we do and ask him to bring good out of it. We can ask God to use our prayers to increase his kingdom, to use us to bring people to know him, to banish fear and sorrow, to build up the broken-hearted and bring home the lost. We can '*work enthusiastically*' at the work of prayer, for it is never useless.

We can also devote our work for God to him, whether that is clearly connected to the life of the church – an area of a church's groups or ministries – or our everyday activity, where God has placed us as disciples – being an employee, raising children, in our extended family, being a caring neighbour and a godly citizen.

Whether easy or hard, whether seen or unseen, when we seek to serve God, it has eternal value. It will be rewarded, so we can stand firm when opposed and trust him to use what we offer.

"*Abba*, Father"

Because you are sons, God sent the Spirit of his Son into our hearts, the Spirit who calls out, "Abba, Father." (Galatians 4:6)

We particularly remember the giving of the Holy Spirit at Pentecost. The name derives from the word for 'fiftieth' for it was 50 days after Easter that the Christians witnessed the outpouring of the Holy Spirit on all the followers of Jesus gathered in Jerusalem (Acts 2:1-41).

As Jesus had promised, God sent his Holy Spirit - power from on high (Acts 1:5-8) - and lives were changed. The disciples experienced this powerful joy in spontaneous praise and worship, in joyful and bold witnessing to Christ Jesus and to the salvation available to all who call on his name with faith. They experienced deep confidence that Jesus is the Messiah, that all God's promises pointed to him, that sin was defeated at the cross and how the grave could not hold Jesus so, similarly, it will not hold any who belong to him. All this is the work of the Spirit, and he still does this work now!

Today's verse is a reminder that the very Spirit sent by God is 'the Spirit of his Son', the Spirit of Jesus himself. Father, Son and Holy Spirit cannot be divided but are three Persons as one God.

The Father sent the Son to save us, in person, in the flesh, through his life, death and resurrection.

The Father sends the Spirit to make that salvation effective for us; we trust the Son for ourselves, so we can experience this salvation. The Spirit awakens a new love for our true heavenly Father; he gives us assurance that now we are truly sons and daughters of God. His power is not just great in measure, but also personal as he works in us; we are transformed and filled.

So the Spirit we receive as a Christian is the same Holy Spirit as Peter received, the Spirit of Christ. And he prompts our hearts, our innermost beings, to respond back to God's love with the same words of intimacy that Jesus used: "*Abba*, Father."

May we know this gift from God, the deep joy of belonging, the security and love of being sons and daughters of our Father, because of the Son and by the Spirit.

God's abundance

Be filled with the Spirit. (Ephesians 5:18)

In the Goldsmith household, we are forever running out of something: bananas, eggs, toothpaste, chocolate mousse (yes, we have particular favourites). If we run out of coffee, urgent shopping trips are made. But this is the nature of food and drink supplies, they run out! We use them, we get some more, we use those.

But we don't 'use' the Holy Spirit. He isn't a resource that we can run out of. It's like saying a small flower could use up the water of the Amazon river. God's Holy Spirit is forever bringing God's life, direction, love, comfort, joy and more into our lives and he will not 'run out'.

Today's verse reminds us that although we are already rich in Christ, fully accepted and loved through Jesus, we are called to continually turn our attention to God. We are to 'go on being filled' with the Spirit. It is not a one-off once-and-for-all experience at conversion, but an ongoing experience of God.

There is more to God and more available from God than we can possibly imagine. His goodness is abundant and far more than we even ask for. Let us keep being filled as we go back to the fountain of life, for God is a generous Giver.

Stand strong

Finally, be strong in the Lord and in his mighty power. Put on the full armour of God so that you can take your stand against the devil's schemes. (Ephesians 6:10-11)

Can you imagine being a football player but choosing not to put your boots on? Or a skier without skis? Or a violinist joining the orchestra without a bow?

It would be odd, possibly amusing, intriguing perhaps, or even dangerous (downhill skiing without skis risks life and limb; the bow-less violinist would survive the ordeal).

What would we make of a soldier entering battle without protective armour? In the war in Ukraine, the lack of winter kit for Russian soldiers and the inadequate armour on their vehicles has been an echo of their situation in WW2 and it will cost lives.

Ephesians chapter 6 is a Sunday school favourite for drawing, making and wearing the armour of God. We explore what God offers us for spiritual warfare. But it is far more than a lesson just for children. God has provided us with protective armour for spiritual life (mostly defensive too, the sword of the word of God being the vital exception). Would it be odd for soldiers to merely admire the kit and not make use of it as they head into battle?

The apostle Paul offers us the source of our life and hope in the midst of ongoing spiritual battle: ultimately, it is God's mighty power, and his battle. But we also hear the strident call not to neglect the battle kit, the armour of God.

We easily forget that we are in a battle. If we are with Christ and in Christ, we are already on the battlefield for the sake of our soul, the church and the kingdom. So let's keep rooted in faith and God's word, in prayer and the Spirit's power, in holy lives and firm faith.

He is all we need and has all we need. Let's heed the call.

God at work in you

Continue to work out your salvation with fear and trembling, for it is God who works in you to will and to act according to his good purpose. (Philippians 2:12-13)

The Christian life can be really difficult. That shouldn't surprise us, Jesus made it clear that we should expect hardship and opposition to our faith. He spoke of the world as lost, sinful, dark – one where sin and suffering still leave their mark – yet a world loved by God. Our own hearts – our inner beings – still have the evidence of our old nature, even as God is making us new and more like Jesus (Romans 8:29).

This is how the words of Scripture are such an encouragement: we are not on our own. It is not up to us to 'fix' ourselves, to improve ourselves by a 10-step programme of trying harder or religious duties, or to 'Be better' without fresh help or power to do so. That would be exhausting, probably depressing. Ultimately it wouldn't work either. No, the gospel is not 'Go and do better', but 'Look what God has done!'

Now, by faith, we have the company of Christ Jesus by the Holy Spirit. We have a role in our spiritual growth – 'work out **your** salvation' – to grow in our faith, hope, understanding and knowledge by leaning on God. But we are not alone: 'for it is **God** who works **in you**.'

Each day, each step of our spiritual life, we can rely on God to be at work in us and for us, 'according to his good purpose'. Especially when it seems tough, when prayer is hard work, when we are hurting, or facing opposition or prone to apathy; let's look to the Lord. Let us recognise again God's loving presence and his activity for our good.

We are his work in progress, his beloved handiwork. May we rest on him today, take note of how he is at work in us, and ask him to show us his good purposes.

Citizens of heaven

But our citizenship is in heaven. And we eagerly await a Saviour from there, the Lord Jesus Christ. (Philippians 3:20)

Have you ever felt you don't belong somewhere? Maybe in a job, or a group, or at a party, or in a country? It can be discouraging, upsetting or lonely. I've spent time in jobs that I didn't enjoy, been to parties where I haven't known anyone, and lived overseas where I felt a bit lost!

It is a natural and good human desire to want to belong, to feel at home and to seek security. We are drawn to a sense of welcome, to pursue joy and to foster our own peace of mind wherever we find ourselves. In all these ways, what a blessing good friends, loving family and a vibrant, healthy church can be!

Today's verse reminds us that in a real sense every Christian is a stranger in a foreign land (1 Peter 1:1). We don't fully belong in this world; we already have the rights and responsibilities of another world. We belong in God's kingdom, we're citizens under his divine rule, enjoying his protection and care, and paying attention to his words and ways. One day we expect to be there with him, in his kingdom of a renewed heaven and earth.

Sometimes this will mean we feel out of sorts with the ways of this world, but that's ok – we know who we belong to. Our Father is in heaven, and his kingdom is real, growing and good. His Spirit is with us now.

So while we wait and watch for the kingdom to come, we can seek to live faithfully and with hope. We can rest in his security and love, eagerly awaiting the day that our Saviour comes from there to here! When heaven arrives on earth, we will truly belong, but we can enjoy being its citizens already.

God's rule, our responsibility

To this end I labour, struggling with all his energy, which so powerfully works in me. (Colossians 1:29)

There are threads that runs through the whole Bible, through the life of every major character and episode in both Old and New Testaments. One such thread is that God is unceasingly at work and in control but our human efforts, activities and lives also make a difference. Two strands run side by side – God's rule and our responsibility. The two 'sides' are unfathomably different in their relative power and wisdom, yet God says that what we do matters.

We are not the Ruler of history, not even over our own life. God is. Divine sovereignty runs through the Bible, over the lives of Abraham, Jacob, Joseph, Moses, Rahab, Deborah, Hannah, Elijah and David. Even the life of Jesus reflects God's divine plan and Christ's human role. We live under God's rule but can also experience his mighty power, 'all his energy', powerfully at work in us.

We can make an eternal difference, because God can use us. He uses our words and prayers, our acts of kindness and our professional skills, our finances and our wisdom, our homes and our hands to bring about his kingdom purposes. Divine sovereignty means God is ruling but also working in us.

This gives our lives great dignity, for they are in God's hands and full of potential in his plans. The apostle Paul grasped this; he trusted God was at work, so he 'laboured', he 'struggled', exerting his physical, mental and emotional resources to serve God. Our lives have great value but we are also called to make a difference, to serve with what God has given us.

May we know the assurance of God with us and for us, trusting that his power is at work through our efforts, but also with true confidence that even our small and unseen works make a difference in his purposes. So we press on!

Wardrobe change

Therefore, as God's chosen people, holy and dearly loved, clothe yourselves with compassion, kindness, humility, gentleness and patience. Bear with each other and forgive whatever grievances you may have against one another. Forgive as the Lord forgave you. And over all these virtues put on love, which binds them all together in perfect unity. (Colossians 3:12-14)

One of the great joys in the church is when we celebrate someone's baptism. For our church, we have a baptistry, a pool set into the floor that we uncover and fill with water for a baptismal service. Hopefully warm water; if the heating system fails, the act of baptism is all conducted at a higher speed.

Baptisms are powerful acts. They include a verbal testimony by the person as to how Christ has saved them and called them, perhaps some aspects of how he changed them. It might include how God broke into, or spoke into, their life in new or surprising ways and has then led them on a new path following Jesus. Every story is different. The encouragement to the church and the joy in the goodness of God shared by the believer and those who are gathered is a precious and faith-strengthening experience.

There is also an important practical aspect of baptism: bringing a spare set of clothes. We don't sprinkle people, we immerse them. They will be properly wet! They never fail to come up out of the water soaked and smiling, they are then wrapped in a towel and hugs as we sing (loudly) in praise to the God who saves, calls and changes lives. Eventually they (we) go and get changed.

The wardrobe change is also a reminder of what God is doing in every Christian. He is at work to remake and remodel our character. We are saved by grace, saved from sin and also saved for a new life. That new life is to become more and more like Jesus. We are to seek after these new clothes, deliberately put them on in our dealings with one another, to 'bear with' and 'forgive' too.

The top layer, the overcoat of Christian character, is love. It tops them all and covers a multitude of wardrobe malfunctions. God is at work to dress us in some beautiful clothes.

Let us look to Christ, lean on him, rejoice in him, and see how he will transform us from the inside out.

Godly ambition

Make it your ambition to lead a quiet life, to mind your own business and to work with your hands, just as we told you, so that your daily life may win the respect of outsiders and so that you will not be dependent on anybody. (1 Thessalonians 4:11-12)

Our world is a noisy, busy place at times. We are surrounded by physical noise and the busyness of traffic, people, news and social media, by the expectations and pressures of others, and by the varied demands of the day.

Sometimes it can feel like we are struggling to keep up, or that it's just a bit too busy.

What if God's assessment is a great "Well done" for simply a life well lived, 'a quiet life' of minding your own business and doing good work? That sounds like a very refreshing alternative to the high-achievement drama of the life modelled in advertising, films, celebrity magazines, self-help books and social media.

The world of Instagram, Facebook and the rest has many positives and immense potential for good, including in evangelism, discipleship and fellowship. But the online world can also become a major joy killer and a distraction from God's best. It can make us compare our life with the great fun others are having (Fear Of Missing Out), even if we know that online life isn't always a true reflection of reality.

In God's grace, he can equip us for our work and he honours us as we do our best even if we don't get noticed or it seems mundane. He sees and values it.

In God's purposes, sometimes we have times of being at the centre of attention, having a public profile or a particular status in work or the community, and we can lean on him there too.

But don't underestimate the value of a quiet life in God's eyes, or its power in his hands. We are saved by faith alone, but a new life relying on him has potential to lead others towards that saving faith by its quiet lack of fanfare, by its steady approach to doing good work where God places us, or by its unobtrusive concern for others without meddling or fuss.

This won't gain hundreds of 'likes' or make the front page of news, but God delights in ambitions like these. That is where peace, joy and affirmation lie: in pleasing God and not the world.

Always joyful

Be joyful always; pray continually; give thanks in all circumstances, for this is God's will for you in Christ Jesus. (1 Thessalonians 5:16-18)

A distinctive feature of Christian faith, a unique and attractive quality, is joy. Not merely happiness when life is good, not a superficial frivolity that pretends life is all going well, but a heart that is touched by the goodness of God even in times of hardship or suffering. Perhaps especially during such times. Joy emerges, it rises up within us, most strikingly in those times when we might least expect it.

Does Paul's instruction sound completely unrealistic?

Joy cannot be manufactured even if it can be displayed with pretence. We might put on a good show to those around us, but God knows our hearts. Real and true joy springs out of the Christian in times of delight in God, over his good work, in the enjoyment of good things in this life (love, sunsets, food, people, intimacy, music, sport, etc.), and in gathered worship as we praise and thank him.

The surprise is that joy also rises to the surface in the 'worst of times too': not the joy of dancing and singing perhaps, but the settled heart which trusts that God is still good, that he holds and loves us in his steadfast loving care, and that our soul is safe even when our tears fall and plans fail.

Jesus spoke in the Sermon on the Mount of rejoicing when we suffer for the sake of his name, from siding with him (Matthew 5:11-12). There is joy in knowing we are in the company of Jesus facing ridicule or persecution, and counted worthy to be seen as his.

The apostle James tells us to consider it 'pure joy' when we face trials, for they deepen our faith and train us in perseverance (James 1:2). God brings us joy as we experience being carried and protected through hard times.

It was for the joy before Jesus that he endured the cross, scorning its shame (Hebrews 12:2). Joy sustained him, the joy of our salvation and bringing us to the Father. Our future joy can be fuel on our journey, reminding us of God's promises of our future hope.

All of this is impossible without faith. It seems absurd and unrealistic. Yet with God nothing is impossible. Joy is a gift, a fruit of the Spirit, and he can grow this fruit in all circumstances. He delights to bring us new joy, so let us continue – as Paul says – to pray and give thanks in Jesus, and notice the joy from him.

The morning star

And we have the word of the prophets made more certain, and you will do well to pay attention to it, as to a light shining in a dark place, until the day dawns and the morning star rises in your hearts.

(2 Peter 1:19)

God sent his Son into the world to bring light into darkness, to overcome the darkness, and to rescue people from a kingdom of darkness into the kingdom of light (Colossians. 1:13; John 3:19). The world is a dark place but the light of Jesus is greater.

But where does that light shine? And how do we experience his light?

The apostle Peter writes that God has spoken. He has spoken through the word of God, 'the word of the prophets' (the Old Testament) and now in his own time through the apostles (the New Testament). God has spoken and he tells us 'you will do well to pay attention to it' – read it, heed it, obey it, trust it.

This 'paying attention' lets the light of God shine into our own lives and through our lives into the world. God's word is like a light revealing his own goodness, beauty and wisdom but also showing us the way to live, as a light and lamp for our own path (Psalm 119:105).

Our own personal experience is of Christ himself; 'the morning star', a stunning image of the Messiah, Jesus. He rises in our hearts as we receive God's word which points to Christ the living word.

May God's light rise up within us, that inner transformation of our hearts. May this rising star banish the darkness of fear, guilt and sin and fill us with his bright hope, peace, love and light. May we pay attention to his word and through this, encounter Christ afresh.

I am coming soon

I am coming soon. Hold on to what you have, so that no one will take your crown. (Revelation 3:11)

The repeated message of the Bible is that history is running on God's timescale, that empires do not last. All earthly powers and institutions are temporary and will be held to account, as will we all individually. This can be a great comfort in the midst of news cycles of war, violence, corruption and persecution across the world. It gives us a fresh perspective on events that can be distressing, but we can know that God has seen them too.

The Book of Revelation was written to reassure and encourage us. It is not written to confuse us or as a strange set of puzzles, despite how it has been ignored or portrayed at times. The great reassurance of today's verse is from the Lord Jesus Christ, speaking to his church who were facing imperial persecution from Rome, with pressures and temptations to 'go with the flow' in their world. We face less persecution but varied pressures and temptations to blend in or conform.

Then and now, Jesus says, "I am coming soon." History has a climax, an end, and he sees and knows the times we live through. We need not fear or be shaken, for Christ rules. And we will stand before him when he comes.

'Hold on to what you have, so that no one will take your crown.' As Jesus spoke to his church then, he encourages us today to recognise that he is coming and calls us to faithfulness, to loyalty to God and his word, and to guard our hearts. We are to do so, despite pressure to give in, to please ourselves or to wander from his ways.

He is coming soon. He is able to keep us from falling and to keep us on the way. May we ask for his help today, take comfort that he is with us, and be assured that he will return.

I stand at the door and knock

Here I am! I stand at the door and knock. If anyone hears my voice and opens the door, I will come in and eat with him, and he with me.

(Revelation 3:20)

The last Book of the Bible, Revelation, has some of the most vivid images of God's 'appearance', of heaven, and of his activity in the world now and at the end. It can be confusing or even intimidating but it need not be. Revelation is also filled with real assurance, with clear words and images meant to encourage us, which of course is why the apostle John was given his vision and why he recorded the words in the first place. The visions were not given to confuse the church but as a means of encouragement, hope and fresh strength from God so we might persevere in faith despite suffering, opposition and evil in this world.

One such striking image is plain to understand: Jesus awaits our response as if he stands at the door of our house, our home.

He wants us to invite him into our lives, to welcome his presence, with the intimacy and deep friendship that sharing a meal suggests. He is not simply dropping off a parcel of 'spiritual feelings' or advice; he wants us to invite him to make his home with us, to 'abide' in him (John 15:4).

So today, may we hear his voice and recognise the desire of Jesus, Lord of all, to make his home in our lives. But each of us is first called to hear, to repent (v. 19), to believe and then let the Lord in. When we do, he will delight to be with us always.

15

GOD WHO SPEAKS

Then Jesus said, "He who has ears to hear, let him hear."
"Others, like seed sown on good soil, hear the word, accept it, and produce a crop—thirty, sixty or even a hundred times what was sown."
(Mark 4:9, 20)

One of the most memorable and compelling of Jesus' parables is the parable of the sower – or should that be 'of the soil', or 'of the seed'? For a very simple story, it is multi-layered and full of rich insights, as we would expect from the greatest Teacher of all.

The heart of the parable is this: God's word has life-transforming power. When received, growth is irresistible. Lives reflect this powerful change and growth, so does the kingdom of God. Where this word is received – the living Word of the Lord Jesus who brings the kingdom of God and the written or announced word of the gospel – there is a rich harvest.

In the Sermon on the Mount, Jesus spoke of his word being received and put into practice as being like someone who builds their life upon rock, on solid ground, and who can then know spiritual security that endures the storms of life.

The word needs to be told, to be shared and to be proclaimed. It is also given to be believed, trusted and obeyed. God's word is then the instrument for his good purposes, as the Holy Spirit applies it and brings it to fulfilment.

The following 12 reflections only begin to touch on the goodness, power and scope of God's word in action and how it reflects God's will for us. Some of them help us reflect on what his word is rather than what it does, and therefore how we should respond to it and honour the One who speaks.

May we seek after 'ears to hear' and for our lives to be good soil that lets the word take root and bear fruit. May we build our lives upon this very good foundation.

Genesis 1:3	Words of power
Numbers 23:21	Words of blessing
Deuteronomy 30:19-20	Words of life
1 Kings 22:14	Only these words
Psalm 119:105	Words for our path
Jeremiah 23:28-29	Words with impact
John 15:9-10	Words to obey
Ephesians 4:11-13	Words for the church
1 Thessalonians 2:13	Not our words
2 Timothy 4:2-4	The word for all seasons
Hebrews 4:12	Living and active word
Revelation 22:7	Final word

Words of power

And God said, "Let there be light," and there was light. (Genesis 1:3)

At some point, every parent dreams of such power: you ask a child to do something and they do it. This is the timeless challenge whether they are 2 years old or teenagers. (Perhaps when they are older too…) Typically, our words don't have much power.

Sometimes human words carry real authority and we recognise that power. For example, we consent to giving elected officials, police officers and magistrates a degree of civic power. Within the armed services, rank implies a degree of real authority over others. When we sign a consent form prior to surgery, our signature indicates we have the power to decide and also give medical staff the authority to go ahead.

The opening chapter of the Bible begins with God. He is the focus of all scripture; it is his story and his sovereign plan, and the first and key action of God is to speak. His words are such that they are completely effective in power. He only needs to speak and the words become or bring about reality: *"Let there be light," and there was light.* Awesome power, revealed through his words.

As we open up our Bibles and recognise afresh that God himself has inspired all these words, that he stands behind the written text with his own completely good purposes through them, let us recognise his power in his word. He still speaks; his words still have transforming power. If we embrace them, we can expect to see and know his good work in our lives. By his Spirit we can experience growing delight in realising that he speaks to us and his promises are for us, this same Spirit teaching us to listen and obey.

God's words have lost none of their power. May we have ears to hear and hearts open to whatever he would say to us in each day.

Words of blessing

"The LORD their God is with them; the shout of the King is among them." (Numbers 23:21)

One of the most unlikely sources of words, of a speaking voice, in the whole Bible is found in this episode (Numbers 22:1-24:19). The false prophet Balaam, driven by greed and status rather than truth and service, has plenty to say – for a price. In the service of a foreign king, he heads off on his mission having been instructed to speak words of curses over God's precious people. However, his journey is brought to a sudden halt when his donkey will go no further. The donkey has seen an angel of the Lord with a drawn sword blocking the way and leaves the path. Ironically, the prophet, the seer, cannot see as well as his beast of burden. At each turn that the donkey takes, receiving repeated beatings from angry Balaam, the angel blocks the way again. Eventually the poor donkey lies down.

Frustrated by this still-unseen problem and the delay, Balaam is then confronted by a voice. His donkey speaks! The animal complains of the abuse it is receiving, Balaam threatens to take a sword to it, still not realising that an angel bears a sword towards him. In our day, false prophets should beware God's judgement and be mindful that the Lord stands with his people.

This episode ends with what is arguably the even more unlikely voice speaking truth: Balaam's. This conniving, self-serving man who couldn't recognise the purposes of God until his own donkey brought him up short had been employed to curse God's people. But God had other plans. Balaam could only say what the Lord commanded.

Balaam could only bless God's people, for these are the words God gives him. God's word can only be for our good. Even when it is words of warning. His words of judgement are good, for God's justice is perfect. Balaam's words are remarkable for whose mouth they come from but he recognised their source: the Lord God Almighty.

God speaks over his people, the 'shout of the King' is amongst us, so we are defended from outside attack and threats. God will still speak amongst his people to challenge our sins and wrong paths, but in loving kindness, for he disciplines those he loves as a Father over his children. But to those who curse or come against his own, he stands resolutely with us.

It can only ever be for our good to listen to God's word. The Lord is intent on blessing his people, despite all opposition.

Words of life

"Now choose life, so that you and your children may live and that you may love the LORD your God, listen to his voice, and hold fast to him. For the LORD is your life." (Deuteronomy 30:19-20)

The Book of Deuteronomy is a recap of Israel's recent history and in particular, God's dealings with them. It calls them to truly *learn* from what they have seen, endured, received and heard.

Moses has been at the heart of these momentous events, beginning with the contest with Pharaoh and Egypt's gods whom Yahweh, the living God of Israel, said he would destroy. Moses's adventure began by hearing God's voice from a burning bush – the call of God to obey, to serve and to lead as God's instrument of rescue for his suffering people. Moses then stood before Pharaoh recounting the warnings from Yahweh, but the Egyptians failed to listen. Finally, all those who heeded the warnings on the Passover night and were shielded from God's wrath were delivered from death and from the grip of slavery, escaping from Egypt in the great exodus. Listen, and live.

Led into the wilderness, Israel were fed and protected by the Lord, shown the way by his fiery presence, and instructed as God spoke his Law – his divine will for them – to Moses. God's words from that mountain top were given to shape their relationship with the Lord and with one another, to govern their civic, moral and religious lives, and to cover a host of topics ranging from handling debt to national security to health and safety. God's words were clear, practical, life-saving and life-shaping.

As Moses reaches the end of his travels and his life, within sight of the long-awaited Promised Land, having navigated the many tough challenges of leading God's people through a wilderness and numerous episodes of temptation, sin, fear, doubt and warfare, what does Moses call them to do?

'Choose life, ... listen to his voice, and hold fast to him.'

Life from God, life with God, is essentially linked to heeding what he says. Moses has seen and heard enough to know how central this is. The life of God's people thrives when God's words are listened to and truly received, embraced and obeyed as being good. Moses's successor received the same primary instructions to know a 'successful' life (Joshua 1:7-8).

These are words of life. God has spoken. May we have choose well and listen to his voice.

Only these words

But Micaiah said, "As surely as the LORD lives, I can tell him only what the LORD tells me." (1 Kings 22:14)

In a sporting contest, the players and officials are meant to submit to the rule of the referee or umpire. They often argue with decisions, some famously so (John McEnroe), but there is at least an expectation that the umpire's word is final and decisive. Similarly, in a court of law, the judge or magistrate has the final say; after all the witnesses, evidence, arguments and deliberations have concluded, they pronounce the outcome, the verdict.

Referees, umpires and judges have been given authority, so when they speak we are accustomed to listen and expected to comply. Their words carry weight. If someone else popped up during a match or at the end of a trial and spoke, they would reasonably be ignored and possibly locked up!

The prophet Micaiah understood this clearly. It wasn't his place to offer his *own* words to the audience, whether to the king before him or a congregation. He wasn't the source of spiritual wisdom and life. His words didn't carry any ultimate weight at all. They could potentially be empty, false, irrelevant or misguided words. Or they might be genuinely fascinating, immensely entertaining, come across with rich insights and deep personal connection; they could be a delight for the listeners to hear.

But that wasn't the prophet's concern – he wanted only to speak what God had told him. Those words matter, they have weight, only they bring life and steer away from death, only his words are wholly good, true, trustworthy and sufficient to lead us to salvation from God.

God still speaks. He has given us his word. In some countries, people risk their lives to receive or read a Bible, such is its value. May we faithfully preach, teach and submit to his words alone. May we hunger for his word and give his voice priority – recognise his authority – to speak to us.

Words for our path

Your word is a lamp to my feet and a light for my path.
(Psalm 119:105)

Have you ever been somewhere so dark that you can barely see your hand in front of your face? Or perhaps so dark that you can't see anything?

If there's a powercut in the evening, you might have that momentary scramble for a phone, a torch or even candles. It can be fun for a short time, unless you're in the middle of cooking a meal!

The darkest place I can remember was in a Welsh cave on a school field trip. Deep underground we were told to switch off our headtorches. It instantly became utterly, completely dark. Pitch black. We could *feel* the walls and floor, *hear* the underground streams and people around us, *sense* the enormity of rock above us, but could not *see* a thing. Light is good!

As we navigate life, God's word is given to us for the way ahead. '*Your word*', says the psalmist, is our guide. It is a lamp and a light for the path of life.

Sometimes we are just given enough for the day, for the immediate situation, for the demands or hopes of the moment; 'a lamp to my feet' only shows the next step, not the whole journey. Our heavenly Father knows what we need, we can ask for our daily bread but not meals for a year. He typically speaks into the particular shape of our current situation. We might want more, sometimes we are granted insight into future direction or long-term horizons, but that's unusual.

However, even if the light of his word only illuminates a short span, we know that the light will be there for the whole way: *a light for my path*. God's word is sufficient, powerful and good in each day, in each season of life, in any circumstance, and to continue to lead us in our life with Christ, even into eternal life. Its particular words and its enduring promises are both to bring God's good light onto our way, dispelling darkness of doubt, fear, and ignorance of God, and helping us walk confidently with him.

Psalm 119, the longest of Psalms, is an epic celebration of God's word. May we receive its light and seek after the path of life it illuminates. May we hear its comfort in our hurts. May we pay attention to keep on the straight path. May we trust the one who knows the way ahead.

Words with impact

Let the prophet who has a dream tell his dream, but let the one who has my word speak it faithfully. For what has straw to do with grain?" declares the LORD. "Is not my word like fire," declares the LORD, "and like a hammer that breaks a rock in pieces?" (Jeremiah 23:28-29)

I once worked in an engineering role that brought me up close to high-speed cutting machinery and the fierce presence of forging furnaces. In a later job, I was so careful in a laboratory environment where extremely hazardous materials were handled, including chemicals that would burn through mere humans or were very toxic. In another career, the risk was from biohazards. Another role had me programming huge industrial robots – great fun but the speed and power in their movements were unnerving. I lived to tell the tale and can recall many rewarding experiences but learned to be careful.

Standing in a pulpit or opening a Bible seems far less dangerous. And yet … God's word has tremendous power. Wielded faithfully, it is like a fire – purifying and refining us as God exposes sin, error, rebellion, apathy and more. That needs great care, but it's God's good work as part of his redeeming, loving and glorious purposes for us.

God's word can also act like a great hammer, doing the work of demolishing and destroying. It breaks down our idols, our wrong thinking and our false sources of security or identity. It opposes evil and injustice. It does so for our good, as God speaks and reveals what is genuine, true, righteous and necessary for our salvation. He wants our life built on his good foundation and he will not hesitate to make rubble of poor foundations. He is building a good kingdom.

The command of Jeremiah is plain: *speak it faithfully*. This fire and hammer are powerful; do not let the fire be extinguished for lack of nerve or faithfulness in preaching or lack of trust in God for each of us as we read and reflect on it. Do not silence the word where a hammer blow is needed. This is never a call to human anger or an excuse for carelessly bruising others, nor does God discipline us except as an act of love. It is to recognise that God's word is given to deeply impact our lives, to break in where our hearts and heads need powerful spiritual change.

Jeremiah himself was impacted. He spoke of God's word being 'in my heart like a fire, a fire shut up in my bones' (Jeremiah 20:9). He cannot keep it in, it demands to be heard, it shapes lives and nations. May we approach his word open to its impact and with care to let it speak.

Words to obey

"As the Father has loved me, so have I loved you. Now remain in my love. If you obey my commands, you will remain in my love, just as I have obeyed my Father's commands and remain in his love."

(John 15:9-10)

'My commands' and 'My Father's commands': one and the same voice, authority, ways and kingdom. These are the Father and Son's commands.

To obey the words of God is to remain in God's love. To obey the words of God is to show love for God: love is not primarily a feeling but an action and attitude. To love God is not to feel emotionally warm towards him, it is to be devoted, to honour him, to give our loyalty to him and his desires, and to give him due respect and honour in how we live, act and speak. To love God is to worship him – to both declare and reflect his worth.

This is what the Lord Jesus did. He honoured God fully. His life was full of God's word in that it shaped him. We see that most obviously in his teaching. He didn't make up a new message. He applied the existing message, making rich use of the scriptures and underlining that it was all fulfilled in him (Matthew 5:17) and that this word would purify and transform us (John 17:17).

As God speaks into our lives from his word, the promises and ways of God are revealed to us from the Father and the Son by the Spirit. The Spirit helps us understand,; he warms our hearts so we can embrace God's words rather than ignore or criticise them. He grows our faith, hope and love. But his preferred instrument to begin this is to take God's word and let it speak to us, for God speaks today.

How has God's word encouraged you recently? How has it challenged you recently? God loves us too much not to speak into our lives.

The word for the church

It was he who gave some to be apostles, some to be prophets, some to be evangelists, and some to be pastors and teachers, to prepare God's people for works of service, so that the body of Christ may be built up until we all reach unity in the faith and in the knowledge of the Son of God and become mature, attaining to the whole measure of the fullness of Christ. (Ephesians 4:11-13)

The people who Christ raises up to serve the church are gifts to the church.

What is their key resource, their method? It is not technology. It is not a 10-step motivational programme. It is not a religious ritual. It is not a charismatic experience or even spiritual gifts, good though they are. It is not even themselves; they are not the means of bringing God's life to the church. So, what is?

Look at their roles and look at the outcomes. The resource is the word of God with the Spirit's enabling. They are all roles that speak, and the words they offer are not their own but God's. Apostles, prophets, evangelists, pastors, teachers; God's Son sends people, he calls people, to take God's word and speak – to raise up the church in new ways and in new locations (apostles), to speak into God's church and into the world with challenge, encouragement and divine insight (prophets), to proclaim the good news of new life in Christ (evangelists), and to care for, disciple and teach the church (pastors and teachers).

How does God equip his people for works of service? Through his word. How does God build up the body of Christ? Through his word. How does the church enjoy unity, maturity and security? When it is rooted in God's word.

The life, well-being, flourishing and impact of the church rest finally on what God will do. This takes the burden off us. He will build his church, not us. But these things are promised only as the church is faithful to his word, centred on it rather than sidelining it, and active in sharing and teaching it. These are words of life, without which the church loses its way, mission loses its impact and its people lose heart.

Which of these people have been a blessing to you? Perhaps pause to pray for them or pass on an encouragement to them.

Not our words

And we also thank God continually because, when you received the word of God, which you heard from us, you accepted it not as the word of men, but as it actually is, the word of God, which is at work in you who believe. (1 Thessalonians 2:13)

One of the most theologically rich and fascinating religious events perhaps any of us will see in our lifetime, was the coronation service for King Charles III and Queen Camilla. It was full of scripture, including Bible readings, prayers, oaths, exhortations and hymns. The entire event was a Christian service, deeply shaped by God's word and filled with its promises and commands.

As the king was handed a copy of the Coronation Bible, the Archbishop of Canterbury said, "We present you with this book, the most valuable thing that this world affords. Here is wisdom. This is the royal law. These are the lively oracles of God."

The Bible is not just a book. It is certainly not just any book, nor merely the words of human beings. As the apostle Paul told the Thessalonians, it actually is the word of God. It has life-transforming power as the Spirit applies it to our hearts and minds. When we approach what God is saying with humble faith – with 'ears to hear', as Jesus said – we experience its power and truth, how it brings light and life and spiritual food from God.

As Paul said, it starts with receiving the word of God *as* the word of God, not as an opinion piece or religious advice. We are tempted to weigh up this Word against the desires and distractions of our hearts, or the prevailing 'wisdom' of the world, or what seems more comfortable, convenient or popular. This is to forget Who is speaking and forget what he offers – true life, life in all its fullness, a renewed heart, peace from above, the friendship of God, rescue from sin, eternal security and lasting joy.

Perhaps we all need to hear the words which were addressed to an earthly king, but hear them from our heavenly King. Then we will be careful not to give our greatest attention to our own words or those of this world, but look into this most valuable thing that this world affords. Here in God's word may we seek and find wisdom, the way to live, and God's lively life-giving words to us.

The word for all seasons

Preach the Word; be prepared in season and out of season; correct, rebuke and encourage—with great patience and careful instruction. For the time will come when men will not put up with sound doctrine. Instead, to suit their own desires, they will gather around them a great number of teachers to say what their itching ears want to hear. They will turn their ears away from the truth and turn aside to myths.
(2 Timothy 4:2-4)

The Norwegians have a saying which roughly translates as 'There's no bad weather, only bad clothes!' I have a good friend whose father loved to buy clothing for the 'great outdoors' and had a jacket for every conceivable permutation of activity, temperature, level of rainfall, choice of layers and probably altitude. He was thoroughly equipped for any and every season!

The word of God comes to us from the God who made us and who is for his people in every situation. The sweep of scripture shows how he speaks his word into the lives of those facing danger or distress and those seeking him in prayer. His word is also for those enjoying his presence or running from him, delighting in obedience or those who barely know God, and indeed, anyone. He speaks to the lost, the least, the leaders, the followers, to kings and to the poor and to all in between. It is a word for all seasons and for all people.

Paul's command to his apprentice Timothy rings out to preachers in every generation: *preach the Word*, and be prepared to do this regardless of the season. For there will be seasons where it is gladly received, its truth embraced, its ways honoured and its place in the church held as vital. But there will be other seasons where it is sidelined, relegated to a source of advice, its incisive challenges blunted, or flatly disobeyed with other voices allowed to drown it out. But it remains the Word, the truth.

We would do well to observe the seasons we live in and recognise that these words are for our great good. They are good even when they disrupt our thinking or challenge us. The Word leads us to Christ; it must be preached.

The living and active word

For the word of God is living and active. Sharper than any double-edged sword, it penetrates even to dividing soul and spirit, joints and marrow; it judges the thoughts and attitudes of the heart.

(Hebrews 4:12)

When you pass through customs at an airport, there is that section of a wide corridor with two wide passageways: 'Nothing to Declare', and 'Something to Declare'. I always approach it with trepidation, wondering if I have accidentally got something on me that must be declared! Did I buy a souvenir that is illegal? Is chocolate something to declare? (If you have ever travelled into or out of Israel, you may be surprised by what is confiscated.)

What if you were carrying a sword, or **a Bible**?

Today's verse has something to declare: the Word of God, the Bible, is 'living and active'. It has power in God's hands. By the Spirit using it, speaking through it, applying it to our lives, shaping our words and actions, it proves to be a phenomenal weapon. We might also liken it to a surgical instrument.

This cutting-edge word can speak into us in ways nothing else can, into our very being: our will, our decision-making, our desires, our failings, our hopes and fears, our ambitions and doubts. That is real POWER.

'It judges the thoughts and attitudes of the heart.' Let it speak, whether from a pulpit or a phone app. Give God space and time to speak, and it is going to change our lives, to speak deeply into our needs and direction. It points to God, brings us hope, builds up and breaks down. It holds the very promises of God.

This book has demolished empires, overturned corrupt regimes, dismantled powers and authorities. This Word has transformed society, rescued the lost, sustained persecuted believers, given sight to the blind, empowered the oppressed, comforted the broken, shaped the church, and pointed to Jesus.

Something to declare? I should say so. Let this book loose - it cannot be chained - that God might lead, equip and transform his people and declare his words to the world.

Final word

"Behold, I am coming soon! Blessed is he who keeps the words of the prophecy in this book." (Revelation 22:7)

The Bible begins the testimony about God and his purposes in Genesis chapter 1, and there we read that God speaks. His words have power and bring such a good creation into being.

What might we expect the final chapter of the Bible to include? Earnest commands about living godly lives, or reminders of the salvation found in Christ Jesus? How much simpler to say, 'Read this book.' In that way, all the commands, all the promises, all the wonderful truths of the gospel and indeed, the entire testimony of scripture are covered. The verse applies most clearly to John's vision, the Book of Revelation, but surely the teaching of the Bible itself and the example of Jesus is that all scripture is for our good (2 Timothy 3:16-17).

However, we aren't simply called to *read* the Book, but to *keep* it – to keep God's words. It is to be our way of life, the light for our path. The loving entreaty of God towards us is to find life with him, the life from his Son and by the Spirit, and his words lead us to that life. Only his words lead that way, in a world of many other ways, and with our capacity for distracted or indifferent hearts.

In the final chapter of the Bible, we are given clear warnings, stark ones even, not to take any words away or add any more words to what God has said through John. We are not to distort his message of remaining faithful to Jesus, preaching truth, guarding the church from sin and immorality, persevering in prayer, standing firm under pressure, and more. The letters to the seven churches lay out particular encouragements and warnings from the Lord who holds the church in his hands.

This same Lord speaks to us today, to bless us. His words are given to bless us too. They are not to be trifled with or edited to suit our desires. They lead us deeper into a relationship with him, as we read, receive and keep these words.

May you know his favour, joy and love as you hear and follow.

16

"I BELIEVE": THE APOSTLES' CREED

The final eighteen reflections of this collection focus on the Apostles' Creed. It is an ancient statement of the Christian faith, an overview of what Christians believe. It is not exhaustive, it does not list or include everything, and it is not meant to do that. It has, however, endured for its power, simplicity, clarity and breadth as a statement of our faith. It has served to bind the church together, as we affirm our faith when we say it, pray it, proclaim it and trust it.

The Apostles' Creed

I believe in God, the Father almighty,
creator of heaven and earth.
I believe in Jesus Christ, his only Son, our Lord,
who was conceived by the Holy Spirit,
born of the Virgin Mary,
suffered under Pontius Pilate,
was crucified, died, and was buried;
he descended to the dead.
On the third day he rose again;
he ascended into heaven,
he is seated at the right hand of the Father,
and he will come to judge the living and the dead.
I believe in the Holy Spirit,
the holy catholic Church,
the communion of saints,
the forgiveness of sins,
the resurrection of the body,
and the life everlasting.
Amen.

As you reflect on these truths, may these words encourage and strengthen you, and draw you closer to God who is Father, Son and Holy Spirit, and closer to his people.

It begins *"I believe ..."* That is a statement of faith.

We all believe things: we agree or assent to facts. Faith also puts *confidence* in what we believe – in the chair we sit on, the service we pay for, the car we drive. There is a sense in which Christian faith is a call to *wholehearted trust*, not vague or apathetic agreement but something upon which we can build a life.

Christian faith is also personal in that it is *relational:* it brings us (i.e. together, as a people not just you or me as individuals) into a relationship with God. The creed reminds us who he is.

Furthermore, faith is *transforming*: these truths make a difference, they should shape our lives. They should mould our character and priorities, grant us hope and God's peace, help us to do good work and serve others, prompt us to justice and to care for God's world, and not to fear death. But most of all, these words bring us back to God and his gospel, the good news. They remind us to whom we can belong, who made us and saved us, and the living hope we have in Christ.

1 Peter 1:3	I believe in God, the Father almighty
Genesis 1:1	Creator of heaven and earth
John 3:16-18	I believe in Jesus Christ, his only Son, our Lord
Matthew 1:18-20	Conceived by the Holy Spirit
Luke 1:26-35	Born of the Virgin Mary
Isaiah 53:3-5, John 19:16	He suffered under Pontius Pilate
1 Corinthians 1:22-24	Crucified, died, and was buried
Revelation 1:17-18	He descended to the dead
Romans 1:4	On the third day he rose again
Philippians 2:9	He ascended into heaven
Romans 8:34	Seated at the right hand of the Father
Acts 10:42	He will come to judge the living and the dead
John 6:63	I believe in the Holy Spirit
1 Peter 2:9-10	The holy catholic Church
Hebrews 10:24-25	The communion of saints
1 Peter 3:18	The forgiveness of sins
Acts 2:26-28	The resurrection of the body
John 6:47	Life everlasting

I believe in God, the Father Almighty

Praise be to the God and Father of our Lord Jesus Christ! (1 Peter 1:3)

The Apostles' Creed begins: *I believe in God, the Father Almighty.*

The Christian faith is relational. The Lord Jesus Christ does not invite us to a new life based principally on an institution, much less a club. The church is an expression of that new life together, a means of great blessing to us, a source of new and rich relationships, but it is not the very heart of the faith.

Nor does Jesus call us to simply adopt a new set of rules for life – like a 10-step programme to be a better person, although he does call us to holy lives, godly lives, shaped by his word and transformed by the indwelling of his Spirit.

The heart of the calling of Jesus and a distinctive feature of Christianity compared to other religions is this: we are each called to know God, personally – within a relationship described by 'love' – as our Father, as the Son – the Lord Jesus Christ, and as the Holy Spirit.

It was a radical and even scandalous thing for Jesus to refer to God as his Father, using the intimate term of 'Abba', an Aramaic term similar to 'Daddy'. He extended this same intimacy and privilege to his followers, famously in his teaching on the Lord's Prayer: 'This, then, is how you should pray: "Our Father in heaven ..." (Matthew 6:9).

The apostle John began his gospel account with the claim that we can become children of God through faith in Christ Jesus who came from the Father (John 1:12-14).

We can come by faith and through Jesus to God himself, our Father Almighty. His power is beyond understanding, almighty indeed, seen in creation and in history. His mighty power is still evident where we have eyes to see; it is seen in how he steadfastly pursues his wonderfully good promises, faithfully fulfilling them, saving and transforming and sustaining his people. He does this supremely through his Son, the Lord Jesus Christ, and by his Spirit's power. We see his power in the stories of individual believers, in both 'ordinary' and remarkable testimony to God's work. We see it in his care for the church. We see it in the advance of the gospel, in the persecuted church especially, and in answers to prayer.

We can still come to our Father, who loves us and gave his Son for us. He invites us to be secure in his love. We can seek his mighty power through prayer for the sake of the world, the lost, those in need, and ourselves. *Praise be to the God and Father of our Lord Jesus Christ!*

Creator of heaven and earth

In the beginning God created the heavens and the earth. (Genesis 1:1)

The first two lines of the Apostles' Creed state:

> *I believe in God, the Father almighty,*
> *creator of heaven and earth.*

Fundamental to our faith is that God is our Maker. In fact, he is the Maker of all things. As John's Gospel puts it, 'without him nothing was made'. This reminds us of two great, rich truths to build into our lives: that **God is our Creator**, and that **we are creatures**.

God as Creator tells us something of his immeasurable power, his vast reach and (for want of a better word) his imagination. Have you ever tried to paint, write a poem, compose a song, scribble a picture, design a spreadsheet, lay out a flower bed, arrange a room in your home? These are just examples of creativity. We are all creative in various ways. But consider God's creativity!

He 'painted' on a canvas so large as to be beyond our understanding and displaying immeasurable power in so doing. He wrote his character of beauty, variety and goodness into creation. He laid it out in such a way that we might flourish, enjoy it, grow things, have families, be able to understand something of it and make use of that knowledge, and recognise him to some degree through his creation.

He still stands over his creation, calling us to be good stewards of the physical world, to honour our Creator. It is all his work, some of it is spoiled, like a garden with thistles and thorns, but still bearing great beauty, vitality, potential and goodness.

What of us? As creatures, this reminds us that we are fragile. We will be hurt, tired, get ill, even die. The Lord knows. We are also finite; we are not God, and it's good to recognise that and rejoice in the true freedom of being his, letting him be God. We can rejoice in letting him rule and direct our steps, finding our true value in being his and not determined by the world's skewed values. We can trust our days into the Creator's hands.

We are creatures, vulnerable yet also immensely valuable. God loves his people. Creatures, but by faith we are also **children of God**. And Jesus entered this creation, a reminder that all human life is precious, and creation is to be honoured.

Let us rejoice and find our rest today, as creatures, as children, enjoying creation and the Creator.

I believe in Jesus Christ, his only Son, our Lord

The third line of the Apostles' Creed begins a new theme, a new focus, and this central section is all about **Jesus**.

I believe in Jesus Christ, his only Son, our Lord

Perhaps the most famous verse of the Bible is John 3:16. Jesus is speaking about himself; he is the only Son of God:

*"For God so loved the world that **he gave his one and only Son**, that whoever believes in him shall not perish but have eternal life. For God did not send his Son into the world to condemn the world, but to save the world through him. Whoever believes in him is not condemned, but whoever does not believe stands condemned already because he has not believed in the name of **God's one and only Son**."* (John 3:16-18)

Here is the great distinctive heart of Christianity: Jesus the God-man, the divine Man, the Son of God. Christianity is built on him, focused on him, flows from him and glorifies him.

He is Jesus of Nazareth, a Jewish man born in Bethlehem and raised in Galilee, with parents and siblings. But he is also the one sent from God – the Messiah, **the Christ**, the anointed saving Servant of God.

Being a special messenger from God is not a claim unique to Christianity. Many have claimed to be prophets from God or the gods. Christianity itself has plenty of prophets, those carrying the divine word as messengers. Jesus was more than that – he came to save not simply **with** a message of salvation, but **as** the Saviour in person. His message, his words, carried divine authority in himself.

How could this be the case? Because **he is God the Son, the only Son of God**. One with the Father and Spirit in all eternal glory, majesty and power. Yet – as the Creed continues – one who came in the flesh, as one of us.

John 3:16-18 reminds us that there is no one remotely like him. He is God in the Person of the Son, the one and only, who came as a love-gift from the Father to save through true faith in him. Eternal life is the gift of God, through the Son who perished for us, bearing our sins, so all who trust their sins to him – who 'believe in his name' – will receive this great gift.

To be a Christian is to believe in him and follow him as **Lord, <u>our</u> Lord**. To obey gladly, walking with him in trust, seeking to do his will. Let us give thanks for God's great gift to us, Christ the Lord.

'On Christ the solid rock we stand, all other ground is sinking sand.'

Conceived by the Holy Spirit

I believe in Jesus Christ, his only Son, our Lord,
who was conceived by the Holy Spirit

At this point, the Creed begins to move from the person of Jesus Christ to the foundations of his story, the gospel story, about his life, death and resurrection. There is a historical series of seismic events including those which we celebrate, proclaim and remember at Christmas, on Good Friday, Easter Sunday and at Pentecost. God acted in history and Christian faith is rooted in what God has done through Jesus, to give us confidence in who he is.

This is how the birth of Jesus Christ came about: His mother Mary was pledged to be married to Joseph, but before they came together, she was found to be with child through the Holy Spirit.

Because Joseph her husband was a righteous man and did not want to expose her to public disgrace, he had in mind to divorce her quietly.

But after he had considered this, an angel of the Lord appeared to him in a dream and said, "Joseph son of David, do not be afraid to take Mary home as your wife, because what is conceived in her is from the Holy Spirit." (Matthew 1:18-20)

A claim of Christianity, at the core of our common faith, is that Christ is both human and divine. He is truly the son of Mary (the next line of the Creed) and the Son of God.

These words from Matthew's Gospel recall the incarnation, the birth of Jesus, from Joseph's perspective. He is told that the very beginning of this new life is through the Holy Spirit. The Christ child is 'conceived by the Holy Spirit'. The eternal Son of God takes on human, material, flesh-and-blood form by God's intervention and power.

Even from before birth, from the earliest moment, Jesus was never less than full of God's presence through the Spirit. He is God the Son, he always has been and will be, and it can be no surprise that for him to take on human likeness involved the power of God himself.

Joseph stands in our place in the story in some ways. He does not offer anything by way of initiative, request, power or resources to bring God's Saviour – it is all of God, by God's Holy Spirit. So Joseph cannot boast, and nor can we! Salvation is a pure gift from God, all of grace and not by our efforts, works or merit (Ephesians 2:8-9). The

Spirit brings Christ to life in human form, in human likeness, conceived in Mary his mother.

But Joseph also gives us a model of our response: he is described as 'righteous'. It does not mean perfect, blameless or sinless. It means Joseph sought to live rightly before God; he would have wanted to honour the Law and God's ways. And he listens to and obeys God's words, brought by the angel. In the presence of extraordinary words, of God's presence and grace and wonder, Joseph trusts.

In the Spirit's power, God comes to us, amongst us, in Jesus, and calls us to receive, worship and trust.

Born of the Virgin Mary

I believe in Jesus Christ ...
who was conceived by the Holy Spirit,
born of the Virgin Mary

The centre of Christian faith is Jesus Christ, the Son of God, God the Son. Fully divine, one with the Father and the Holy Spirit.

Yet he is also fully human. One like us, in every way yet without sin.

Matthew's Gospel recounts the announcement of his coming to Joseph and his response. Luke's Gospel tells of the angel's news brought to Mary.

In the sixth month, God sent the angel Gabriel to Nazareth, a town in Galilee, to a virgin pledged to be married to a man named Joseph, a descendant of David. The virgin's name was Mary.

... the angel said to her, "Do not be afraid, Mary, you have found favour with God. You will be with child and give birth to a son, and you are to give him the name Jesus.

... "The Holy Spirit will come upon you, and the power of the Most High will overshadow you. So the holy one to be born will be called the Son of God." (Luke 1:26-27, 30-31, 35)

The Apostles' Creed reminds us of the full ***humanity*** of Jesus. He did not appear as an angelic being, a spiritual force, a vision, merely a message or a set of religious dogma from the heavens, much less a myth. He came into the material world, born as a baby, born of the Virgin Mary, announced by God.

At once, all human life is shown to have remarkable dignity and sanctity – God himself took this form. From before birth through to old age, regardless of physical or mental capacity or strength, or beauty or skills, or achievements or social standing, **all** of human life is sacred, to be honoured and protected, for Christ himself took on our nature. This underpins our Christian compassion and approach to abortion, euthanasia, disabilities and more. Life is sacred.

The eternal Son, the 'Word' of God in person, who speaks with God's power, authority and truth, became a finite, fragile, vulnerable baby dependent fully on his mother Mary to bring him into the world and then nurtured by her. The 'Word became flesh' (John 1:14) and dwelt among us, growing up experiencing friendship and family, work and celebrations, compassion and indifference, love and hostility. He knew, as we do, hunger, thirst, fatigue, sorrow and pain, alongside the blessings in this life that we enjoy. So he can sympathise with us in our humanity and in our spiritual struggles too, for he endured temptation even, far more than us for he resisted it fully.

The humanity of Jesus is also essential for our salvation. Only God is sufficient in power and authority to bear our sin, only he is sufficient to endure all its weight and penalty, and to represent himself in heaven's court. So the Saviour had to be divine, as one with God. But only a human being could represent us and go in our place to the cross. Only a fully human yet sinless Saviour could be our substitute, bearing humanity's sin, able to bring healing and peace and forgiveness to us.

Jesus stands in our place as both God the Son and the son of Mary. The divine Man, Jesus of Nazareth.

> Let earth and heaven combine,
> Angels and men agree,
> To praise in songs divine
> The incarnate Deity,
> Our God contracted to a span,
> Incomprehensibly made man. (Charles Wesley)

We praise him indeed.

He suffered under Pontius Pilate

I believe in Jesus Christ ...
who suffered under Pontius Pilate

He was despised and rejected by men, a man of sorrows, and familiar with suffering. Like one from whom men hide their faces he was despised, and we esteemed him not. Surely he took up our infirmities and carried our sorrows, yet we considered him stricken by God, smitten by him, and afflicted. But he was pierced for our transgressions, he was crushed for our iniquities; the punishment that brought us peace was upon him, and by his wounds we are healed.
(Isaiah 53:3-5)

Finally Pilate handed him over to them to be crucified.
(John 19:16)

For all of human history, the name of Pontius Pilate will be remembered. What he was like or what he achieved in life is of little significance apart from this: he presided over the final hours of the life of Christ Jesus. And these hours, under his authority, were the darkest hours of history.

This line of the Apostles' Creed is not about a Roman governor whom history records as being prone to instigating acts of violence in an unruly corner of an ancient empire. The Creed reminds us here not only of the suffering of Jesus, but also that the gospel is grounded in history. It happened.

Consider this: Christianity is set upon the acts and words of God in history, amongst particular people and places, on actual land, with words and deeds recorded. From Joseph's fall and rise in Egypt to the rescue of the slaves under Moses. From words from heaven at Sinai to Joshua's conquest. From the chaos of the Judges to the rise of David the shepherd-king. From idolatry and exile to the searing warnings and promises of prophets – all this happened in history, written by men from God, recorded for us as lessons for faith and hope and as warnings from the past (1 Corinthians 10:6-11).

So too, the gospel events of Jesus Christ are rooted in history and written for us; Jesus born under the reign of an emperor, suffered and crucified under the jurisdiction of Pontius Pilate. A historical, true faith, centred on times and places. Bethlehem. Nazareth. Jerusalem. Gethsemane. Calvary. A garden tomb.

Consider his sufferings, for this is what the Creed asserts. That Christ the Innocent One bore our sufferings as he bore our sins on the cross. But before that, he endured beatings, humiliation, accusation and the gross injustice of false witnesses and a parody of a trial.

Jesus Christ gives witness to the truth, as he did before Pilate, that truth matters, that justice matters, that God is familiar with suffering, hardship, insults and pain.

We can look to him with confidence for he knows us and our needs. We can look in humility and gratitude, for he endured for us. We can find assurance as we work and pray for justice, that he stood up in the face of all injustice and his kingdom will come in full.

Crucified, died, and was buried

I believe in Jesus Christ ...
who was crucified, died, and was buried.

Jews demand miraculous signs and Greeks look for wisdom, but we preach Christ crucified: a stumbling block to Jews and foolishness to Gentiles, but to those whom God has called, both Jews and Greeks, Christ the power of God and the wisdom of God.
(1 Corinthians 1:22-24)

The climax of the mission of Jesus was not a place of prestige, honour or fanfare in the eyes of the world. It wasn't a victory parade like a Roman emperor returning from battle with gold, fame and prisoners to the adulation of the people. It wasn't a religious ceremony with crowds of joyful worshippers singing, dancing and praying.

The climax was the place of shame – a cross – and the place of death – a grave.

Jesus went from the very highest place, heaven's glory at the side of God the Father, to the very lowest place: the scandalous, horrific, reviled punishment of crucifixion. Reserved for slaves, for rebels, for enemies of the state. A place of utter disgrace, of extreme humiliation and pain. Unmentionable in Roman society, yet the King of Kings stooped down in surrender there, in our place.

He was **crucified**. The central focus of the apostles' preaching, and the symbol of Christians since, is a place of barbaric execution. Why? Because of the One who died there, not in miserable defeat but in glorious victory. God's loving, saving purpose led Jesus to bear our sins – yours and mine – and defeat evil. He was crucified for us.

He **died**. His body was broken, his blood poured out, that we might be forgiven. His life was given that all who trust in him might have eternal life. The blow of God's wrath fell on the Shepherd that the sheep might be spared (Matthew 26:31; John 10:11). By his wounds we are healed.

He was **buried**. The body of the Lord was laid in a borrowed tomb, honouring him in death. He would not need it for long.

We *believe* these things. We *boast* in his saving death, even as others find it foolish or look for something else. Why such confidence? Because here is God's love, God's mercy, God's power, God's wisdom. God revealed. May we find great confidence that he has done this for us, and bow in humility as we remember that he would come down so low to save us. None are out of reach.

He descended to the dead

I believe in Jesus Christ ...
was crucified, died, and was buried;
he descended to the dead.

When I saw him, I fell at his feet as though dead. Then he placed his right hand on me and said: "Do not be afraid. I am the First and the Last. I am the Living One; I was dead, and behold I am alive for ever and ever! And I hold the keys of death and Hades."
(Revelation 1:17-18)

Christians affirm that Jesus died; he fully experienced death. So the Apostles' Creed states that explicitly, not just that '*he was crucified died, and was buried*' but that he went where we cannot yet see or experience in life; *he descended to the dead.*

This was not a fleeting moment of unconsciousness on the cross. He did not resuscitate. He had died physically, from a combination of violent traumatic injuries, blood loss, dehydration, excruciating pain and finally perhaps the inability to breathe. Jesus died for our sins, at the hands of his enemies. So then he entered the realm of the dead.

He descended. The Bible depicts the shadowy place, *Sheol*, to be 'down' just as we go down into a grave, whereas heaven is 'above'. However, Jesus descended to the dead not as only a victim himself of death but ultimately as the **Victor** over it.

Christ Jesus entered death without a stain on his own soul for sin had been conquered, the curse undone, the debt paid in full, the charges cancelled, the devil defeated. Justice satisfied, wrath endured, love demonstrated, salvation won. So death could not and would not hold him.

As he declared to the apostle John in the divine revelation, "I am the Living One; I was dead." He had been there but could not be held or overcome by death. "I hold the keys of death and Hades." He holds all authority over that realm too. For the departed faithful and those who die in their sins, Jesus rules. He will save and judge. And for those in him, death will NOT have the last word.

"Where, O death, is your victory? Where, O death, is your sting?"

The sting of death is sin, and the power of sin is the law. But thanks be to God! He gives us the victory through our Lord Jesus Christ. (1 Corinthians 15:55-57)

Hallelujah!

On the third day, he rose again

On the third day he rose again

Who through the Spirit of holiness was declared with power to be the Son of God by his resurrection from the dead: Jesus Christ our Lord. (Romans 1:4)

As you read through the book of Acts – the Acts of the Apostles, or the Acts of the Holy Spirit, either would be a fitting title – you can't fail to notice what the focus of the apostles' preaching is. Their message has a laser-like focus on the death and resurrection of Jesus. The two events are tied together; one explains and expands on the other. Two glorious realities, central to our faith.

Death could not hold him; he is – as Jesus says to the apostle John – the Living One (Revelation 1:18). He is the Author of life, the light of life; he cannot be conquered by the darkness of death or sin. So he truly died, Jesus died in his human flesh and blood. But the Son of God is unconquerable so God the Father demonstrated his power and lifted him from the grave. He is now alive, gloriously so, forever.

But why is this the focus of the apostles' message?

Because this is not merely another miracle – like feeding a vast crowd, walking on water or healing the sick. It is the ultimate miracle in the life of Christ; to overcome not merely death in a partial, temporary way but to conquer it fully and forever. He had raised Lazarus and others, who would then die again later in the natural course of their life, but Jesus will never die. He has eternal life, he is eternal life, he brings eternal life for all who believe in him as their Saviour and follow him as their Lord.

It is not merely victory over death. It is vindication, demonstration, that the cross was indeed the victory over sin and evil, not a mere act of great love or sacrifice. The resurrection proves who Jesus is: Saviour and Lord, the Son of God, the Living One.

The empty grave and the physical, visible appearances of the risen Christ Jesus are God's great YES to all his promises: every promise of God, every claim of Jesus, is given divine approval and the sign of guarantee by what happened on that Easter day.

That is why they preach and why we do. **That** is why we sing and pray. **That** is why faith is grounded in God's solid hope, not on wishful thinking or merely our performance. It rests on what God has done in Christ. We can have hope of new life now and forever, for Christ is alive. He has risen.

He ascended into heaven

I believe in Jesus Christ...
he ascended into heaven

Therefore God exalted him to the highest place and gave him the name that is above every name. (Philippians 2:9)

The Apostles' Creed includes the story of Jesus' life from eternity to eternity. A story that tells us who he is, what he has done, what he will yet do and how we are caught up in that story as he saves, serves and leads us.

Jesus 'descended' in his incarnation, coming down from heaven's glory into the vulnerability, lowliness and humility of his humanity. He descended from glory to the place of shame and suffering on the cross. He descended to the dead. This was the downward part of his journey, to the lowest and darkest places of all; he came down so we can know him in his humanity and to reveal the Father.

He went down to the cross and grave so that we need not fear but have hope, so we need not be trapped in sin nor have to face judgement on our sins, so we might be saved and have eternal life.

From there he rose up from death into new and glorious life. Vindicated by the Father, empowered by the Spirit, he rose up from the tomb, stepping out into the light and into the garden and into the lives of his grieving, despairing and doubting friends (and the women who believed!) He appeared to many – in person – still inviting people to faith, to enter the kingdom, to repent and believe.

40 days later, he rose up again, ascending into heaven, returning to God's immediate presence and to his rightful place above all powers and authorities. Above all reputations, earthly status and honour, Jesus is incomparably the highest and greatest of all.

The ascension is only recounted in the first chapter of Acts, the details are frustratingly sparse there, but the fact is assumed and alluded to often. Jesus reigns in heaven with God the Father.

The focus of the Acts account is that Jesus is received into heaven – God's great approval of the Son is beyond question! But it also declares that he will return from there. Personally, visibly, decisively.

Our great hope now is that Jesus, Lord of all and King of Kings, is also our great high priest. He rules from a throne of grace, ever ready to hear us and minister to us with his grace and mercy. Heaven is close at hand and so is the Lord of heaven. Ascended, exalted, yet by his Spirit always with us.

He is seated at the right hand of the Father

I believe in Jesus Christ ... seated at the right hand of the Father

Who is he that condemns? Christ Jesus, who died—more than that, who was raised to life—is at the right hand of God and is also interceding for us. (Romans 8:34)

Jesus is at the right hand of the Father in heaven. His is a position of glory, authority, power and dominion which none except God can fathom. No earthly or evil power can contend with his.

From there, ***Jesus intercedes for us***. He speaks for those who are his brothers and sisters by faith. He speaks on our behalf to God the Father, and his words are heard if we are belonging to Christ, if we are in Christ, the beloved Son.

The story we have to tell, the good news of Jesus, is of God come to us as one of us – a human being, God in the flesh. He lived the life we couldn't live before God, revealing God's very good news and the kingdom, inviting us in through him. He died the death we deserved for our sins, rose to a new and glorious life for us, and returned to heaven as our exalted Saviour and King. It doesn't end there though. He wasn't finished.

What is Jesus doing now? He prays for us. He prays for all those who belong to him, for all who rest their lives and hopes on his saving work and great promises. He looks with love on God's adopted children, reminding us we belong, and he intercedes for us!

It's as if Jesus takes every promise from the Bible over God's people, reads it back to the Father and applies it to us, saying "They are mine, they are with me." He claims all the promises of salvation for his own people. All the promises of encouragement, blessing, comfort, wisdom, protection, fruitfulness and of knowing God's love – Jesus prays these over us. He prays that we might know them, and so we will not let guilt, condemnation, shame or sin's power have any grip on us. "Who is he that condemns?" Answer: for those in Christ, no one, for **he** speaks for us.

All our prayers – he brings them before the Father, with the Spirit's power, to bring our needs before God. If you knew that Jesus Christ was in the room or chair next to you, praying for you, drawing your heavenly Father's attention to your very needs, would you be more comforted or confident? Yet he is nearer still than that!

Christ is at God's right hand, yet by his Spirit he is also right here, always, and claiming all God's promises for us, for you and me.

He will come to judge

I believe in Jesus Christ ...
and he will come to judge the living and the dead.

"He commanded us to preach to the people and to testify that he is the one whom God appointed as judge of the living and the dead."
(Acts 10:42)

The final line of the central section of the Apostles' Creed points us forward to the future activity of Jesus. He lived, died, rose up to new life and ascended to heaven as our exalted Saviour and King. He reigns in heaven now, interceding for his own. He will come again, on a day only known to the Father, with power and great glory to judge the living and the dead.

His return will be as Saviour and Judge, God has appointed Christ alone as worthy of these roles. He is worthy for the perfect obedience of his life and death, worthy for the greatness of his sacrifice for us, worthy for his victory over sin and evil. 'He alone is worthy' is the song of heaven which we can join in now (Revelation 4:11, 5:9-12). Whatever we see on the news or experience in our lives, there is one absolutely worthy to stand above it all and judge rightly, to save and to judge on God's behalf.

We long for justice in this world. Justice and righteousness are the two terms in the Bible for everything being made right, good, whole, clean, straight, true and holy. We long for right relationships in our families and with our friends. We long for justice for the vulnerable, for innocent victims of war or crime, for goodness and mercy to be the hallmarks of society. We long for an end to despots and dictators, to cruelty and abuse, to corruption and lies, to all that is vile or ungodly, to all that destroys our planet or distorts God's good ways. We long for God's kingdom to come, as the Lord's Prayer teaches us to pray.

We long for this. How much more does God feel for this, for the ravages of sin, selfishness, pride and so on? A world in rebellion. Yet in his patience and purposes he waits, allowing space for repentance and sustaining his people, still working by his Spirit for good in countless ways.

Christ Jesus will return. This will be a day of judgement and of salvation. As Christians we can have confidence that we will be judged by the one who knows us, who sees the cross of Christ and our response to the Son. That is the basis on which we are judged, and for those in Christ there is no condemnation (Romans 5:1).

His judgement will be perfect, in every way; a sobering reality when many deny him, ignore or distort his words, and ridicule his ways; a great joyful assurance for those of us who know him and for the persecuted church today who stand faithfully under great pressure.

We have this assurance that the goodness of God in justice and salvation is coming, in person. So stand firm, have hope, and be thankful.

I believe in the Holy Spirit

I believe in the Holy Spirit

"The Spirit gives life; the flesh counts for nothing. The words I have spoken to you are spirit and they are life." (John 6:63)

Jesus believed in the Holy Spirit! Some say this for themselves, meaning they believe simply that the Holy Spirit *exists* but Jesus was wholly trusting in the Spirit's power and presence, in the activity of the Spirit. He sends the same Spirit to all who believe today.

This is who the Spirit of God is: God's power and presence in person. In complete harmony with the Son and the Father, the Spirit brings life to God's people. Jesus said this plainly: 'The Spirit gives life.' Spiritual life is a miracle, a supernatural act of God, to raise those who are spiritually dead to new life.

We can't do this ourselves by any amount of behavioural change, self-improvement, education or religious rites: 'The flesh counts for nothing.' In other words, human work won't do it, only the Spirit brings life, and the Spirit points us to Jesus the author of life. He is our Teacher, enabling the Bible to speak into our lives with transformational power. He is the one who grows our godly character, refining and pruning us. He is the one who sustains the church, opens people's eyes to faith, guards the faithful, and empowers us in mission and service.

This third and final section of the Apostles' Creed is focused on the ongoing ministry or activity of Jesus Christ by his Spirit and in the Church, and on his future promises for us. The first section is about the Father, the second and most extensive is about the Son, the third begins with the Holy Spirit.

Everything we see of God now, in our lives, the church or the world, is by the Spirit. He is a gift from the Father and Son, sent to bring us life from God in all its fullness for now and eternity, sent to bring a harvest for God's glory. He points us to God's true words – may we pay close attention to them, for the Spirit leads in complete harmony with scripture, the words of life.

Ask God to grant you the Spirit's presence in a deep way today. What would God say to you – to comfort, challenge, encourage or direct you? Be still, wait, watch and pray.

The holy catholic church

I believe in the holy catholic church

But you are a chosen people, a royal priesthood, a holy nation, a people belonging to God, that you may declare the praises of him who called you out of darkness into his wonderful light. Once you were not a people, but now you are the people of God; once you had not received mercy, but now you have received mercy. (1 Peter 2:9-10)

The church is a body, the body of Christ, a people united in their belonging to God. The church is God's 'idea', a remarkable, enduring, precious people of faith. This line of the Creed focuses on this body united. The next line emphasises our part, our fellowship together.

Ancient Christian creeds affirm the belief in 'one holy, catholic and apostolic church'. The Apostles' Creed picks up two of these defining characteristics: the holiness and catholicity of the church. There is only one true church (across the world and throughout history), for all its many denominations and shapes and sizes, and that is the church of Christ. This church is also apostolic – it is built on the teaching of the apostles' teaching, which in turn is built on the Old Testament and the good news of the gospel, all pointing to Christ. The Church is built on God's word. If a local church isn't true to this word, it is not a true church.

One holy church

We are a people belonging to God who is Most Holy, so we too are made holy because we belong to him, 'a holy nation'. We are precious in his sight and the church is to be honoured because it is God's holy church. The wellbeing of the church, our unity, our faithfulness, our love for one another and the stranger, our integrity in holding to God's word – all of these matter not simply for our sake or for effective mission and service, but because the church is holy: it is God's. The letters to the seven churches in Revelation 2-3 are a mix of stark warning and glorious encouragement to the church today in our holy calling.

Holiness also reminds us that we – the church – are being transformed into the likeness of Jesus. The Spirit is the power in the church, in the lives of every believer. He works in the midst of preaching, praying, discipleship, worship, fellowship and evangelism, to change us to be more holy, more like Jesus. He equips the church with love and knowledge; he brings spiritual growth. He enables us to be a light in the dark world, to be salt as a distinctive people. Where the church fails to shine God's light of his sacrificial love for people and the truth of his word, or fails to be distinctive against the backdrop of the world and society around it, it is then no longer the church as God intends.

One catholic church

This is not a reference to the Catholic Church centred on Rome but the catholic church (little 'c') meaning the universal church. The church everywhere, in every nation or culture or denomination or language or building is THE church of Christ. Where Christ is worshipped faithfully, in Spirit and in the truth, there is the church (John 4:23-24). This is the church universal or 'catholic' with Christ as the head of his body. We are not uniform (all the same) but we are united in Christ: in Spirit and in truth.

Wherever we live, we are called to be God's people, to honour the church, pray for it and actively encourage one another in it. God loves his church!

The communion of saints

I believe in the communion of saints

And let us consider how we may spur one another on toward love and good deeds. Let us not give up meeting together, as some are in the habit of doing, but let us encourage one another—and all the more as you see the Day approaching. (Hebrews 10:24-25)

There is no place for the 'lone ranger' Christian, the isolated believer, in God's purposes. We might live alone, work alone, feel alone, but we are never truly alone for the Lord is with us. However we are also called to gather with God's people regularly, as far as it is possible for us. If we cannot gather physically, we can still connect in other ways and meet with a few. The Lord's body is meant to be joined up!

We are made to be part of this new life together, part of the body of Christ – the church – where we can sing and pray, sit under God's word together and share bread and wine. We can belong and grow, give and receive, share and encourage, spurring one another on in love to do good for the sake of others. This is the focus of the Apostles' Creed affirmation: *I believe in the communion of saints.*

The 'saints' in the Bible are simply Christians. Every Christian is a 'holy one', we are saints of God. Many of the letters address the church in this way (e.g. Romans 1:7). You don't need a statue, a flag or a papal decree to become a saint! All God's children are holy, saints in his eyes.

We believe in the 'communion' of the saints, our real spiritual belonging in the body of Christ. We belong in him and to one another, being built together as a dwelling for God's Spirit (Ephesians 2:22). We are the household of faith, God's field, the flock of his pasture, branches of the true vine, the family of faith, his army, partners in the gospel, the elect from the world, those in Christ, a chosen people. Every part is valued, every believer is called to be rooted in Christ and under his Lordship but also joined together in the body.

God sees his church, visibly gathered but also scattered through the week, across the world and throughout history. Some are in heaven already, many are on earth. Visible or – for now – invisible to our eyes, this is God's great host, held together in God's love and power: the communion of saints.

May you know his love over you and the life and love of God expressed to you from belonging in the church.

The forgiveness of sins

I believe in the forgiveness of sins

For Christ died for sins once for all, the righteous for the unrighteous, to bring you to God. (1 Peter 3:18)

See what God has done. Christ Jesus died for sinners to bring us to God.

This very short statement in the Apostles' Creed summarises the breadth and depth of the New Testament teaching of how Christ rescues us. Here is the great achievement of Christ Jesus on the cross, that through faith in him we have forgiveness of sins.

This is what true faith, faith in God, rests on: what God has done in and through Jesus Christ. This is how Christianity has endured and transformed lives, because at its heart is the power of God and not the activity, piety, prayers or devotion of human beings – as precious as they can be in God's hands.

Christ died for sinners to rescue us and bring us home. This is the answer to our times of doubt, to days when we wonder if God's love is real, to seasons of sorrow or apathy, or when our own sin looms large in our conscience; Christ has done it, he died for sins once for all, the righteous for the unrighteous. The unrighteous = all of us. Christ died for you, for me, for us all.

He did this to bring us to God, to open the way to the Father. Today, by faith in Christ as we genuinely turn from sin and trust him to forgive, lead and rescue, you and I have full access to our heavenly Father. The way is open. The door will never be closed again. The 'welcome' sign is cross-shaped for Jesus has cleared the way and opened the door.

Forgiveness is expressed in the gospels and in the New Testament in various ways – as an effective and priceless sacrifice, as a colossal debt cleared or penalty paid, as victory won, as complete cleansing, as a relationship with God reconciled, as the guilty pardoned, and all at great cost. The outcome is the same: sin is cancelled, fear of death is overcome, and new life with God is ours.

May you know this assurance of your Father's loving welcome today, the joy of Christ's complete work to wipe out the penalty of your sins, and the confidence of belonging. He has done it.

The resurrection of the body

I believe in the resurrection of the body

'Therefore my heart is glad and my tongue rejoices; my body also will live in hope, because you will not abandon me to the grave, nor will you let your Holy One see decay. You have made known to me the paths of life; you will fill me with joy in your presence.' (Acts 2:26-28)

"Christians, we are one day nearer to heaven!" I've seen this a few times and it has often made me pause. We will all die. How do I face death? How are others doing so?

The verses today capture something wonderful of the Christian hope, our hope in life and in death. The words come from the apostle Peter's appeal to the crowds at Pentecost, probably his first ever sermon (what a debut!), and here he recites the words of King David from Psalms 16 and 110. Peter makes the bold claim that Jesus died and rose from the dead, he was not 'abandoned to the grave', and so **we** can have the same hope.

That hope is not just for heaven, or for the new creation of heaven and earth which will be united and restored, the ultimate home for God's people. No, that hope is for now too, to bring us joy even today. David sings of a glad heart, of words of rejoicing – surely the overflow of a person confident of God's goodness now.

This joy is in life and in death, what he knows now and will have before God:

'You have made known to me the paths of life; you will fill me with joy in your presence.'

God is with us and will not abandon his own. He leads us into the paths of life, of eternal life, of life with him. Paths of security, peace and hope. Finally, these paths lead into his presence with great joy. With a renewed, restored, recognisable body. As Christ was raised bodily and physically, so will our bodies also be redeemed in the new creation.

We are one day nearer that face-to-face presence; the hope is real, home awaits. Ask him to lead you in his paths today.

Life everlasting

I believe in ... life everlasting. Amen

"I tell you the truth, he who believes has everlasting life." (John 6:47)

Jesus is emphatic. 'Truly, truly, I tell you: he who believes in me has eternal life.' Eternal life from God is decisively and uniquely linked to a true faith in Christ Jesus as Saviour and Lord. It comes from God and as a gift of grace to those who believe. Nothing more can be added, an encouragement to all. Nothing less will suffice, a clear direction or correction to many.

The Apostles' Creed begins with declaring faith in God from whom all life comes, our Father and Creator. It then affirms our great confidence in our rescue to new life by God through Christ the Son. This new life is by the Spirit and amongst God's people.

The Creed closes with this statement of faith in life everlasting with God – life begun now but to be enjoyed forever.

Our Christian hope is not 'eternal life' meaning merely an unimaginably very long life. To many that sounds really boring, it's also incomprehensible. God stands outside of time and space, so how would eternity look without time? Perhaps a better way to approach it is to think of 'the life of eternity', the life of God, an unbroken and everlasting life in that sense. Life that is to the full, undiminished and untarnished, brimming with joy, untouched by sorrow or pain or death, in the presence of God's love and light always without end, with joy unlimited. Everlasting, eternal **life**.

Jesus said he came to bring life in all its fullness (John 10:10). This is the life of Christ in us, our life as a brand new creation from God; we are spiritually alive. This everlasting life begins when we become a Christian; we are born again (John 3:3). We can enjoy this life in part now, tasting and seeing that the Lord is good even in the midst of tears or trials. We will enjoy God's new life in us to the full one day, beyond death, in glory with him and God's people.

This is our hope, firm and secure. The Apostles' Creed ends with '**Amen**', for this is not merely a statement of faith but a prayer of praise and thanks to God for who he is, what he has done and how we can receive from him. It is used in corporate worship but is also for our personal response.

May this prayer be yours and this life be your confident hope too.

ABOUT THE AUTHOR

 Andrew Goldsmith is married with two children and is currently serving as Senior Pastor of Ampthill Baptist Church.

He has been in ministry for over 15 years with an emphasis on Bible preaching and teaching to enable everyday discipleship, as we seek to follow and honour Jesus in all of life. He also enjoys creatively engaging in apologetics (explaining and defending Christianity, trying to clear the big questions out of the way) and helping people connect with Jesus through the Bible. He loves working with other leaders and churches united around the gospel, and he's an Associate of LICC (licc.org.uk).

Prior to pastoral ministry he worked in industry and academia in the area of medical engineering, developing replacement hip and knee joints.

His previous books include:

Formation Groups: Transforming Disciples

Big Questions

Bomb Disposal: Dealing with the Seven Deadly Sins

Light in our Lockdown

He also posts online, mostly pictures of books and trees.

 @rev_andrewg   *andrew_goldsmith*

Printed in Great Britain
by Amazon

26921130R00175